THE
EVERYTHING®
THEODORE ROOSEVELT
BOOK

Dear Reader,

I met Theodore Roosevelt several years ago in a college classroom. Well, I didn't meet him in the true sense of the word. TR was the subject of the class, not a member. But, after the semester ended, I vowed to learn more about his life because he was such a fascinating character. Doing the research for this book gave me the chance to do that and pass some of what I learned on to you.

The course was "The Politics of Theodore Roosevelt." As the title implies, the emphasis was on his political philosophies and method-ologies. There was not much about his personal life included. That is a drawback when you are trying to learn about the total person. So I learned more about his private life to create a more complete profile of the man and his personality, rather than a string of dates and facts, which is the bane of most readers.

Now, several years after the course ended, I have completed that proj-ect. I share it with you. Hopefully, you will be as happy as I am to "meet" TR and gain an insight into his life and legacy.

Arthur G. Sharp, MA

Welcome to the EVERYTHING® Series!

These handy, accessible books give you all you need to tackle a difficult project, gain a new hobby, comprehend a fascinating topic, prepare for an exam, or even brush up on something you learned back in school but have since forgotten.

You can choose to read an Everything® book from cover to cover or just pick out the information you want from our four useful boxes: e-questions, e-facts, e-quotes, and e-ssentials.

We give you everything you need to know on the subject, but throw in a lot of fun stuff along the way, too.

We now have more than 400 Everything® books in print, spanning such wide-ranging categories as weddings, pregnancy, cooking, music instruction, foreign language, crafts, pets, New Age, and so much more. When you're done reading them all, you can finally say you know Everything®!

QUESTION
Answers to common questions

FACT
Important snippets of information

QUOTE
Words of wisdom from experts in the field

ESSENTIAL
Quick handy tips

PUBLISHER Karen Cooper

DIRECTOR OF ACQUISITIONS AND INNOVATION Paula Munier

MANAGING EDITOR, EVERYTHING® SERIES Lisa Laing

COPY CHIEF Casey Ebert

ASSISTANT PRODUCTION EDITOR Jacob Erickson

ACQUISITIONS EDITOR Hillary Thompson

ASSOCIATE DEVELOPMENT EDITOR Hillary Thompson

EDITORIAL ASSISTANT Ross Weisman

EVERYTHING® SERIES COVER DESIGNER Erin Alexander

LAYOUT DESIGNERS Colleen Cunningham, Elisabeth Lariviere, Ashley Vierra, Denise Wallace

Visit the entire Everything® series at *www.everything.com*

THE
EVERYTHING®
THEODORE ROOSEVELT BOOK

The Extraordinary Life of an American Icon

Arthur G. Sharp, MA

Foreword by Dr. William N. Tilchin,
Editor of the *Theodore Roosevelt Association Journal*

Avon, Massachusetts

*To the Roosevelt family, whose public service
over the centuries has made the United States
a better place in which to live—sometimes.*

An Everything® Series Book.
Everything® and everything.com® are registered trademarks of F+W Media, Inc.

Published by Adams Media, a division of F+W Media, Inc.
57 Littlefield Street, Avon, MA 02322 U.S.A.
www.adamsmedia.com

ISBN 10: 1-4405-2729-6
ISBN 13: 978-1-4405-2729-6
eISBN 10: 1-4405-2765-2
eISBN 13: 978-1-4405-2765-4

Printed in the United States of America.

10 9 8 7 6 5 4 3 2 1

Library of Congress Cataloging-in-Publication Data
is available from the publisher.

This publication is designed to provide accurate and authoritative information with regard to the subject matter covered. It is sold with the understanding that the publisher is not engaged in rendering legal, accounting, or other professional advice. If legal advice or other expert assistance is required, the services of a competent professional person should be sought.

—From a *Declaration of Principles* jointly adopted by a Committee of the American Bar Association and a Committee of Publishers and Associations

Many of the designations used by manufacturers and sellers to distinguish their products are claimed as trademarks. Where those designations appear in this book and Adams Media was aware of a trademark claim, the designations have been printed with initial capital letters.

Historical image research and restoration by Steven Wynn.

*This book is available at quantity discounts for bulk purchases.
For information, please call 1-800-289-0963.*

Contents

Acknowledgments

There is a plethora of information about TR's life available through a variety of online sources, published books, his own writings, etc. These sources are available in a "one-stop" format now. Thanks are due to the people who have assembled them all in one place and facilitated the research process.

The Top 10 Facts about TR's Life

1. TR had dogs that climbed trees to hunt cougars and lynxes on his ranch in the Dakotas. He was fond of revealing stories about such animals to his children.

2. It was not unusual for TR to carry guns for protection when he was on the campaign trail. Unfortunately, he was not packing one the night he was shot in Milwaukee in 1912.

3. TR did not believe that children should play sports if it meant jeopardizing academics. He was a firm believer in "study first, play later."

4. As far as TR was concerned, the only good novels had happy endings. And if the heroes had to die, they had to do so nobly and worthily—just as people should spend their lives.

5. On his expeditions, TR carried a vial of morphine with which to end his life if necessary. He almost used it on his River of Doubt trip.

6. Even though TR was an advocate of a strong navy, he was always bored when out at sea.

7. TR was a sickly person when he was young. But the worst malady he suffered was homesickness, especially after he married Edith and traveled away from his home and family for long periods of time.

8. TR was not fond of campaigning and talking to people who expected speeches from him at every stop. He especially did not like people telling him things about nature that he already knew, just to impress him.

9. There was no better place on earth for TR than Sagamore Hill at Oyster Bay, New York. It was especially appealing when his family was there, since he valued family above all else.

10. TR had very little use for news reporters while he was in the White House and advised his children to simply ignore them in the hopes that they would go away.

Foreword

HISTORIANS ARE ASKED PERIODICALLY to rank U.S. presidents. In recent decades, such surveys have tended to place Theodore Roosevelt as the fourth greatest president—behind Abraham Lincoln, Franklin D. Roosevelt, and George Washington. While the #1 ranking for Lincoln (who, with incomparable poise and skill, literally preserved the United States as a country during its time of maximum peril) would be difficult to contest, Theodore Roosevelt, who served as the twenty-sixth president from 1901 to 1909, may very well be deserving of the #2 ranking. True, Franklin Roosevelt (TR's fifth cousin) successfully confronted two crises, the Great Depression and the Second World War, that were far graver than any danger faced by America during TR's era. But FDR's foreign policy from 1933 to 1939 indirectly facilitated the growth in power of Nazi Germany, whereas TR demonstrated an extraordinary capacity to anticipate international crises and to act to forestall them. Theodore Roosevelt was by far the foremost environmentalist president in U.S. history. He was the first great domestic reformer among twentieth-century presidents. And TR's foreign policy was extremely well-conceived and well-executed and was based on farsighted principles—broadly defined U.S. interests, formidable deterrent power, and Anglo-American solidarity and preeminence—that would guide U.S. presidents from World War II to the present day.

Beyond his accomplishments as the nation's chief executive, Theodore Roosevelt is an enormously interesting historical figure. He was both an avid outdoorsman and a prominent American intellectual. He read voluminously, and his output as an author of high-quality books and essays on a very broad range of subjects was extremely impressive (plus he wrote well over 100,000 letters during his sixty-year lifetime). He was a devoted husband and a loving father actively engaged in the upbringing of his children. Before and after his presidency, his career included periods as a state legislator, as a Western rancher, as a historian, as a U.S. Civil Service commissioner and then a New York City police commissioner, as assistant secretary of the navy, as a military officer fighting in Cuba during the Spanish-American War, as governor of New York, as vice president of the United States, as a big-game hunter in Africa and a few years later an explorer of uncharted territory in South America, as the founder and leader of a new national political party, and as a newspaper editorialist. To all of these activities and responsibilities TR brought his powerful, effervescent, irresistible personality. As the subtitle of this book suggests, he was, deservedly, "an American icon." He has been immortalized on Mount Rushmore—and through the enduringly beloved teddy bear.

In *The Everything® Theodore Roosevelt Book*, author Arthur G. Sharp provides an excellent starting point for individuals desiring to become acquainted with the life and achievements of Theodore Roosevelt, as well as a useful reference source for Roosevelt aficionados seeking to plug holes in their knowledge. (Those looking for ongoing exposure to the latest and best writing on TR are additionally encouraged to become members of the Theodore Roosevelt Association [P.O. Box 719, Oyster Bay, NY 11771; *www .theodoreroosevelt.org*].) By producing this volume, Arthur Sharp and Adams Media have made a truly valuable contribution to the field of Theodore Roosevelt studies.

—WILLIAM N. TILCHIN

Introduction

WHEN THEODORE ROOSEVELT—OR TR, as he is referred to in this book—died in 1919, he was a medical marvel. He was deaf in one ear, blind in one eye, had a swollen ankle and a bullet in his chest . . . in short, he was not a healthy man. To him, these afflictions were part of the process of living, and a person who could not overcome obstacles would never succeed. That is the central theme of this guide.

This book is a compendium of facts about TR's life drawn from a variety of sources, including his speeches, articles, and books. You can interpret the facts according to your knowledge and experience. It is impossible not to draw a picture of TR based on the myths and truths of his life. Historians have been doing that for years, yet TR remains as much a mystery to readers and researchers today as he did when he was alive.

The brainteasers located at the end of each chapter add a bit of amusement to the study of TR and the world around him. They are also educational. They demonstrate and define the people and situations with which TR dealt in his lifetime and enhance the central message of the book: He is a historical figure worth studying because of his eclecticism and enthusiasm for life.

No one book can tell the full story of a man like Theodore Roosevelt. He was a complex man, and complex personalities require a lot more analysis and explanation than personalities of the average person. And, since it is difficult to measure historical figures without studying their public and private sides, this book examines both. In its final form, it is simply a snapshot of TR, which can be cropped, adjusted, or otherwise fine-tuned.

The trick is to figure out what made him tick. He was the ultimate enigma wrapped in a puzzle. This book unravels a bit of the mystery surrounding him and provides insights into his life that will give you a deeper understanding of the substantial contributions he made to world history.

Admittedly, this book raises as many questions about why TR did what he did and how he did it as it provides answers to his behavior. If you want answers to those questions, you are encouraged to seek them on your own. The chapters include some sources you can refer to for more information, and each source is a pointer to more. Following those sources will help you fill in the inevitable "blanks" that dot the pages of overviews such as this one.

Like most historical figures, TR did not exist in a bubble. He lived among and worked with other people who helped shape the world around them. Many of the people you will meet in these pages had profound effects on TR, just as he did on them. Sometimes those effects were positive; sometimes they were not.

TR suffered through the same vicissitudes of life in every facet that most people do. He enjoyed victories; he endured defeats. Victories and defeats aside, he could not abide people who sat life out. TR was a motivated man who believed in deeds, not thought. Thus, some critics have looked at him as a hard person to live with. Despite such suggestions, he was neither a demon nor a deity. Theodore Roosevelt was a mortal. Perhaps he accomplished more in life than a lot of other people do, but he was still a mortal—albeit an enigmatic one at times.

Yes, as TR proved, individuals can succeed regardless of societal status, physical challenges, political adversaries, and other factors that shape their lives. The challenges that TR overcame to earn his success are an inspiration to people everywhere. He was a role model, and his legacy reflects that.

Everyone can learn something from Theodore Roosevelt's life; these pages are a great place to start the process.

CHAPTER 1

Inaction to Action: TR's Pattern for Life

" . . . a man must be respected for what he made of himself."

History begins anew every time a baby is born. There is no way to predict how each newborn is going to change history or whom the change will affect. Only history can tell that. Certainly, Theodore Roosevelt's birth on October 27, 1858, led to some radical changes in world history. They began in his early years as he established the patterns in his life that shaped him into one of the world's most dynamic and enigmatic leaders, and created a legacy that endures almost a century after his death.

A Man of Action

Theodore Roosevelt was a self-made man. The shaping process began, as it does with any self-made person, when he was a child. TR recognized early in life that if he was going to be successful, he would have to earn whatever he achieved—if he lived long enough to achieve it. Even though he had been born into a privileged family, nobody was going to give him anything. That was not the Roosevelt family way.

QUOTE

A woman who lived next door to the Roosevelts told TR's friend and biographer Jacob Riis that she saw the young boy hanging from a second-story window one day. She alerted his mother, and then prepared to catch TR as he fell. She told Riis, "If the Lord had not taken care of Theodore, he would have been killed long ago."

For the Roosevelts, the road to success required action and perseverance. Inaction was not an option. TR learned that lesson in large part due to his parents' and siblings' influence.

The future U.S. president's childhood was not ordinary by any stretch of the imagination. He suffered from health problems that no family's name or wealth could prevent. Yet, neither he nor his family members ever used those problems as an excuse for failure or weakness. Instead, he—and his father in particular—used them as a challenge and a steppingstone to what he called a "strenuous life," a phrase TR used often as he developed physically, mentally, and emotionally.

"Bamie"

Young "Teedie," a nickname he acquired early, was the second child born to Theodore Roosevelt Sr. ("Thee") and Martha Bulloch Roosevelt ("Mittie"). By the time he arrived on October 27, 1858, in the family's New York City brownstone at 28 East 20th Street, his older sister, Anna, was almost four years old. Anna, born on January 18, 1855, was destined to play a significant role in TR's life.

Anna and TR had two major things in common. Like him, she had to overcome serious health problems. And they were both full of seemingly boundless energy despite their ailments.

Anna, known as "Bamie," a play on the Italian word *bambina* (little girl), or "Bye," suffered from a spinal ailment. As a result, she wore confining corrective steel braces in her childhood.

The braces did not slow her down. Her disdain for them explains how she acquired her nickname. Anna came and went so fast at times that people were not sure they actually saw her. They got used to saying, "Hi, Bamie. Bye, Bamie."

Elliott

The next young Roosevelt, Elliott, "Ellie" or "Nell" for short, was born sixteen months after Teedie, on February 28, 1860. That was ideal for them both from a playmate standpoint. Elliott and TR were close as children. But their lives eventually went in different directions, as Theodore developed into the best-known and most successful of the four siblings and Elliott became the pariah. No one could have predicted that in 1860, though.

Elliott and TR were highly competitive as children. Elliott served as TR's best man at his first wedding. Sadly, Elliott started drinking alcohol when he was young. Eventually, he was ostracized from the family. He survived a suicide attempt at age 34, but died a few days later. That was a sad day for the Roosevelt family.

"Conie"

The fourth child, Corinne, joined the family on September 27, 1861. She, too, played an important role in TR's life—especially after his first wife died. "Conie," as she was known, formed a friendship with the Roosevelts' next-door neighbor, Edith Kermit Carow. Edith, who was born on August 6, 1861, only a few weeks before Corinne, also befriended TR. Eventually, their friendship turned into marriage.

The close family relationships among the Roosevelt children, and their love and respect for their parents, were significant factors in TR's development. The same close family relationships blossomed among TR's children after he became a father.

A Civil War at Home

There was a bit of strife between his parents over the Civil War. For the most part, though, family life in TR's early years was harmonious—especially after the war ended.

Theodore Sr. was a lifelong New Yorker and a Union supporter. Like her future husband, Martha was a native of the North, at least technically. She was born in Hartford, Connecticut, on July 8, 1835, but she and her mother moved to Savannah, Georgia, when Mittie was only a few months old.

FACT

Mittie's mother was visiting a stepson in Hartford and taking a respite from the stifling heat of their Savannah home when Mittie was born. They stayed in Hartford for a few months before returning to Georgia. Ironically, Bamie was buried in Farmington, Connecticut, just a few miles away from Hartford.

Mittie's family members, the Bullochs, were at heart "dyed-in-the-wool" Southerners. As a result, Thee's and Martha's political allegiances became an issue when the Civil War began in April 1861.

Theodore Sr. worked for the Union, although he never served on active duty in the military. Rather, he paid a replacement to serve in his stead, which was legal at the time. That was one of the few aspects of Thee's life that he regretted.

ESSENTIAL

TR learned early history and political science lessons from James Bulloch, who moved to England after the Civil War and became an ardent Tory (conservative). Bulloch could not abide the liberal statesman William E. Gladstone. TR sometimes defended Gladstone, much to Bulloch's dismay. TR was trying to understand both sides of an argument, which became the norm for him.

In all fairness, Theodore Sr. may have avoided active military service in an effort to keep peace in the family. Instead, he served as an allotment commissioner for New York, tried to persuade soldiers to send part of their wages to their families, and traveled to Washington, D.C., to visit President Lincoln and lobby Congress for programs to support the Union troops in the field and their families.

Martha placed her loyalties with the Confederate States of America out of concern for her brothers, James Bulloch, a Confederate agent in England, and Irvine Bulloch, an officer with the Confederate Navy. Irvine was the youngest officer aboard the vaunted commerce raider CSS *Alabama*, which succumbed to the U.S. Navy sloop-of-war *Kearsarge* in an historic battle off Cherbourg, France, on June 19, 1864. He was credited with firing the last gun aboard *Alabama* just before it sank.

Both brothers survived the war, as well as the Roosevelt family.

Early Health Problems

Thee and Mittie must have wondered after the birth of their second child if they would ever have any healthy children. Anna contended with her spinal problem. Teedie developed asthma and other ailments as a child. As a result, he often slept in a chair or sitting up in bed.

Theodore Roosevelt, about four years old

TR's breathing problems grew so severe at times during the night that his father would take him for horse rides in an attempt to open his airways. The relief was temporary, but TR did not let his persistent ailments get him down. He may have been weak physically, but he did not let that get in the way of learning.

At times, the family left New York City just to find places where TR could breathe. Even that did not always help. Corinne remembered times when he suffered tremendously, even in summer weather. But, she observed, his asthma attacks were never as bad in the summer as they were in the winter.

To compound his problems, TR was nearsighted. He joked that the only things he could study while learning about nature "were those I ran against or stumbled over." His eyesight never improved. Later in life, he lost the sight in one eye in a boxing match. In one sparring session, his partner hit him so hard below the left eye that he lost sight in it. He kept the blindness a secret and went about his business despite the impairment. He did not reveal it to anyone for a long while afterward.

Developing an Interest in Natural History

TR was an inquisitive child. Since he was ill and indoors so often, he had to find ways to occupy his time. One activity was to study nature. He developed an interest in natural history that he never lost, whether it was through books or field experiments.

Studying birds and animals and their role in nature provided a mental getaway from the rigors of whatever avenue he was pursuing at various stages of his life. He shared the knowledge he gained with the rest of the world, and provided the results of his scientific research to museums and educational institutions.

In a way, TR's bad health was beneficial. It contributed to his early interest in natural history. Because he was limited at times to nontaxing physical activities, he developed a fondness for the subject—starting with a dead seal.

FACT

One of the first books TR read intensively was David Livingstone's *Missionary Travels and Researches in South Africa*. Livingstone's discussions of ants fascinated him. TR kept pestering everybody in the family to answer his questions about ants. Finally, Bamie had to do some research and answer his questions to give the family some peace.

The Seal of Approval

One morning, while on an errand, TR saw a dead seal at a market. He started asking questions about where it came from and how it died.

If there was one thing TR knew how to do, it was ask questions. He was a naturally curious boy. Somehow, he connected the dead seal to the adventure novels of the Irish-born writer Mayne Reid, and the seal became an obsession with TR.

TR visited the dead seal often. He measured it frequently, took notes regarding its carcass, and continued to ask questions about the animal. One day, the seal was gone, but TR found and kept the head. It ended up in what he called the Roosevelt Natural History Museum.

TR's parents encouraged his natural history studies. A family chambermaid did not. He and two of his cousins established their natural history museum in his room, which did not get the chambermaid's seal of approval. They had to move it and other specimens they had gathered to a new location in an isolated part of the house.

Hooked on Natural History

From that point on, TR was hooked on natural history and planned to make it his life's work, with his father's help. Thee gave TR permission to take lessons in taxidermy when he was thirteen years old. His teacher, John G. Bell, had accompanied famed naturalist James Audubon on an expedition to the western section of the country. Even though Bell did not know much about science, he taught TR how to stuff and mount animals. That skill came in handy in TR's later years as he expanded his big-game hunting horizons.

That same summer he expanded his collection of books on mammals and birds and read them thoroughly. That led him to collecting specimens of the critters mentioned in the books, which almost led to disaster due to his poor eyesight.

Hunting Guns and Eyeglasses

TR had an old hunting gun, which he described as a "breech-loading, pin-fire double-barrel, of French manufacture." The Roosevelts were living at Dobbs Ferry, New York, at the time, a few miles up the Hudson River from New York City. Rural Dobbs Ferry was an ideal hunting ground for him.

His gun was an excellent piece for "a clumsy and often absent-minded boy." The cartridges tended to stick at times when he tried to fire the gun, which led to misfires. As a result, he said, "[I] tattooed myself with partially unburned grains of powder more than once."

Finally, his parents stepped in to help him. That fall, he received his first pair of eyeglasses. His corrected eyesight allowed him to read more, shoot better, collect more specimens, and expand his knowledge of natural history.

Thee recognized early that TR was an avid learner. He watched with pride as his first-born son practically taught himself the basics of taxidermy and built his own wildlife museum. TR caught and killed animals, studied and stuffed them, and displayed them in his personal collection.

Writing about Insects

Not only did TR prepare specimens for posterity, but he recorded rigorous notes. One of his first "published" works was a paper titled "The Natural History of Insects," which he wrote when he was only nine years old.

ESSENTIAL

TR never lost his love for animals, a love that his children inherited. In 1902, when he was in the White House, his family menagerie included "a puppy of the most orthodox puppy type," a terrier, a Chesapeake Bay dog, a macaw, a piebald rat, a flying squirrel, two kangaroo rats, and a pony. TR was as much a zookeeper as he was the president at the time.

Of course, Thee understood that TR's interest in natural history was laudable and beneficial, but it alone could not serve as the foundation for a well-rounded education. The young man needed to study math, history, geography, foreign languages, and other subjects, which were best left to professional teachers. That was a dilemma for Thee.

Thee's Misgivings

He did not believe that TR was prepared from either a health or a physical standpoint for a regular school. The next best alternative, in his opinion, was homeschooling. Thus, Thee assumed the dual role of parent and school superintendent. That was both a benefit and a drawback for TR.

Thee employed several tutors, including TR's maternal aunt, Annie Bulloch, and a French governess.

For a few months, the youngster attended a school run by Professor John McMullen, Thee's former tutor. TR acquired his early education mostly through homeschooling—which put him automatically at or near the head of his class.

Portrait of Theodore Roosevelt Sr.

Portrait of Martha Bulloch

Mittie and Annie related stories from their own childhoods to entertain and educate the Roosevelt children. They recounted their lives on the Georgia plantations, related tales of hunting fox, deer, wildcats, and other animals, and spun stories of their long-tailed driving horses, Boone and Crockett. When TR grew older, he founded a hunting club named after those two horses.

More to Education than Classroom Training

Thee could provide the subject background for a classical education and moral training. But he could only go so far in providing the social skills that complemented the coursework. Granted, TR had friends and a family network who helped him develop socially. But most children of his age attended private schools where they received well-rounded educations, developed complementary social skills, and participated in competitive physical activities.

In those respects, TR's homeschooling was a detriment in his early years. Even he recognized, albeit much later, that he was not the most mature young man in New York City for the first few years of his life.

His homeschooling did provide some benefits that were above average. Whereas some students had to study geography through books, TR got to

9

study it up close and personal. The family traveled through Europe twice, in 1869 and 1870, and through the Middle East in 1872–1873. That beat reading books as far as TR and his siblings were concerned.

Moral and Religious Training

Thee did not neglect his oldest son's moral and religious training. Since he was a firm believer in religion and morality, he made sure to include liberal doses of both in his children's training.

FACT

The Roosevelt children said prayers with their father every morning on a sofa. They made a game out of it. The children called the space between Thee and the arm of the sofa the "cubby-hole." Whichever sibling occupied it on any given morning was the favorite child—on that day at least. The others were "outsiders"—until the next morning.

As part of the regimen, Thee took TR on tours of the city so he could gain some knowledge of New Yorkers' living conditions and gain a feel for the plight of the people who were unfortunate enough not to be Roosevelts. He also inculcated religious lessons into the young boy.

Part of TR's assignments involved memorizing stories from the Bible. Thee believed in literally practicing what he preached, and he instilled that lesson into TR. He demanded that TR stay active in the religious arena—and in all other aspects of life.

TR never forgot his early religious training. He switched denominations at different stages of his life, but he thanked God regardless of which church he sat in. He had a lot for which to be thankful.

Building the Body

The word "inaction" was not in Thee's lexicon. He hammered into his children the idea that laziness was a bad habit that he would not tolerate. He pushed physical activity as a remedy for laziness, especially for TR.

Theodore Roosevelt at Harvard Boat House, circa 1877

Thee encouraged the youngster to exercise regularly and take boxing lessons to build himself up physically. He built an in-house gymnasium for TR where he could work out. The activity paid off.

The changes in his physique became more noticeable as he grew older. By the time TR entered Harvard, he was a much stronger and healthier-looking person than he had been a few years earlier. His father's investment in what he called the "strenuous life" had paid off.

"Muscular Christianity"

Although Thee encouraged his son's interest in science, he taught him the values of Muscular Christianity by taking him on his missionary rounds. He insisted that TR memorize Bible stories and taught him the principles of patriotism and manly valor. He chastised laziness, demanding constant action.

QUOTE

The term "Muscular Christianity" appears occasionally throughout literature, often with no explanation. A deranged preacher in Robert B. Parker's Western novel, *Brimstone*, set in the 1880s, told a marshal advising him of trouble, "An armed and muscular Christianity cannot be defeated." The author did not explain that it was an actual movement that affected TR's childhood.

By the time TR was ready to leave his New York home and enter Harvard, he had matured mentally, spiritually, morally, and physically—although he was still not as robust as he needed to be to survive on his own. He continued his development process at Cambridge.

1-1 Which character in a major novel and movie was allegedly based on TR's mother?

A. The Wicked Witch of the West
B. Scarlett O'Hara
C. Jane Eyre
D. Dolly Madison

1-2 Fraulein Anna, who tutored the Roosevelt children in foreign languages while they were in Dresden, helped them with two languages. One was French; the other was:

A. Chinese
B. Hungarian
C. Russian
D. German

1-3 What was the explorer David Livingstone's nationality?

A. Scottish
B. Norwegian
C. Paraguayan
D. English

1-4 David Livingstone was presumably lost on an African expedition in 1864. A search party led by Henry Stanley found him, which resulted in a famous question/quotation. It was:

A. "Dr. Livingstone, wherefore art thou?"
B. "I regret that I have but one life to give for my country."
C. "Dr. Livingstone, I presume?"
D. "How many fingers am I holding up?"

1-5 "Dime novels" in the 1880s were so named because:

A. the best known author of such novels was Neil Dime.
B. anyone needing a break while reading one could "stop on a dime."
C. they cost ten cents originally.
D. they became popular after the release of H. G. Wells's novella *The Dime Machine*.

1-6 TR's parents encouraged him to read novels when he was a child.

A. True
B. False

ANSWERS

1-1. B: Scarlett O'Hara was the female protagonist in Margaret Mitchell's novel Gone with the Wind.
1-2. D
1-3. A
1-4. C: Stanley found Livingstone alive and well on November 10, 1871, after looking for him for eight months.
1-5. C: After a while, the label "dime novel" encompassed a variety of publications.
1-6. False: Even though they preferred that he read books of an educational nature, he managed to read some books that might have been considered "dime novels."

CHAPTER 2

From Home to Harvard

"All this individual morality I was taught by the books I read at home and the books I studied at Harvard. But there was almost no teaching of the need for collective action, and of the fact that in addition to, not as a substitute for, individual responsibility, there is a collective responsibility."

The transition from home to Harvard was difficult for TR. He was used to the informal homeschool environment at the family home and to his limited circle of friends. TR found that Harvard was an unforgiving place for him at first. He adapted, but slowly. Once he learned that there was more to college than studying, he began to develop his mind, body, and a wider circle of friends. Eventually, he graduated with high honors, a healthy attitude, a widely expanded store of knowledge—and a soon-to-be wife.

Entering Harvard

In his early teens TR was not prepared to enter Harvard. He needed a considerable amount of preparatory schooling before he could begin his studies there. TR recognized the value of a college education, especially if he wanted to accomplish everything he had in mind. For him, that meant an opportunity to pursue his studies in natural history. His stay at Harvard sidetracked him from achieving that dream.

QUOTE

TR believed firmly in a college education. He had a quaint way of saying that it opened up a door or two for anybody, whether for good or for bad. TR advised, "A man who has never gone to school may steal from a freight car, but if he has a university education, he may steal from the whole railroad."

TR possessed a lot of knowledge, much of which he had learned from practical experience. That alone was not going to get him into Harvard. He realized that. He explained, "I could not go to school because I knew so much less than most boys of my age in some subjects and so much more in others."

He was well versed in science, history, geography, German, and French. He needed to strengthen other liberal arts subjects. So he worked with a tutor his father hired to start his preparation for an Ivy League education.

After the family returned from a tour of Europe in the winter of 1872–1873, Thee employed Arthur Cutler, a recent Harvard graduate, to work exclusively with TR. Cutler developed a program for his student, designed to strengthen the academic areas in which he was most lacking, such as mathematics and classical languages, specifically Latin and Greek.

A Demanding Taskmaster

The program Cutler designed was meant to take three years to complete. TR was equal to the challenge. He worked six to eight hours a day and finished the curriculum in two years. By that time he had polished his mathematics, Greek, and Latin skills to the point where he did well enough on the Harvard entrance exams to gain admittance.

A look back at his entrance exams shows that even then TR demonstrated a predilection for choosing subjects that interested him. He focused on subjects like mathematics and placed very little emphasis on the classics. His strategy worked. He was one of the few freshmen in his class at Harvard to take advanced mathematics courses.

Cutler may have been TR's superior in academic skills, but not in physical strength. In 1879, on a hiking trip in Maine, they climbed Mt. Katahdin with a guide, Bill Sewall. Normally, the climb up the 5,268-foot mountain took days. Even though TR was carrying a 45-pound pack, he made it to the top. Cutler did not.

Cutler did wonders preparing TR for a big step in his life.

Muscular Christianity and Masculinity

TR may have been ready for Harvard, but there was some question as to whether Harvard was ready for him. He arrived at the college with an air of smugness and condescension that his fellow students found difficult to tolerate. Worse, he found it difficult to break his ties with Thee, which complicated his life on campus at first.

Thee espoused some eccentric ideas that redounded badly on his family at times. One of them was his belief in Muscular Christianity as it related to masculinity—and Harvard.

The Roosevelts were devout Christians. TR never lost his belief in God or Christianity, and his religious fervor pushed away some of his classmates when he arrived on campus. He may have agreed with Thee when it came to religious beliefs, but father and son differed when it came to sexism.

Men and Morals

Thee believed that men were the stronger and more moralistic gender. TR always saw women and children as strong people who could benefit from the support of males. Thee carried his belief about male superiority over into the religious realm. His connection between the two worlds led to problems for TR.

In Thee's mind, men were becoming emasculated by the mid-nineteenth century—at least in New York City. He theorized that one way to restore their disappearing zest for life and morality was to build up their bodies, which he thought would be good for TR. Thus, he was a strong proponent of Muscular Christianity. After all, Muscular Christianity advocates averred, Jesus Christ was morally pure and physically fit. His advocates should follow suit. That philosophy fit well into Thee's "private trainer" program for TR.

FACT

The Young Men Christians Association (YMCA, or simply the "Y") is not much older than TR. It was established in England in 1844 to provide young men with an alternative to pubs and brothels. The first YMCA in the United States opened in Boston on December 29, 1851, which was ideal for the students at Harvard College.

Thee began pushing TR almost from birth to strengthen his body through constant physical activity. He thought that what was good for TR was good for the rest of his children, the young people of New York City, and beyond. Thee used his philanthropic bent to promote Muscular Christianity and build a better, more masculine world.

Some of TR's fellow students at Harvard believed that he pushed the Muscular Christianity concept too far. They viewed his focus on the "strenuous life" as a bit bizarre, even though some of them marveled at his physical prowess. Stories of his athletic endeavors, energy, and enthusiasm for just about everything abounded.

Pushing the Physical Bar

TR developed a passion for boxing at Harvard. He engaged in bouts with classmates both in the ring and outside. Frederic Almy, the secretary of TR's class of 1880, related an event that occurred during the controversial 1876 presidential campaign between Republican Rutherford B. Hayes and Democrat Samuel J. Tilden.

As Almy recalled, there was a torchlight parade in progress when a person on the sidewalk near TR made a derogatory comment. TR reacted violently and rashly.

Almy said that he "reached out and laid the mucker flat." That was uncharacteristic of TR for two reasons: He was not prone to solve arguments through physical means, and he had not developed a great fondness for politics at that point.

Another classmate, Richard Welling, related endurance contests they took part in.

QUESTION

What was the outcome of the 1876 presidential election?
The presidential race in 1876 was marred by controversy. Tilden won the popular vote and had a lead in the electoral count, 184 to 165, with twenty disputed votes uncounted. After a protracted legal and political battle, the disputed votes were awarded to Hayes. Incidentally, Hayes was the first president to graduate from law school (Harvard Law School, 1845).

Good Skates, but Not Good Skaters

Welling, like TR, was a physical training devotee. One extremely cold afternoon the two young men went skating on a local pond. Neither one was particularly adept at skating. Under ordinary circumstances they would have hung up their skates, gone inside, and warmed up. But neither would admit that they were close to suffering frostbite.

QUOTE

Philip M. Boffey, who wrote an article about TR's life at Harvard, cautioned, "So many legends have grown up around Theodore Roosevelt that it is hard to sift fact from fiction. A host of friends, classmates, and distant admirers have felt obliged to produce anecdotes about this 'locomotive in human pants,' thus swelling the collection of stories over the years."

TR kept asking Welling, "Isn't this perfectly bully?" Welling did not think so, but he would not say anything to destroy TR's feigned enthusiasm. He just agreed. The test of wills continued. Finally, well into their third hour of skating—at least as Welling reported—TR suggested they stop. It was one of the rare times that TR found himself on thin ice and gave up—if he did.

A Loud Attention-Grabber

Another criticism of TR at Harvard centered on his penchant for grabbing attention. He occasionally broke the unwritten rules of decorum that suggested students should be quiet when passing each other in the halls or on the grounds. And he was always running when everyone else was walking.

Perhaps some of his classmates might have thought he was trying to gain attention. But, that was simply the way TR did everything: full speed ahead, which helped him earn respect from his classmates.

TR was not a big man when he entered college. He was about five feet nine inches tall and weighed 135 pounds. To him, size did not matter. What he lacked in size he made up for in stamina and courage. TR used those assets to gain the respect of his classmates.

He did not play on any intercollegiate teams, but he did participate in sports. One of his favorite activities was boxing. He would take on all comers in sparring matches or tournaments. TR did not win any championships, but he won some of his classmates over to his side.

In March 1879, TR won a match in a lightweight boxing tournament at Harvard. As it ended, the referee called "Time." Just as TR dropped his hands, his opponent punched him hard in the face. The crowd protested and screamed, "Foul." TR allegedly told them to quiet down. "He did not hear," TR explained. That indicated his sense of fair play.

Tragedy Strikes

Halfway through TR's stay at Harvard, a major tragedy occurred. On February 9, 1878, his father died of stomach cancer. That was a bitter blow for the young man, who had enjoyed a close relationship with Theodore Sr. for almost twenty years. TR made no bones about his admiration for his father. He said, "I never knew anyone who got greater joy out of living than did my father, or anyone who more whole-heartedly performed every duty; and no one whom I have ever met approached his combination of enjoyment of life and performance of duty."

Thee had opened TR's eyes to the fact that not everybody lived as well as the Roosevelts did. Thee made sure that his family visited people in all strata of society. On Thanksgiving or Christmas Day he sometimes took TR and his siblings to dinner at places like the Newsboys' Lodging House or Miss Slattery's Night School for Little Italians, both of which he had a hand in establishing.

The Newsboys' Lodging House was one of Thee's pet projects. He was also active in getting orphaned and homeless children off the streets and out of the city. He arranged as often as possible to get them placed on farms in the West.

FACT

Thee helped form the Children's Aid Society in New York City, which built institutions for homeless children and originated "orphan trains" to transport them to the western part of the United States. For a while, Thee visited the Newsboys' Lodging House every Sunday night and sponsored dinners there. TR picked up temporarily where he left off after he graduated from college in 1880.

Thee's death affected TR deeply, but he continued his studies. Despite the fact he claimed that he did not learn much of value at Harvard, he did well academically there.

A True Liberal Arts Education

TR did occasionally enter classrooms. They were not his favorite places on campus, though. He admitted that he did not have much interest in the academic side of the school, which was the primary reason he enrolled at Harvard.

TR's avowed purpose in attending Harvard was to study natural history. Once he arrived on campus, he discovered that the curriculum was not geared toward the sciences. It was, after all, a liberal arts college. He compensated through physical activities and a perfunctory interest in the courses that were available.

One of his favorite professors was A. S. Hill, who taught English. TR developed a fondness for Elizabethan poetry, much to the amusement of some of his classmates.

History was also a favorite subject of his. It stimulated his interest in politics, as one of the topics on which he concentrated was the Federalist Papers. Later in his political career, he often used them as a starting point for solving problems.

Books over Studies

One of TR's major accomplishments during his time at Harvard was his authorship of *The Naval War of 1812*, although TR belittled it later. He completed it years later when he was in law school.

He noted in his self-deprecating fashion, "Those chapters were so dry that they would make a dictionary seem light reading by comparison." Readers did not agree with his assessment after the book was published.

TR commented that the chapters he wrote represented "purpose and serious interest on my part, not the perfunctory effort to do well enough to get a certain mark." He revealed, "Corrections of them by a skilled older man would have impressed me and have commanded my respectful attention."

There is no telling what direction his education would have taken if that had happened. History turns on such little events.

Our Young Folks

Although TR was an avid reader, textbooks were not his favorite source of knowledge. He said he learned more from his favorite magazine, *Our Young Folks*, than he did from any textbook he ever read.

TR claimed that everything in the magazine "instilled the individual virtues, and the necessity of character as the chief factor in any man's success—a teaching in which I now believe as sincerely as ever." The magazine taught him the "right stuff," which shaped his life.

QUOTE

TR believed "All the laws that the wit of man can devise will never make a man a worthy citizen unless he has within himself the right stuff, unless he has self-reliance, energy, courage, the power of insisting on his own rights and the sympathy that makes him regardful of the rights of others."

TR did not discount completely the value of the textbooks he used at Harvard. He acknowledged that he learned something from them, but they were merely supplementary to the other books he had read at home prior to entering college. It was from all those books combined that he learned the individual morality that he applied in every phase of his life.

A Photographic Memory

TR may not have had a high opinion of textbooks or the lessons that complemented them, but he read them. They contained new thoughts and ideas that intrigued him. That explained why he read as many books as he did throughout his life and what facilitated the process.

He possessed two valuable assets to help him satisfy his reading habit: a photographic memory and the ability to speed-read.

FACT

It was amazing to some people how much and how fast TR could read and retain. He could read a page while other people were reading a sentence or repeat stories from a newspaper he had just put down as if he were still reading it.

TR could easily read two or three books a day. When TR traveled, he always took along a sufficient number of books to educate and amuse himself with. He also used reading as an escape—and he read some esoteric material at times.

A classic example of his retreat into books occurred in the hours leading up to TR's nomination as vice president at the 1900 Republican Convention.

He was sitting quietly in another room, impervious to all the excitement. He was relaxing by reading *Thucydides*. His companion at the time, Albert Shaw, said he "was not reading the book as much as he was living it."

TR's ability to read quickly and absorb information made him one of the most intellectually talented presidents in U.S. history. Some of his predecessors may have been more versed in the classics, but TR was better equipped to digest facts on issues that mattered to statesmen, such as military history and affairs, economics, and business statistics. His experience at Harvard helped him develop his reading, concentration, and retention skills.

TR's Attention Span

Charles William Eliot, the president of Harvard when TR was in attendance, recalled his remarkable power of concentration. Although TR confessed that he rarely saw Eliot, the president knew about him.

TR lamented the lack of science courses at Harvard. Ironically, Eliot is remembered for expanding the range of courses during his tenure and offering undergraduates unlimited choices in selecting from the list. He wanted them to discover their "natural bents" and pursue them into specialized studies.

Eliot stated that "the intellectual power which most attracted the attention of his [TR's] companions and teachers was an extraordinary capacity for concentrating every faculty on the work at hand, whether it were reading, writing, listening, or boxing."

He added that TR "would read by himself in a room half-filled with noisy students without having his attention distracted even for an instant; indeed, he would make no answer to questions addressed directly to him, and did not seem to hear them." That was a talent that TR never lost.

There Is More to College than Studying

TR became a "joiner" at Harvard. When he wasn't boxing, engaging in endurance contests, or studying, he was participating in a club activity of some sort. He was connected with *The Advocate*, Harvard's undergraduate journal of fiction, poetry, art, and criticism, and the O. K. Society, a group of the publication's editors, which included him.

At various times he was a member and vice president of the Natural History Society, the Art Club, the Finance Club, the Glee Club, the Harvard Rifle Corps, and the Harvard Athletic Association.

His position as editor reflected TR's enthusiasm and penchant for challenging authorities. In 1916, on the fiftieth anniversary of the publication's founding, Albert Bushnell Hart, then head of the government department at Harvard and a classmate of TR's, talked about the newspaper in 1880. He noted that those were turbulent days.

FACT

TR was by far the most honored member of the Harvard Class of 1880 when it came to advanced degrees, honorary degrees, and society memberships. Only one classmate came close: Albert Bushnell Hart. His resume included a PhD in history, an LLD, honorary degrees from Tufts (1905) and Western Reserve (1907), and a LittD. He became a professor of history and a member of the Massachusetts Historical Society.

Hart hastened to add that it was not because TR was editor. Rather, he said, "The entire board was a fighting organization, with definite ideas of needed reforms and a positive manner in urging them."

Social Climber

TR also joined the Hasty Pudding Club; the oldest collegiate social club in the United States; the "Dickey," the nickname for the Institute of 1770, the oldest club at Harvard; and the prestigious Porcellian Club (The "Pork"). The Porcellian, a men's-only group, was the last club a student could join prior to graduation. For that reason, it was called a "final club."

Membership in such clubs, particularly the "Dickey," drew charges of snobbery from some of TR's classmates. "Dickey" members often ate off campus in small groups, away from school activities. TR did the same thing. He was not particularly concerned at that point about what other students thought of him or his eating habits. He was simply doing the right things to establish his place in the Harvard caste system and his college legacy.

Some of the clubs to which he belonged were offshoots of his interests, e.g., the Natural History Club, the Harvard Rifle Corps, and the athletic association. He was in the Glee Club as an associate member, which indicated that it was not one of his primary interests. He did prioritize his club activities.

A Cluttered Room

The clues to what clubs TR was mostly interested lay in the paraphernalia in his room. Among the items he had there were a rifle, a hunting kit, and trophies from his hunting expeditions. He also had live turtles and insects in the room.

QUOTE

One of TR's classmates, Mark Sullivan, remembered when "a particularly large turtle, sent by a friend from the southern seas, got out of its box one night and started toward the bathroom in search of water." TR did know how to create excitement in his college living quarters.

Even though TR belonged to many clubs, he was never overextended. He rarely attended meetings of some of them. TR needed some time to study. He was an unorthodox student, but he still did well when it came to grades—sometimes.

Graduating with Honors

Somehow, TR completed his studies in the allotted four years at Harvard and graduated Phi Beta Kappa, which recognizes and encourages scholarship, friendship, and cultural interests at the undergraduate level. That was not easy, considering that he had failed a couple of courses along the way and did not write an honors thesis.

Not surprisingly, TR's best grades were in natural history, where he averaged in the high eighties and nineties. He failed two courses, Greek and French. His grade averages for the four years were 75, 87, 82, and 78, for an overall average of 80.5. There is no telling what he could have done if he had applied himself.

There is some discrepancy about TR's overall average at Harvard. Estimates range from 80.5 to 87. Regardless, he graduated magna cum laude (with great honor) and finished in the top tenth of his 174-member class, although he was not sure if it was the tenth of the whole number who entered or of those who graduated. Either way, TR had a college degree—and an achievement to be proud of.

Theodore Roosevelt, Harvard graduate, circa 1881

TR's Most Remarkable Friend

TR developed a few friendships at Harvard. The most cherished friend, however, was a young lady named Alice Hathaway Lee, whom he met on October 18, 1878. She changed his life forever. Soon, she became his primary interest. He found himself chasing two goals at a time: his degree and a wife.

2-1 When did the first YMCA in New York City open?

A. 1748
B. 1812
C. 1852
D. 1865

2-2 U.S. President Rutherford B. Hayes's wife Lucy was nicknamed "Lemonade Lucy" because she:

A. ran a lemonade stand to earn extra money as a child.
B. refused to serve alcohol in the White House.
C. invented lemonade.
D. grew lemons in the West Wing.

2-3 Thee Roosevelt established a Newsboys' Lodging House in New York City because he:

A. was not satisfied with the delivery of his daily newspaper, so he wanted the newsboys to live closer to his house.
B. wanted a place available for newsboys who had no other place to sleep.
C. needed a place for TR to stay after he completed his paper route every day.
D. thought newsboys were all living under terrible conditions at their own homes.

2-4 Who or what was Thucydides?

A. a form of thistle found in the western Badlands
B. a bird discovered by TR on a trip to Egypt
C. a Latin word for suburban road
D. a Greek historian best known for writing *The History of the Peloponnesian War*

2-5 The Hasty Pudding Club at Harvard is named for:

A. the first meal club members ate at a meeting.
B. the need for staff members to serve food quickly at a club meeting.
C. Harold H. Hasty, the founder of the club.
D. Haste Tea, the beverage of choice at early club meetings.

2-6 Richard Saltonstall played a major role in TR's life. He:

A. beat TR for the intramural boxing championship at Harvard in 1877.
B. commanded the SS *Oyster Park* during the Spanish-American War.
C. introduced TR to Alice Hathaway Lee.
D. developed the "Saltonstall" diet that was popular in the 1890s.

ANSWERS

2-6. C

2-5. A: Hasty pudding, mentioned in the song "Yankee Doodle," is a traditional American dish made from grains or corn and cooked in milk or water.

2-4. D: He wrote The History of the Peloponnesian War, which documented the fifth-century B.C. war between Sparta and Athens.

2-3. B: Many of the newsboys in New York City in the late 1800s were homeless orphans who lived on the streets when they were not hawking newspapers.

2-2. B

2-1. C: The first YMCA in New York City opened in September 1852 at the Stuyvesant Institute on Broadway.

CHAPTER 3

Law School at Columbia

"Far better is it to dare mighty things, to win glorious triumphs, even though checkered by failure than to rank with those poor spirits who neither enjoy much nor suffer much, because they live in a gray twilight that knows not victory nor defeat."

When TR graduated from Harvard, he faced a dilemma common to his peers: what to do with the rest of his life. Even though Thee had left him a comfortable inheritance, TR did not want to live off it. He returned to New York City to study law at Columbia University. For one of the few times in his life, he started something he did not finish. What seemed to be a bad choice at first led to a promising career in politics.

Learning to Recognize Opportunity

Perhaps the most glossed over period of TR's life is his brief stop at Columbia Law School. He accomplished some wonderful things in the short time he was there, but they were not connected to his presence in any classrooms. Yet the lessons he learned at Columbia contributed to his success as he became more accomplished later in life.

TR's choice of law school was based more on a need to find a profession than on a passion. He admitted freely that he did not have to go to law school, or any other type of school, after completing his studies at Harvard.

QUOTE

Money was not an issue for TR. As he put it, "I had enough to get bread. What I had to do, if I wanted butter and jam, was to provide the butter and jam, but to count their cost as compared with other things. In other words, I made up my mind that, while I must earn money, I could afford to make earning money the secondary instead of the primary object of my career."

The money Thee had left TR provided him with a cushion to fall back on. He could have idled away his time in leisurely pursuits if that had been his preference. But TR was a Roosevelt. That was not what Roosevelts did.

The family tradition was to meet social responsibilities. TR honored that charge. But his decision to pursue a profession was not easy. He looked at the future, as well as the present, when deciding what to do. That helped steer him toward Columbia Law School, which turned out to be a secondary pursuit.

A career in law would satisfy his desire to work in a field that allowed him to treat the work as more important than the money he earned performing it. So he entered Columbia Law School in 1880, filled with enthusiasm and idealism. Both faded quickly.

Avoiding the Law

Once TR began his studies at Columbia, he realized his heart was not in the program. The most significant thing he learned there was that the law was too often on the wrong side of the business and political spectrums, at least as far as his youthful idealism perceived it. That was an eye-opener for TR, and the realization changed his life goals—and ultimately many other people's lives.

QUOTE

TR noted, "When I left Harvard, I took up the study of law. If I had been sufficiently fortunate to come under Professor [James Bradley] Thayer, of the Harvard Law School, it may well be that I would have realized that the lawyer can do a great work for justice and against legalism." He labeled Thayer "the greatest Professor of Law Harvard ever had."

The young, idealistic TR believed that the *caveat emptor* side of both the law and business seemed repellent. It did not, in his view, make for social fair dealing. The words "fair deal" had been—and continued to be—important to TR throughout his life.

In his view, the law ruling transactions between sellers and consumers should have struck a balance between the two: both should have profited mutually. But what he heard from professors and what he read in law books weighted the balance in favor of the sellers, which to him was an injustice. That realization dampened his interest in becoming a lawyer.

TR did not want to engage in a curriculum or a profession that ran contrary to his personal beliefs. He transferred his energy from studying law to completing what was to become his first published book, *The Naval War of 1812*, and working on behalf of the consumers he believed were getting a raw deal instead of a fair deal.

At Columbia, TR became more interested in politics than the study of the law. *The Naval War of 1812* was published in 1882, the year he should have received his JD degree. He decided the law degree could wait. TR dropped out of law school to work for justice as it related to his vision of the law.

Becoming a Dropout

TR left Columbia in 1881. He did not walk away without a plan or because he had learned enough about the law in one year to make him an expert. TR had reached a point at which he wanted to engage in politics. TR may not have graduated from Columbia Law School with his class, but the *New York Times* reported he "studied law in the office of his uncle in this city, and was admitted to the bar." It did not always require completion of formal studies to attain a goal.

Entering politics was not a new idea for TR. He had begun developing an interest in politics while he was at Harvard. By 1881, TR felt that the time was right to transfer his desire into action. Some of the things he learned while at Columbia, which had nothing to do with the study of law, pushed him in that direction.

In TR's opinion, the job of "doing good" for others placed a lot of pressure on politicians who, at some point, would be forced to step aside at least temporarily and pursue another line of work. That belief was one of the reasons he entered Columbia in the first place.

TR bravely entered politics without another occupation to fall back on. Eventually, the pressure he talked about became a self-fulfilling prophecy. Before that happened, he threw himself into his first political job: New York state assemblyman.

Republican by Default

TR learned that the only political party open to him was the Republicans, due to two factors: He was considered an aristocrat and the Democrats were too rough for a young man of his upbringing. Consequently, he started attending meetings of the Twenty-First District Republican Association. He recalled, "At that day, a young man of my bringing up and convictions could only join the Republican party, and join it accordingly I did." He may have been labeled a Republican, but he manifested democratic tendencies throughout his lifetime.

His friends looked at his dabbling in politics with disdain. Powerful businessmen and lawyers with whom he was acquainted scoffed at him because they considered politics beneath their dignity. Their role was to let rougher men do the grunt work while they used their influence to grease the wheels of government to get things done.

TR never forgot their cavalier attitude toward politicians and the general public in general, for whom he worked so diligently. TR may not have known much about the ins and outs of politics in 1881, but he did know how to ingratiate himself with the right people. He sensed that if he became close to the leaders at the lower levels of the party, they would think of him when the right opportunity came along. His strategy worked.

The more TR became embroiled in the machinations of politics, the more law school became a distant memory. Politics pushed the practice of law to the back of TR's career path.

Turn Off the Machine

The lessons TR learned in his first foray into politics served him in good stead throughout his government career and justified his decision to leave law school. One of the first things he learned was that a politician could buck a machine and still come out ahead. He proved that when he became embroiled in an internal power struggle between his good friend and party stalwart Joe Murray and the Republican boss at the time, Jake Hess.

ESSENTIAL

> Murray was working his way up through the party structure at the time, and he "adopted" TR as his protégé. Hess also had a soft spot for TR. At the time, one of the few things Hess and Murray had in common was their recognition that the young Roosevelt was an up-and-coming star in the Republican Party. TR got caught in the power struggle between Hess and Murray, and played the game to perfection.

The issue that won Hess and Murray over to TR's side was trivial. It concerned a nonpartisan approach to street cleaning. TR backed the method in defiance of the "machine." He and the faction that was against the street cleaning practice, led by Hess and Murray, forced a vote on the idea. They all knew that TR did not have a chance of winning the vote.

As expected, his side drew about 6 votes of the 300 to 400 cast. TR recalled that he accepted the results in a good-humored fashion. But they did not change his attitude about bucking the machine to fight for something in which he believed. Murray in particular took note of that.

The First Step in TR's Political Career

As the 1881 elections approached, the Republicans were looking for a candidate for assemblyman from their district. Murray saw an opportunity for TR to run for office. Hess did not agree with Murray's proposal to nominate TR, who he believed was too young and inexperienced. Murray prevailed.

FACT

TR was surprised to get the nomination for assemblyman. He recalled, "I had at that time neither the reputation nor the ability to have won the nomination for myself, and indeed never would have thought of trying for it." If Murray had not nominated him, the course of history might have been altered.

Hess joined Murray in the effort to get TR elected. Once the campaign began, TR injected himself into it full bore, which was the only way he knew to accomplish something he wanted. The law degree he had sought was deferred—for 127 years.

Two Law Degrees Are Better than One

Eventually, TR received his law degree—several, in fact. Harvard granted him an honorary LLD in 1902. The University of California, Berkeley, followed suit a year later. He did not waste the trip to California.

The day after he accepted the degree, TR departed for a tour of Yosemite Park with John Muir. The two men would work together afterward on conservation issues.

The honorary degrees TR received from Harvard and Berkeley were among a handful he gathered over the years. He was not a great fan of honorary degrees. Sometimes he could not turn them down without offending his friends, which TR was always loath to do.

A Bit of Chicanery

In 1918, TR's longtime friend, Flavel S. Luther, the president of Trinity College in Hartford, Connecticut, invited TR to deliver the commencement address at the school. Luther was aware of the former president's bias against honorary degrees, but he was sure TR would not turn one down from Trinity. So he offered a two-for-one deal.

TR suggested that Flavel confer an honorary degree on his friend Russell Jordan Coles, a naturalist and sportsman from Virginia. Flavel agreed to present Coles with the requested degree at the June 1918 commencement, as long as TR would deliver an address the day before. Even though TR was not in the best of health at the time, he agreed to the deal.

Not only did Flavel award Coles with an honorary degree, but he conferred one on TR as well. Still, TR did not have a law degree, honorary or otherwise. He received one in 2008.

A Law Degree 127 Years Later

Columbia finally got around to presenting TR with a law degree—almost a century after his death. At a September 25, 2008, reception ceremony in New York City, the school presented an LLD to its former student. It also granted one to Franklin Delano Roosevelt on the same day.

FACT

TR and his distant cousin Franklin Delano Roosevelt had one thing in common: both left Columbia Law School before they completed their degrees. The school conferred JD degrees on both Roosevelts posthumously. They became official members of the classes of 1882 and 1907, respectively.

There is no telling how TR would have felt about receiving a law degree. He was never fond of receiving honors that he had not earned. He felt that a young man should set his sights on something he truly wanted and believed in, and that using law school as a stop-gap measure was a wasted opportunity. His ambivalence was apparent when his son Theodore Jr. was deliberating between entering the Army or Naval academy or pursuing a civilian profession.

TR wrote to his son in a January 21, 1904 letter:

The result would be that at twenty-five you would leave the Army or Navy without having gone through any law school or any special technical school of any kind, and would start your life work three or four years later than your schoolfellows of to-day, who go to work immediately after leaving college. Of course, under such circumstances, you might study law, for instance, during the four years after graduation; but my own feeling is that a man does good work chiefly when he is in something which he intends to make his permanent work, and in which he is deeply interested.

Those words came straight from TR's heart—and from his own experience of using law school as a time filler. He might not have agreed with the administrators at Columbia when they got around to granting a law degree.

A Few Kind Words

Columbia Law School Dean David M. Schizer had kind words to say about the Roosevelts in 2008. "We are pleased to commemorate the Presidents Roosevelts, two of the most remarkable and distinguished lawyers ever to train at Columbia Law School, and celebrate their connection to our storied history," he said. The honor came too late for TR to appreciate.

Even though TR had never completed his law studies, he had learned some valuable studies in the pursuit of his degree. He proved that not all law has to be learned from textbooks—especially as it pertains to the administration of social justice.

QUIZ

3-1 TR graduated Phi Beta Kappa from Harvard. Phi Beta Kappa is:

A. a type of hat he wore at graduation.
B. a term derived from the Greek initials of the motto "Love of learning is the guide of life."
C. the easiest award for a college student to earn.
D. restricted to Harvard University students only.

3-2 Franklin Delano Roosevelt suffered from what debilitating disease?

A. measles
B. malaria
C. polio
D. mumps

3-3 How many terms did Franklin Delano Roosevelt serve as president of the United States?

A. four
B. two
C. three
D. one

3-4 Theodore Roosevelt's son Theodore chose to attend the U.S. Military Academy in West Point, New York, based on his father's advice.

A. True
B. False

3-5 John Muir founded which well-known conservation association?

A. Audubon Society
B. Kit Carson Group
C. Sierra Club
D. YWCA

ANSWERS

3-5. C
3-4. False: Young Theodore graduated from Harvard, as did his three brothers.
3-3. A: He was serving his fourth term when he died on April 12, 1945.
3-2. C
3-1. B

CHAPTER 4

Serving in the New York State Legislature

"I put myself in the way of things happening; and they happened . . . During the three years' service in the Legislature I worked on a very simple philosophy of government. It was that personal character and initiative are the prime requisites in political and social life."

Republican Party leaders gave TR a chance to enter politics in 1881, a job for which he was untested. The three years he served as a New York state assemblyman alerted him to the corruption that ran rife in the state and taught him that fighting it could lead to political suicide. On the positive side, he learned the value of bipartisan politics. Overall, the three terms he served in Albany curbed his idealism and prepared him for his later political offices at the city, state, and federal levels.

First Run for Office

New York City Republican leaders saw something special in TR when he entered politics after graduating from Harvard. They gave him the opportunity to run for office as an assemblyman from Manhattan's Twenty-First District. (The Assembly was the lower house of the New York State Legislature.) TR had no sooner entered the race than the bosses began wondering if they had created a monster.

The young candidate got off on the wrong foot with his future constituents in the early days of his first campaign. Hess and Murray accompanied TR on his campaign stops along Sixth Avenue. They thought it would be helpful for him to visit some of the tavern owners in the area, since they wielded considerable influence. The bosses quickly wished they had started somewhere else.

ESSENTIAL

At the time TR began dabbling in politics, saloon-keepers in New York City wielded a considerable amount of political power. They had cozy relationships with politicians and police officers, and bribes changed hands among them in return for licenses, special favors, and good deals with brewers, the types of relationships TR wanted to end.

They introduced TR to saloon-keeper Valentine Young in the first tavern they entered. Mr. Young seemed a bit belligerent to TR, which he thought was strange. TR believed that as an assemblyman he would be in a position to help tavern owners. Young apparently felt that he would be telling TR what to do. That was political lesson number one for TR.

Working at Cross Purposes

Young opined that the fees for tavern licenses were too high and that he expected TR to lower them and treat the liquor business fairly. TR informed Young that he would treat the liquor business as fairly as he treated everyone else. He was, after all, a believer in a "fair deal" for everyone. And, TR announced, he thought that liquor license fees were too low, and he would try to raise them.

FACT

The idea of a "fair" or "square" deal was a cornerstone of TR's politics. He worked to ensure that all competing interests affected by his programs and policies received some benefits. He tried hard not to favor labor over and management, consumers over businesses, developers over conservationists, or vice versa.

Hess and Murray were aghast. They had not gotten beyond their first campaign stop and TR had already made an enemy. They hustled TR out of the tavern, escorted him over to Fifth Avenue, and advised him that they would campaign for him on Sixth Avenue. Their plan worked. TR won the election and moved to Albany.

The Youngest Legislator

When TR started his career as an assemblyman at age twenty-three, he was the youngest legislator in the state of New York's history. He began his first

Theodore Roosevelt in the New York Legislature

term like a whirlwind, which was a harbinger of the future. Before TR ended his three years in the Assembly, he set a record for having introduced more bills into the Assembly than anyone else.

The four bills he introduced within the first forty-eight hours of his initial legislative session demonstrated his primary interests and sincerity for reform. They focused on water purification, aldermanic election reform, finance reform for New York City, and judicial reform. He learned quickly that the number of bills introduced was not important. The true measure of a legislator's effectiveness lay in the number that passed.

Only one of TR's first four bills received any attention. The Legislature passed a modified version of the aldermanic election reform bill. The numbers accomplished one thing, though. He earned some respect from a group of similar-minded independent young

Republicans bent on reform and notice from a prominent *New York Times* legislative reporter, George Spinney, who decided that Roosevelt made good copy. Other journalists followed his lead.

QUOTE

George Spinney joined the *New York Times* staff as a legislative reporter in 1879 when it was a politically independent newspaper. In 1893, when the *Times* announced it would officially become a Democratic newspaper, an editorial writer for the *Memphis Commercial* said, "The *Times* was originally the bitterest Republican paper in the country." That was helpful for TR in 1882.

The unofficial Republican reform group elected TR its de facto leader. With their encouragement and Spinney's news coverage, the dynamic TR began his quest to produce reform. It did not take long before TR justified their faith in finding a good story.

First Attack on Corruption

TR learned about a group of high-level New York state politicians who were involved in a ring of corruption with railroad magnate Jay Gould. The politicians included the state's Attorney General and Supreme Court Judge Theodore Westbrook.

FACT

In the late 1860s, railroad developer Jay Gould named Tammany Hall boss William Tweed a director of the Erie Railroad. In return, Tweed arranged favorable legislation for him. That irritated the citizens of New York, but the state Legislature did not address the resulting corruption. Gould also had a controlling interest in the New York City elevated railroads after 1881.

He approached Republican Party leaders and asked them if they planned to address the corruption. They said they did not, and they would be happy if he did not either. Rather naively, TR vowed to do it himself.

On April 6, 1882, TR delivered a speech in the Assembly that made members of both parties cringe. He demanded that the Assembly investigate the dealings between Gould and Westbrook—and impeach the judge. The Assembly failed to act.

TR Versus Westbrook

Undaunted, Roosevelt continued to convince the Assembly that it was in its best interests to end the corruption and impeach Westbrook. Veteran legislators countered that it was in his best interests to let the matter drop.

TR alleged that Judge Westbrook's rulings in a recent railroad scandal had cost legitimate investors so much money that his decisions threatened their livelihoods. He accused the judge of being a co-conspirator. The Legislature was outraged. Newspapers picked up the story and made the legislators so uncomfortable that they were almost forced to investigate Westbrook.

TR would not back down. Day after day he spoke in the chamber about the need for an investigation. Eventually, the Legislature, spurred by the growing number of newspapers carrying stories about TR's persistence and the resulting negative publicity, voted 104 to 6 to begin an investigation.

The investigation came to nothing. There were no charges brought against Judge Westbrook. The committee that conducted the investigation delivered its findings to the Legislature, which voted 77 to 35 against impeachment.

The results disappointed TR and the citizens of New York state, but they magnified his reputation as a brash young legislator seeking reform in their best interest. He did not let up in his reform efforts.

Although TR did not accomplish all he set out to do in his first year in the Assembly, he did earn a reputation as a young politician who would not back down from anyone—including his own party leaders—in his quest for reform. Even though he had been sent to Albany to represent his district in Manhattan, he was there to fight for all New Yorkers.

From Legislator to Leader

The voters of his district were supportive of TR after his first year's performance. They re-elected him in 1882, expecting more of the same from him. He did not disappoint them.

TR began his second year in a stronger power position in the Assembly. The Republicans put forth his name for the Assembly speakership. Since the Democrats held a majority, he became the minority leader. Regardless of his position in the Assembly, he continued to pursue reform, which he knew many of his colleagues opposed.

QUOTE

In his January 26, 1883, speech at Buffalo, New York, "The Duties of American Citizenship," TR said, "Nothing is more effective in thwarting the purposes of the spoilsmen than the civil service reform. To be sure, practical politicians sneer at it." He considered himself practical, but he never sneered at reform, civil or otherwise.

TR had to fight his battles against corruption on two fronts. He estimated that at least one-third of the members of the Legislature were corrupt. As a result, he had to fight corruption from within the Legislature and among the outsiders who were trying to influence representatives to pass bills in their best interests. TR fought hard, along with a phalanx of friends from both parties, against both groups.

TR kept up the pressure against corruption on all fronts, while introducing bill after bill to establish a park in New York City, lower taxes for New Yorkers and raise them on certain businesses, strengthen laws governing child abuse, and change machine politics. Not all passed, and he did not always succeed in his reform attempts, but he never stopped trying.

The three years TR spent in the Legislature provided him with some valuable lessons about morality, chicanery, constitutionality, and political principles in general. During that time he grasped the connection between business and politics, which he later made a habit of severing. The lessons played a subsequent role in how he conducted his affairs in his politically appointed and elected positions.

Working for Social Justice

Roosevelt was re-elected as state assemblyman by a two-to-one margin in the 1882 elections and nominated on January 1, 1883, to stand as the

Republican candidate for Assembly speaker. Although he lost to the nominee of the majority Democrats, Roosevelt served as minority leader.

By the beginning of his second term, TR was feeling more comfortable in the Assembly. Quickly, he introduced a civil service reform bill to enhance job seekers' chances for acquiring government jobs. The legislation was modeled on a similar bill, the Pendleton Civil Service Reform Act, passed by the United States Congress in January 1883.

FACT

The Pendleton Act addressed political patronage at the federal level. It mandated that government jobs had to be awarded on the basis of merit, introduced competitive exams for civil service jobs, and made it illegal to fire or demote government employees for political reasons. The law also created the United States Civil Service Commission to enforce the mandates.

One of TR's strongest allies in enacting his proposed legislation was the New York state governor, Grover Cleveland. The two men formed an unholy and unpopular alliance early in Cleveland's tenure, even though TR was a Republican and Cleveland was a Democrat.

Despite their differences in political philosophy, Roosevelt and Cleveland were both committed to honest, efficient government. Cleveland privately discussed strategy with Roosevelt and publicly endorsed the bill, which passed both houses and was signed into law in May 1883.

Another early 1883 bill that highlighted the connection between Cleveland and Roosevelt reduced fares on New York City's elevated trains from ten cents to a nickel. Jay Gould had instituted the increases in an effort to make the city's failing railway system solvent. The legislators, including TR, voted to reverse the hikes, because Gould was unpopular. The governor vetoed the bill—one of eight vetoes he delivered in his first two months in office.

The governor's veto was as unpopular among legislators as Gould. Yet, he had a valid reason for vetoing the bill. He believed it was unjust, since the fee hike was necessary. Cleveland also argued that legislatively changing Gould's franchise violated the contract clause of the U.S. Constitution. Newspapers sided with the governor.

The governor's veto convinced TR to take a second look at the bill. He acknowledged voting for it originally even though he believed it was wrong. But he voted for it more to punish Gould than anything else. After careful consideration, he realized that Cleveland was right. He voted to sustain the veto, which the Legislature sustained. The governor had taught him a valuable lesson: People's first impressions are not always the right ones. There were other lessons TR would learn as he matured politically.

Touring with Gompers

One of the men who influenced TR most in his formative years was Samuel Gompers, a young man who had experience making cigars in New York City tenements, where he lived. He attempted to get a bill passed in the New York State Legislature that would protect the women and children making the cigars. He persuaded TR to tour the tenements where the cigars were being made. The tour—and Gompers—had a profound effect on TR's life.

TR was no stranger to the city tenements and the poverty and squalor that were associated with them. As a child, he had accompanied Thee on his visits to city slums often. His visit with Gompers heightened his desire to alleviate the cigar makers' conditions. He got the chance, but the attempt ultimately went up in smoke.

The Cigar Makers' Union introduced a bill into the Legislature seeking to ban the manufacture of cigars in tenements. TR was appointed to a three-member committee to investigate the conditions in the tenements. He learned a valuable lesson about the role of political influence in legislations.

One other member of the committee said he had to vote for the bill because he represented labor interests. A second said his orders were to vote against it because he represented businesses. But he told TR he did not care personally one way or the other which way the vote went.

Another Change of Heart

Initially, TR was against the bill. After he toured the tenements, he changed his mind and supported it. He was not sure that Governor Grover Cleveland would sign it, though. The governor was not sure either.

The Cigar Makers' Union pleaded with TR to convince the governor the bill was needed. He did, and Governor Cleveland signed it. Ultimately, a Court of Appeals declared the bill unconstitutional, much to TR's chagrin.

The Court of Appeals based its decision on the fact that one home in which the cigars were made was an ideal spot for the process. They labeled the law an assault upon the "hallowed" influences of "home." The outcome of the case taught TR "the courts were not necessarily the best judges of what should be done to better social and industrial conditions."

TR said later that this decision completely blocked tenement-house reform legislation in New York for at least twenty years. In fact, he emphasized, it was one of the most serious setbacks the cause of industrial and social progress and reform had ever received.

But, as so often happened in TR's case, the setback turned into a victory of sorts. He learned more about playing the political game and impressed Governor Cleveland. The two would work together closely again, despite their different political affiliations.

The Third Year Is Not a Charm

TR was elected to a third term in the 1883 election. His constituents still supported him. The Republican Party did not. They conspired to remove him from any leadership position in 1884 because he was stepping on too many toes. That did not stop him. As a consolation prize, the leaders appointed him to the Cities Committee. That worked in his favor.

Democrats and Republicans alike looked to TR for floor leadership in the Assembly. He ended up with more power than he would have had as the official House leader and learned a valuable lesson from the situation. He commented, "As so often, I found that the titular position was of no consequence; what counted was the combination of the opportunity with the ability to accomplish results."

TR's 1883 re-election victory as assemblyman gave him the opportunity to change the role of the aldermen in New York City. He deemed it the most important challenge of the term. TR saw it as a chance to get the citizens of the city involved in politics to their benefit.

ESSENTIAL

In the mid-1880s, aldermen in New York City had the power of confirmation over the mayor's appointments. The real power lay in the hands of the ward bosses, who controlled the aldermen. TR and his allies in the Assembly believed that if they could reduce the aldermen's power, they would eliminate a critical step in the appointment process and give ordinary citizens a stronger voice.

Take That, Mr. Young

The appointment to the Cities Committee opened the door for him to pursue the reform he thought was so badly needed in New York City. The 1884 session had no sooner started than TR introduced three bills into the Assembly: one to raise liquor license fees by a large margin, one to weaken the city's borrowing power, and another to increase the mayor's authority and accountability.

The first one was a throwback to his first campaign visit to Valentine Young's saloon on Sixth Street, which had ended so badly; it failed. The second one passed. The third created a controversy when he introduced it, and it got TR and Governor Cleveland into hot water again—on the same side.

The Reform Charter Bill, as it was called, upset the political machine leaders in New York City because its intent was to weaken them and to increase citizens' chances of electing a reform mayor. That intrigued Governor Cleveland, who had been elected largely on his strength as a reformer. His support of TR's bill drew the ire of Tammany Hall, which supported aldermanic chicanery. The battle lines were drawn once again.

FACT

There was a definite need for aldermanic reform in 1884. Several members of the Board of Aldermen were involved in a scheme to help entrepreneur Jake Sharp acquire a Broadway railroad franchise at a noncompetitive price. In exchange, they received kickbacks (called "boodles") and acquired the nickname "The Boodle Board."

TR delivered an eloquent speech to support passage of the Reform Charter Bill that drew praise from almost every newspaper in New York. The bill passed, and he and Governor Cleveland became Tammany Hall's "Co-Enemies Number One." That did not bother either man. It simply demonstrated that they were accomplishing what they were elected to do: enact civil reform.

One More Controversy

As TR's third term in office ended, he became embroiled in one more controversy that involved Grover Cleveland indirectly and the 1884 presidential election. Again, he did not endear himself to his party.

TR was selected as a delegate to the Republican National Convention in Chicago in 1884. The party nominated James G. Blaine as its candidate. TR opposed the nomination, as did many other Republicans. One of them was George William Curtis, an ardent reformer of the civil service at the federal level, who noted in a statement after the convention ended that TR would play a major role in politics in the future.

James G. Blaine was the leader of the "Half Breed" faction of the Republican Party in 1884. He was accused of graft and corruption in the granting of railroad charters in the late 1800s, which earned him nicknames like "The Continental Liar from the State of Maine" and "Slippery Jim." He won the nomination but lost the election.

A faction pushed for the party to back the Democrat candidate, Grover Cleveland. TR refused their entreaties to join them. As much as he had enjoyed working with Cleveland in New York, he could not break from his party. The incident shook his idealism in the political process.

Disillusionment with Politics

The prescient Curtis had this to say about the young Theodore Roosevelt:

> Later the nation will be criticizing or praising him. While respectful to the gray hairs and experience of his elders, none of them can move him an iota from convictions as to men and measures once formed and rooted. He has integrity, courage, fair scholarship, a love for public life, a comfortable amount of money, honorable descent, the good word of the honest. He will not truckle nor cringe, he seems to court opposition to the point of being somewhat pugnacious. His political life will probably be a turbulent one, but he will be a figure, not a figurehead, in future development— or, if not, it will be because he gives up politics altogether.

Curtis was right on all points. Despite his success as an assemblyman, TR grew disillusioned with politics and changed career paths, albeit temporarily. It was another two years before he ran for office again. The choice to step aside was not of his own making.

TR's decision to take some time off from politics was not due entirely to his experiences in the Legislature or at Chicago. His self-imposed respite was hastened by a personal tragedy: the death of his wife, Alice Hathaway Lee, on February 14, 1884.

QUIZ

4-1 TR admired Alexander Hamilton because they both:

A. lived in New York at one time.
B. believed in a strong central government.
C. enjoyed Beethoven symphonies.
D. fought duels with men named Burr.

4-2 A ward boss in New York City:

A. ran the emergency ward at Bellevue Hospital.
B. was in charge of children at the city's orphanage.
C. warded off the evil spirits often found at City Hall.
D. gathered votes and handed out patronage positions in the city's voting districts.

4-3 A "boodle" is a:

A. child's stocking
B. breed of dog
C. Dutch word for bribe money
D. slang term to describe a proposed law

4-4 Labor unions were strongly in favor of TR during his three terms as a New York state assemblyman:

A. True
B. False

4-5 An assemblyman in the New York Legislature in the 1880s was allowed to vote only for bills that affected his district:

A. True
B. False

4-6 TR represented the Twenty-First District of New York City. Which of the following statements is *not* true about the district:

A. It was the richest district in New York City.
B. It was called the "brownstone district."
C. It had a maximum age restriction on elected state representatives.
D. TR was the youngest assemblyman ever elected from the Twenty-First District.

4-7 Samuel Gompers was born in which country:

A. England
B. Ireland
C. United States
D. Hungary

4-8 Tammany Hall was:

A. a political organization.
B. a nightclub singer in New York City.
C. a building where the New York assemblymen met in the 1870s.
D. the mayor of Peekskill, New York, when TR was police commissioner.

4-1. B

4-2. D

4-3. C: The term was applied often in New York City in the 1800s, most often to the 1884 Board of Aldermen, which was particularly susceptible to bribes.

4-4. True: According to a union report, he voted for twenty important labor issues as an assemblyman.

4-5. False: They could vote on every bill that was presented.

4-6. C: There was no maximum age limit in any district of the city.

4-7. A: Gompers was born in London, England, on January 27, 1850.

4-8. A: The Tammany Society began as a patriotic and charitable organization in New York City in 1789. In 1798, Aaron Burr transformed it into a political organization. Eventually, Irish immigrants seized control, and trading votes for benefits became a standard practice. When William Tweed took over in 1868, he began a statewide reign of extreme corruption that lasted into the early 1900s.

ANSWERS

CHAPTER 5

A Significant Person Exits Theodore's Life

"The light has gone out of my life."

TR met the first love of his life, Alice Hathaway Lee, in October 1878 while he was a junior at Harvard. She delayed their marriage plans, at least until he graduated. But the star-crossed lovers married on October 27, 1880. The happy couple moved to New York City, where they lived while he started his career and won a seat as a New York state assemblyman. Sadly, Alice died after giving birth to their daughter. Her death sent him into a deep depression, and instigated a major life change.

Thank You, Richard Saltonstall

Near the beginning of his junior year at Harvard, TR visited the home of his classmate Richard Saltonstall in Chestnut Hill, Massachusetts. He always remembered the exact date: October 18, 1878. Saltonstall's cousin and next-door neighbor, Alice Hathaway Lee, was there. Later, TR wrote, "As long as I live, I shall never forget how sweetly she looked, and how prettily she greeted me." This love was a new experience for him.

Their meeting would change his life dramatically. It affected everything he did from then on—at least for the next four years.

Alice Hathaway Lee

Alice Hathaway Lee Roosevelt

What caught TR's eye was a statuesque young lady about five feet seven inches tall, an inch or so shorter than him, with light brown hair and blue eyes. She had barely turned seventeen when they first met. Within a month of meeting Alice, TR decided he was going to marry her.

Alice possessed both inner and outer beauty and intelligence to match. Her nickname, "Sunshine," captured her demeanor perfectly as far as TR was concerned. She certainly brought a lot of sunshine into his life.

Like TR, Alice came from a large family. She was the second of six children. The first five were girls. Her only brother, George Jr., was not born until 1871. (He, too, graduated from Harvard, with the class of 1894.) TR and Alice Lee had anything but a whirlwind courtship. She dragged it out much longer than TR preferred.

A Long Courtship

Although TR had fallen in love immediately, Alice took her time deciding how she felt about him. It may have been because of her youth. He was almost three years older than Alice. Or it might have been because of his somewhat odd appearance at the time. He was thin, pale, sported long hair and a mustache, and wore eyeglasses.

The real reason she demurred is anyone's guess. But, while she "shined," he pined.

QUOTE

> TR filled pages of his diary with accounts of his love, their activities, and the lengths to which he would go to see her. He wrote in his diary on February 3, 1880, "Snowing heavily, but I drove over in my sleigh to Chestnut Hill, the horse plunging to his belly in great drifts, and the wind cutting my face like a knife."

TR just could not believe his luck. He wrote in his diary a few months after he met her, "It seems hardly possible that I can kiss her and hold her in my arms; she is so pure and so innocent, and is very, very pretty. I have never done anything to deserve such great fortune." He decided to push his luck and her, too. TR did everything he could to get her to marry him.

As soon as TR met Alice his interest in his studies and campus activities dwindled. There were two pieces of solid evidence that he was in love: he let Alice call him "Teddy" and he interrupted his naturalist expeditions.

Most of TR's family members called him "Teedie" when he was a child. The nickname did not follow him to Harvard. Alice started calling him "Teddy." He confessed later that he was never fond of that nickname, but she could have gotten away with calling him a lot worse because he was so much in love with her.

Lovestruck

Alice was also responsible to some degree for his diminished interest in ornithology. TR wrote a letter in 1879 to his close friend and Harvard classmate Henry Davis Minot to tell him about his new romance and that he had not done any collecting of specimens to think of that year. That was a startling admission from TR, who had been addicted to natural history since his very young days. And he did things that were out of the ordinary even for him.

TR attended club meetings rarely after he met Alice. Occasionally, he took her with him. At one Hasty Pudding gathering he pointed Alice out to a group of people and vowed that he was going to marry her, even though, he said, "She won't have me."

He turned the staid old Porcellian Club on its ears when he ushered Alice in for lunch. That was reportedly the first time any member had brought a woman into the club.

FACT

According to historian David McCullough, Henry Davis Minot was TR's only close friend at Harvard. (See McCullough's book, *Mornings on Horseback*.) Minot dropped out of Harvard in his sophomore year, ostensibly due to a nervous breakdown, but actually because of the lack of morality he perceived in the student body. He became a railroad executive and died in a train wreck on November 14, 1890, at age thirty-one.

It was unorthodox, but TR specialized in doing things that had never been done. Red tape, bureaucracy, tradition, anti-female rules . . . nothing stood in the way of love—or much of anything else—as far as TR was concerned. When he wanted something, he went after it. He kept up the pursuit; she continued to put him off.

Love Grows

In June 1879, TR proposed to Alice. She procrastinated for months. Finally, at the beginning of 1880, she agreed to marry him. He spent February 13, 1880, with the Lee family at their home in Chestnut Hill. The next day the couple announced their engagement.

A July 4, 1880, entry in TR's diary showed that his love was growing day by day. He wrote, "Not one thing is ever hidden between us. No matter how long I live I know my love for her will only grow deeper and tenderer day by day; and she always will be mistress over all that I have."

TR returned to Cambridge to announce their engagement. One of the first people TR told was Henry Minot.

He sent a letter to his old friend and asked him to keep the engagement secret—which TR could not do himself. He said, "I write to you to announce my engagement to Miss Alice Lee; but do not speak of it till Monday. I have been in love with her for nearly two years now, and have made everything subordinate to winning her; so you can perhaps understand a change in my ideas as regards science, etc." He could not wait for the wedding.

First Marriage

The wedding day finally arrived. TR and Alice Hathaway Lee were married either at the Unitarian Church in Brookline, Massachusetts, or at the Lee's home, depending on conflicting historical accounts. In any case, they married on October 27, 1880—his twenty-second birthday.

Among the guests was TR's childhood friend Edith Carow, who would also attend his second wedding a few years later—as his second wife.

TR's wedding to Alice was the greatest birthday present he could have received, but the joy was short lived. The happy couple moved to New York City to take up residence as he started his career. They lived happily there—but not forever after. It started well, however.

ESSENTIAL

The conflict in the wedding site is indicative of the reportage of many of the events in TR's life: different people saw and/or heard events differently, remember different dates, etc. That is true of historical events in general—and explains why there may be a few differences in facts between this book and other sources.

A Short Honeymoon

Alice and TR spent their first night together in Springfield, Massachusetts, then honeymooned for two weeks at the Roosevelt home at Oyster Bay, Long Island. That was a long respite for the energetic TR, who needed to be working. He had begun his studies at Columbia Law School and his interest in politics was growing—as was his love for Alice.

Following the wedding, TR put into perspective the balance between his love for Alice and for nature. He wrote:

I do not think ever a man loved a woman more than I love her; for a year and a quarter now I have never (even when hunting) gone to sleep or waked up without thinking of her; and I doubt if an hour has passed that I have not thought of her. And now I can scarcely realize that I can hold her in my arms and kiss her and caress her and love her as much as I choose.

The hunt was over; TR had married the woman he loved.

After TR was elected to the New York State Assembly in 1881, he spent a lot of time in Albany carrying out his legislative duties. He wrote letters to Alice during his times away and invited his friends and fellow politicians into their home in New York City often.

They were living at the family home on West 57th Street in New York City so Mittie and his sisters could provide Alice with company. He came home for weekends to help out. It was a happy time for TR—until Valentine's Day, 1884.

A Daughter Is Born; Two Mothers Die

When TR began his third term in the Legislature, Alice was both pregnant and ill. That put pressure on him. But there was added work-related stress he had to contend with as his term began. TR was facing opposition from his own party as he struggled to become the Speaker of the Assembly. While he was in Albany looking for votes, a series of notes and telegrams arrived that sent him scurrying back to New York City.

Only six days before his daughter was born, TR wrote Alice in a letter, "How did I hate to leave my bright, sunny little love yesterday afternoon! I love you and long for you all the time, and oh so tenderly; doubly tenderly now, my sweetest little wife. I just long for Friday evening when I shall be with you again." He did see her shortly, but not under the circumstances he imagined.

QUESTION

What was the cause of Alice's death?
Alice's death was attributed to Bright's disease, a kidney ailment. Today, it is known as acute or chronic nephritis. Sadly, it might have been treatable under ordinary circumstances. In Alice's case, her pregnancy masked the symptoms.

Alice sent TR a note on February 11 to assure him that she was fine and that the doctor was not particularly concerned about her health. Next, she sent him a telegram to announce that they had a daughter, who was born on February 12. Then, he received a telegram advising him to return to New

York City immediately because Alice's health was deteriorating. There, a terrible double tragedy and a moment of joy awaited him. They did not offset one another in his thinking.

When TR arrived at his house on February 13th, he walked into a scene of utter despair. Mittie was dying of typhoid fever in one room; one floor above, Alice was fighting for her life from complications of childbirth and Bright's disease.

There was little that TR could do except shuffle from room to room in a futile vigil for two of the most cherished women in his life. Mittie and Alice Hathaway Lee Roosevelt passed away within hours of each other on February 14, 1884. Alice was twenty-two years old at the time. Mittie was relatively young, too. She was forty-eight.

A Devastating Death

Mittie died first, at approximately 3 A.M. Alice clung to life for another eleven hours. She fought until she drew her last breath in TR's arms at about 2 P.M. It was a bitter anniversary for TR. Not only was it Valentine's Day, but it was the fourth anniversary of his engagement to Alice. It was of little comfort to TR, but at least he was there to hold her as she died.

A few days after Alice died in 1884, TR expressed in his diary his fond memories of the three years they had together: "We spent three years of happiness greater and more unalloyed than I have ever known to fall to the lot of others."

TR was devastated. Two entries in his diary showed his anguish. In one, he wrote a large X and a solitary sentence stating, "The light has gone out of my life." Alice's death left him with a large void that he sought to fill in the only way he knew how: work.

In a second entry, he wrote, "On February 17th I christened the baby Alice Lee Roosevelt. For joy or for sorrow my life has now been lived out."

Burying Alice—But Not the Memories

The family buried Alice and Mittie at a double funeral on February 15, 1884. The ladies were laid to rest together in Greenwood Cemetery. The epitaph on Alice's grave reads, "For joy or for sorrow my life has now been lived out."

In a way, TR's reaction to the double deaths was out of the ordinary. He tried to erase his memories of Alice by destroying any photographs and all correspondence that made any reference to her. He vowed to never speak of her again, even to her namesake and his daughter. For the most part, he managed not to.

TR even declared that he did not want to hear the name "Teddy" again. He could not escape the nickname, though, since he is forever connected with the "teddy bear," which his name popularized. Inadvertently, the "teddy bear" became one of the world's most beloved toys.

FACT

In November 1902, TR went on a bear hunt to Mississippi, but game was difficult to find. Eventually, the hunting dogs cornered a small black bear. Party members asked TR to kill the bear, but he felt it was unsporting and refused. Based on this story, artist Clifford K. Berryman of the *Washington Post* created an amusing cartoon called "Drawing the line in Mississippi." The cartoon delighted readers and prompted several toy makers to manufacture stuffed toy bears named for the president.

Breaking the Rule

TR's refusal to talk about Alice deprived the world of a great deal of knowledge about the happy life they lived together. (Her name is not even mentioned in his autobiography.) But there was a major obstacle to forgetting Alice Hathaway Lee Roosevelt altogether: his newborn daughter, Alice.

TR broke his self-enforced rule not to speak of Alice Hathaway Lee Roosevelt after her death. He wrote of her in a private moment:

She was beautiful in face and form, and lovelier still in spirit; As a flower she grew, and as a fair young flower she died. Her life had been always in the sunshine; there had never come to her a single sorrow; and none ever knew her who did not love and revere her for the bright, sunny temper and her saintly unselfishness. Fair, pure, and joyous as a maiden; loving, tender, and happy. As a young wife; when she had just become a mother, when her life seemed to be just begun, and when the years seemed so bright before her—then, by a strange and terrible fate, death came to her. And when my heart's dearest died, the light went from my life forever.

Enter Bamie

Young Alice was a constant reminder to TR of his first wife. He needed someone to take care of her. He turned to his family once again, as he so often did in times of trouble. His sister Anna stepped in—and TR stepped out.

The social conventions of the time suggested that a widower was not the proper person to raise a young daughter. Even though TR was not above breaking convention on occasion, he chose not to in this regard. Enter Bamie.

Bamie was twenty-nine years old at the time. She may not have known much about child rearing, but she did know that her younger brother needed help, which she provided to his everlasting gratitude.

Bamie had to walk a tightrope with regards to Alice Hathaway Lee Roosevelt's death and TR's refusal to speak publicly of her or let anyone mention her name in his presence. Young Alice did ask him occasionally about her mother, but he always referred her to Bamie. As a result, Alice learned about her mother from her aunt, who became her confidante.

Leaving New York

While Bamie took over the task of raising young Alice, TR sought a way to forget his beloved wife. His way of coping was to erase her memory completely, an impossibility. Her memory would follow him wherever he went. Nevertheless, he tried to escape it.

Not long after the funerals of Alice and his mother, TR left New York to try to forget Alice. The light may have gone out of his life, but it would come back on eventually. It began to gleam again in the Dakota Badlands.

QUIZ

5-1 The "teddy bear" is named after TR.

A. True

B. False

5-2 A city in North Dakota is named after one of TR's close friends from college. Which is it?

A. Saltonstall

B. Welling

C. Minot

D. Moorehead

5-3 Valentine's Day was bittersweet for TR between 1880 and 1884. Why?

A. He could not find the appropriate card to express his love to Alice Hathaway Lee.

B. It was the day he announced his engagement to Alice and the day she and his mother died.

C. He did not like romantic holidays.

D. It was too close to Groundhog Day for his taste.

5-4 Typhoid fever in New York State is:

A. quite common

B. completely eradicated

C. limited to children

D. rare

5-5 It is still possible to leave messages of sympathy on Alice Hathaway Lee Roosevelt's memorial.

A. True

B. False

ANSWERS

5-5. *True: There is a website where people can—and do—leave such messages.*

5-4. *D: Only thirty to fifty cases of typhoid fever occur in New York each year. Most of them are acquired during foreign travel to underdeveloped countries.*

5-3. *B: He announced his engagement to Alice on Valentine's Day, 1880. She and his mother both died on Valentine's Day, 1884.*

5-2. *C*

5-1. *True*

CHAPTER 6

There Is a New Sheriff in Town

"It was still the Wild West in those days, the Far West of Owen Wister's stories, and Frederic Remington's drawings, the soldier and the cowpuncher. The land of the West has gone now, 'gone, gone with the lost Atlantis,' gone to the isle of ghosts and strange dead memories . . . In that land we led a hardy life. Ours was the glory of work and the joy of living."

TR visited the Dakota Territory in 1883, which whetted his appetite for the area. In 1884, after his wife died, he moved there for two years to forget her. TR bought two ranches and immersed himself in the Western lifestyle. He learned a great deal about people's ability to adapt to new circumstances and mended himself mentally, physically, and spiritually. After a disastrous winter ruined his business venture, TR returned to New York with a much healthier attitude about the western United States—and a renewed zeal for life.

TR's First Trip to the Badlands

TR's 1884 trip to erase the memories of his deceased wife was not his first visit to the Dakota Territory. He had been there earlier under happier circumstances, most recently in 1883, when Alice was pregnant and he was looking for some diversion. He got the diversion and unknowingly took a major step in altering his life drastically.

TR arrived in the Dakota Territory for the first time before dawn at the Little Missouri train depot on September 8, 1883. The timing was hardly auspicious. TR had left his beloved wife at home, he did not know anyone in the Badlands—and he did not have a horse. None of those factors bothered him.

TR was a man who was used to adversity and well-equipped to deal with it. As far as he was concerned, adversity in the Badlands was no different than adversity in New York. As events turned out, he was right.

One thing TR had in his favor was a pocket full of cash, which he used to induce Joe Ferris, a twenty-five-year-old hunting guide from New Brunswick, Canada, to help him. The rugged individualists in North Dakota may have distrusted Easterners in general, but they did respect the value of a dollar. Once TR secured Ferris's assistance, he turned to his next goal: acquiring a horse.

Joe Ferris wasn't particularly helpful to TR at first. He was skeptical that the bespectacled, rather unfit looking young man could handle the rigors of Western life. TR changed Ferris's mind almost immediately. In fact, Ferris could hardly keep up with the young Easterner as he looked in vain for the buffalo he had come 1,800 miles to shoot.

He used his considerable powers of persuasion to convince Ferris's brother Sylvane and his friend Bill Merrifield to lend him a mount. They didn't trust this stranger who had just stepped off a train from New York in the dead of night. Again, TR resorted to a cash inducement.

TR offered to buy a horse. That convinced Ferris and Merrifield that he had no intentions of riding off into the sunset with their steed. They lent TR a horse, and the hunt was on.

Not a Good Time for Hunting

Conditions were not suitable for buffalo hunting in western North Dakota in September 1883 as the men set off on the hunt. (Buffalo are known technically as bison, a distinction TR's naturalist side would appreciate.) The weather was rainy and commercial hunters had practically eliminated any buffalo in the territory.

Despite the difficulty TR had in finding live buffalo, he put his time to good use. He and Ferris spent their evenings at the ranch managed for Sir John Pender by Gregor Lang, a recent immigrant from Scotland. While Ferris recovered from the relentless pace of each day's hunt, TR peppered Lang with questions about ranching, life in the West, and politics. Lang's answers intrigued TR. He decided to buy a ranch of his own. First he had to find a buffalo to shoot.

Determination had always been one of TR's strongest characteristics. He had traveled to North Dakota to shoot a buffalo, and he wasn't going to leave without one. It took almost a week of hunting in steady rain, but he finally succeeded.

FACT

When TR, Ferris, and Merrifield closed the Maltese Cross Ranch deal at Gregor Lang's ranch, TR gave them a check for $14,000 (or $12,000, depending on the source). Merrifield asked TR if he wanted a receipt. "Oh, that's all right," TR replied. And these men had been reluctant to lend him a horse only a few days earlier!

TR shot an old bull, which was one of only 1,200 buffalo left in the world. Virtually all the rest were killed by the end of 1884. TR's kill left him with just one more goal before returning to New York: buying a ranch.

Buying a Ranch

TR, not one to pass up what he considered to be a wise investment, offered to buy the herd Lang managed. Lang demurred and suggested that TR approach Sylvane Ferris and Merrifield, who were running the Maltese Cross Ranch for a Minnesota-based company named Wadsworth and Hawley. The three men agreed to a fairly complicated contract that was signed in St. Paul, Minnesota, on September 27, 1883.

According to the terms, Ferris and Merrifield agreed to manage up to 400 cattle on the ranch for seven years at a cost to TR of no more than

$12,000. (Some accounts suggest that he paid $14,000 initially.) At the end of the seven years, Ferris and Merrifield would return to TR 400 cattle or their equivalent in value.

If there were any increases in the number of cattle during that period, Ferris and Merrifield would receive half of them. The contract permitted TR to add cattle according to the same terms as the initial 400 animals. The timing was propitious for him, but the venture ended in disaster several years later.

TR returned to New York, where he was re-elected to the state assembly. Dakota Territory became a memory until Alice died.

TR stayed in New York long enough to clear up some administrative details, then returned to the Maltese Cross Ranch, this time to stay for a while. He sank an additional $26,000 into his investment there.

Pursuing the "Strenuous Life" Anew

TR had been living a rather sedentary life between his graduation from Harvard and his trip to the Badlands. Once he bought his ranch there, he pursued the "strenuous life" again.

TR was happy living the hard life of a cowboy. He made it sound at times like a life of ease and downplayed the work that went into surviving the rigors of the West. He said about his time in the Territory that "It was a fine, healthy life, too; it taught a man self-reliance, hardihood, and the value of instant decision—in short, the virtues that ought to come from life in the open country. I enjoyed the life to the full."

ESSENTIAL

Two of TR's old guides from Maine responded to his request to help him manage the Elkhorn Ranch. William W. Sewall and his nephew Wilmot Dow, neither of whom had any experience working with cattle or ranches, joined him in 1884. Their wives and children arrived shortly thereafter—and practically drove TR out of his own home. Both women gave birth to children there in 1886, which kept the house abuzz with activity at times.

Theodore Roosevelt with Wilmot Dow and Bill Sewall at Elkhorn Ranch, 1886

Part of his satisfaction was the hard work. Another part was the companionship. TR's cattle herd survived the winter of 1883–1884 with no problems. The success of his venture may have lured him into a false sense of security. He acquired his second ranch, the Elkhorn, for only $400 and invited some of his friends from "Back East" to join him there. The value of choosing the right friends paid off once again.

TR discovered cattle ranching at a time when it was becoming popular in the Dakota Territory. During the 1885–1886 season, he owned between 3,000 and 5,000 cattle. He became so involved in the operation that he helped organize the Little Missouri Stockmen's Association. Eventually, he became its chairman and then president. He was also a member of the Montana Stockgrowers Association. His life was going well, but disaster lay ahead.

Life at the Elkhorn

While his friends built new buildings and managed the herds on his two ranches, TR settled into the rigorous life of the Badlands and insinuated himself into the local life. The Elkhorn became his "home" ranch.

TR continued to write while he was at his ranches. He completed *Hunting Trips of a Ranchman* at the Maltese Cross Ranch in 1885 and almost finished *Life of Thomas Hart Benton* the following year at the Elkhorn Ranch. He found it difficult to stay away from his writing, no matter how many cattle had to be fed.

No matter where he was, TR impressed everyone with his willingness to work hard, his ability to pick up the tricks of the cowboy trade, the rapidity with which he adapted to the life, and his transformation from a thin, "four eyed," raw Easterner into a healthy, robust man. Soon, he began a new career: deputy sheriff.

Wearing the Badge

TR learned quickly that a rancher's profits could be crimped by rustlers, horse thieves, claim jumpers, and other criminals, but the West was generally safer than the East. He opined that, "A man has very little more to fear in the West than in the East, in spite of all the lawless acts one reads about." But he did not leave law enforcement to chance. TR became a lawman. He demonstrated respect for the law rather than giving thieves a fair trial and then hanging them.

FACT

Jacob Riis recounted one story that demonstrated TR's respect for law and justice. Local ranchers believed that their sheriff was sympathetic to cattle rustlers, some of whom he had let escape. The ranchers would not confront him. TR did. At one meeting, he accused the sheriff directly of favoring the outlaws and informed him that he had lost the ranchers' confidence and good will. The sheriff did not even defend himself.

TR served as a deputy sheriff for the northern end of Billings County at a time when shootings, stabbings, stealing cattle, and other serious crimes were on the decline. The job did not carry with it a great deal of prestige—or pay. Deputy sheriffs were paid when they made arrests and received travel reimbursement. On a couple notable occasions TR earned considerable amounts of prestige and pay for his exploits.

Law enforcement work taught TR a valuable lesson that he applied to other aspects of his life. It was not an epiphany for him. He had been aware since childhood that he had limitations, especially in the physical arena. The trick, he learned, was to act first and outsmart his opponents.

For example, TR arrested several miscreants who were stronger than him and quicker with weapons. In such cases, he thought ahead and acted faster than the criminal. That prevented him from becoming the victim of physical violence and saved him from the embarrassment of finishing second best in confrontations. TR was a firm believer in the adage "He who hesitates is lost."

Chasing the "Bad Guys"

On one occasion in March 1886, TR, Sewall, and Dow pursued three "bad guys" who had stolen the only boat they had on the ranch. Sewall and Dow quickly built another boat and the chase began. They apprehended the thieves after a harrowing adventure.

The three men did not receive a great deal of reward for their effort. According to TR, "Under the laws of Dakota I received my fees as a deputy sheriff for making the three arrests, and also mileage for the three hundred odd miles gone over—a total of some fifty dollars." That was small compensation for time lost and wear and tear on their equipment.

But TR was not as much interested in the reward as he was in applying justice. That did not change whether he was in New York or North Dakota.

Respect for the Law—and Books

Whether TR was chasing desperadoes or hunting for big game, he never forgot his passion for learning through books. As he prepared for chases, hunting expeditions, or ranch work, he always packed books.

While he was on the boat thief case he had a copy of Leo Tolstoy's *Anna Karenina*. Where many people read Tolstoy to fall asleep, TR read his book to stay awake. After he finished *Anna Karenina* he asked one of the prisoners if he had any books to read. He did: a dime novel. The eclectic TR read that one as well.

FACT

In the fall of 1886, TR went on a trip to the Montana Rockies to hunt the rarest of all American game, the white antelope-goat. He packed blankets, a light wagon sheet, the ever-present camera, flour, bacon, salt, sugar, coffee, rifles and ammunition, a few cooking utensils—and a book or two. He could not go anywhere without them.

TR's career as a deputy sheriff did not occupy a lot of his time. He spent most of his time running his ranches, with the able assistance of his friends and co-workers. They gave him the time to hunt, learn the trade of "cowboy-ing," and fraternize with the hardy people who populated the West and for whom he formed an everlasting romantic picture that he never forgot.

Social Life

TR left time to socialize with the people of the Badlands during his stay. For the most part, his relationships were cordial. Out of necessity, he associated with more males than females. That was due partly to the amount of time he spent on the range with cattle and horses and working the ranch. No doubt the memory of Alice continued to travel with him.

Occasionally, TR had disagreements with local residents. He aggravated local resident the Marquis de Morès to the point where the Marquis challenged TR to a duel. Fortunately, cooler heads prevailed and TR evaded being drawn into a fight due to his penchant for diplomacy.

Two disagreements in particular created tension between the two men. One involved an argument over land rights. The second occurred when TR canceled a cattle sale when the Marquis reduced the agreed-upon price per pound from 6 cents to 5.5 cents after the terms were set. That upset TR's sense of fair play.

The argument that almost led to the duel occurred when the Marquis informed TR in a letter in the summer of 1885 that Joe Ferris had worked to get him indicted after he shot a man, a crime for which he was later exonerated.

Dueling Letters

The Marquis intimated that TR had put Ferris up to it. Based on his suspicion, he wrote to TR, "If you are my enemy I want to know it . . . between gentlemen it is easy to settle matters of that sort directly."

TR got the reference. He had no desire to fight a duel.

Tactfully, TR wrote back that, "Most emphatically I am not your enemy; if I were you would know it, for I would be an open one, and would not have asked you to my house nor gone to yours." That was vintage TR: open and direct. The Marquis accepted TR's response and invited him to dinner. It was incidents like this that led TR to love the West.

Losing the Ranch

As much as TR liked the Badlands, he did not spend all his time there. He returned to New York in the winter to work on various projects that he had let slip while hunting and ranching. There were certain things he was not good at, such as carpentry, and he knew enough to get out of the way when he was not needed.

On one of his trips back East, TR met an old friend of his, Edith Carow, with whom he formed a romantic attachment. That changed any plans he had to settle permanently in the West—if he had ever had any.

For him, the ranches were more investments than homes. Eventually, both were damaged significantly by one of the pieces of life TR loved so much: nature. It was no consolation, but he was not alone in suffering irreparable damage to his Western livelihood.

The problem actually began in the spring of 1886, with a late thaw. The summer temperatures rose as high as 125 degrees, which impacted plant growth. These were ominous signs for the ranchers. To compound matters, there were too many cattle on the land. Overgrazing was affecting the herds adversely. Disaster was a step or two away.

TR had returned to the East in 1886 to run for mayor of New York City and prepare for his second marriage. While he and Edith honeymooned in

Europe, his cattle died in the Badlands. The Roosevelts suffered a significant financial setback, which spelled the end of TR's adventure in Dakota Territory.

The Winter of 1886–1887

All the signs that the winter of 1886–1887 was going to be devastating to the Dakota Territory cattle industry proved true. Blizzards raged across the plains; cattle froze to death everywhere. The ranchers could not feed them.

Cattle were so desperate for food during the winter of 1886–1887 that they were eating tar-paper off houses and climbing snowdrifts to strip twigs from trees. Ranchers found many dead cattle hanging from those trees in the spring. Almost 80 percent of the cattle in Dakota Territory died that winter.

TR returned from Europe in the spring of 1887 and traveled to Medora to check on his cattle. He discovered that more than half of them had died during the winter. He also lost more than half of the $80,000 he had invested. He could not tolerate any more losses.

TR wrote to Bamie and told her he was quitting the business. Giving up anything was a rarity for him. But prudence outweighed his quest for adventure at the time. After all, he did have a new family to consider—and support.

Return to New York

Even though his Western adventure ended badly, TR returned home with fond memories and new ideas. He made up his mind to apply some of those new ideas whenever the right situations arose.

Based on what he had learned about the sturdy Westerners, who had helped him in so many ways, he swore that if he ever got into a war, the men he met in the Dakota Territory "were of just the kind whom it would be well to have with me if ever it became necessary to go to war." That was just what happened when he rounded up his Rough Riders in 1898.

He also learned the value of friendship and loyalty. TR crossed paths often in later years with people he met and worked with in the West. Sometimes he helped them; other times they helped him.

QUOTE

During a campaign stop, one of TR's former Rough Riders made a speech on his behalf. He urged the crowd to "Vote for my Colonel! And he will lead you, as he led us, like sheep to the slaughter!" TR noted that it was neither a tribute to his military skill nor his leadership talent. It did amuse the crowd, though.

Another Lesson Learned

Perhaps the biggest lesson TR learned in his brief stay in the West was the need for conservation. He had experienced reservations about the overstocking of cattle and the resulting overgrazing in the Dakota Territory ever since his arrival—although that did not stop him from investing. His fears were realized in the winter of 1886–1887 when the lack of food for cattle and the harsh weather almost destroyed the ranching industry there.

TR realized that there had to be a balance between human and animal needs and nature's ability to provide for them. The search for that balance became one of his focal issues later in the various political and government offices he filled.

There was a lot of pressure on TR to return to New York City for good. There was no point in staying in the Dakota Territory, since his cattle were all but gone and rebuilding his herds would be costly. Besides, with a new wife and a call from politicians to get him to run for mayor of New York, he did not see a future in the Badlands.

TR opted to return to the home of his birth. He had matured mentally and physically during his hiatus in the West. For him, leaving the land he had learned to love was simply closing another chapter in his book of life. The city and the state of New York—and ultimately the United States—would benefit from his return.

QUIZ

6-1   Owen Wister, TR's classmate at Harvard, is best known for:

A. discovering wisteria on a nature expedition with TR.
B. writing novels about the West.
C. establishing a newspaper in Nevada called *The Virginian*.
D. his wisdom about the Italian bird named the *La teria*.

6-2   TR came close to participating in an old-fashioned duel with the founder of Medora, North Dakota.

A. True
B. False

6-3   TR considered the Russian author Leo Tolstoy a degenerate, even though he was not averse to reading his books.

A. True
B. False

6-4   The contract between William Sewall, Wilmot Dow, and TR regarding their work and payment on the Badlands ranch was never in writing.

A. True
B. False

ANSWERS

6-1. B: Wister, who graduated from Harvard in 1882, is considered the "father" of Western fiction. His best known work is the 1902 novel, The Virginian, which he dedicated to TR.
6-2. True: The two men settled their differences before the shooting began.
6-3. True: In 1890, the United States Post Office Department banned anyone from mailing newspapers containing serialized installments of Tolstoy's novella, The Kreutzer Sonata. Theodore Roosevelt called Tolstoy a "sexual moral pervert."
6-4. True: Sewall believed it was one-sided in his [Sewall's] favor, but it remained unwritten.

CHAPTER 7

TR Learns How to Gain from Losing

"But anyway, I had a bully time."

One of the lessons TR had learned almost from birth was that losses were only temporary. Anyone with the right temperament and a resolve to succeed could—and should—use setbacks as lessons and persevere. A particular event that reinforced that lesson for TR was the death of Alice. But he recovered from it starting in 1885 and used the tragedy as one more steppingstone to a happy family life and successful personal career. As he learned, the two go hand in hand.

New Marriage

Not long after Alice's death, TR met Edith ("Edie") Kermit Carow at his sister's house. It was not long before "Teedie" and "Edie" became romantically involved, as many people had suspected they would when they were younger.

Edith Carow Roosevelt

On November 17, 1885, TR proposed to Edith. She accepted. But he did not make their betrothal public at first. He was afraid that people would think he had not allowed enough time to get over his first marriage. But it was not like he was falling head over heels for someone he did not know. TR and Edith had a long history, which was destined to become longer after Alice died.

TR and Edith were not strangers. They had grown up together in New York City. She was his best friend by proxy and a schoolmate of sorts. His mother invited Edie to "enroll" in the home school taught by the younger

Roosevelts' aunt and governess, Anna. Besides, Edith and Conie, who were born only seven weeks and 109 miles apart (she was born in Norwich, Connecticut), were playmates, so Teedie tagged along with them.

Edie and Teedie shared some special moments in their early years. One in particular was poignant. They and Elliott Roosevelt watched President Lincoln's funeral procession pass by from an upstairs window of the Roosevelt's grandfather's house on Union Square in New York City. The Carows lived nearby on Union Square.

FACT

President Lincoln's body was carried by train through several cities en route to his final resting place in Springfield, Illinois. It was a 1,700 mile funeral procession. At ten stops, his casket was removed from the train for public viewings. New York City was one of them. The funeral procession passed by TR's grandfather's house.

Thirty-six years later, another presidential assassination would play a role in Teedie's life. He would assume the presidency to replace the slain William McKinley, alongside "Spotless Edie."

As a sign of how close TR and Edith were as children, he gave her a pet name based on her penchant for tidiness: "Spotless Edie." Over the years, their friendship developed into a romance, although it took 25 years and a myriad of vicissitudes before they became husband and wife—and she became a future first lady.

Teedie and Edie Go Their Separate Ways

Into their early teens, the childhood friends spent a lot of time with one another. They were often together during summer events at Oyster Bay, Long Island, which was destined to become their home. They did not see one another exclusively, partly because she was three years younger than him. Edie was always on his mind, though.

Young Theodore painted the name Edith on his rowboat when he was sixteen. Their age difference came into play when he left for college.

TR was seventeen years old when he started classes at Harvard. She was fourteen. The age difference was beginning to show. He was in

Massachusetts; she was in New York. He was at Harvard; she was a product of Miss Comstock's Finishing School in New York City. Distance aside, they continued to share two traits in common: They were both serious students and loved books.

A Mystery of History

Teedie and Edie maintained their friendship while he was at Harvard. It changed after his father died in 1878. Exactly what happened is a mystery of history.

QUOTE

There is some speculation that TR proposed to Edith in the summer of 1878, but she said no. He never admitted to that and would not explain what happened to affect their relationship. He did say later, "we both of us had tempers . . . that were far from the best." At any rate, they both moved on with their lives.

Edith attended TR's October 27, 1880, marriage to Alice Hathaway Lee, but after that they drifted apart. They did not have many opportunities to socialize while he was married. They did see each other occasionally when he traveled from North Dakota to New York to visit. All in all, their get-togethers were few and far between until he returned from his North Dakota adventure in 1886—the same year she moved to London with her widowed mother.

TR caught a lot of people off guard, especially close family members, when he announced his engagement to Edith. As their relationship started growing into something serious, Edith showed her practical side when TR told her he was considering a run for mayor of New York City.

Edith's Opposition

Theodore had no sooner returned from North Dakota when he got the political itch again and campaigned for mayor of New York City in 1886. He had some significant opposition: the Tammany Hall nominee Democrat Abram

S. Hewitt; Henry George, economist and reformer, who had moved to New York City from California a few years earlier; and Edith.

She may not have been on the ticket, but Edith was against TR's involvement based on two issues: They were planning a wedding in Europe less than a month after Election Day, and he would have to take office only a few weeks after that if he won, which would cut into their honeymoon. Despite her objections, TR ran—and lost. At least he did not lose Edith.

FACT

Henry George ran as the United Labor Party candidate in the 1886 New York City mayoral campaign. He was best known for his support of the land value tax, a.k.a. "single tax," on land and the founder of "Georgism," the philosophy that everyone owns what he or she creates, but that everything found in nature—primarily land—belongs equally to all humanity.

The race was an eye-opener for TR. His opponents overshadowed him and his supporters practically ignored him. He understood that, and he did not expect to win. He was scheduled to sail to Europe with Edith only four days after the election.

TR had purchased tickets under the name of Merrifield for a transAtlantic voyage aboard the *Eturia*, which was scheduled to leave New York on November 6. That morning, he and "Mrs. Merrifield," actually his sister Bamie, boarded *Eturia* in disguise. They had spent the previous night writing engagement announcements and wedding invitations. He figured that by the time the announcements and invitations reached their destinations, he would be at sea.

TR was right about the outcome of the election, but he had no intention of leaving politics. Many people believed that someone like TR, who came from one of the city's aristocratic families, should not be involved in politics. What could he know about the severe economic depression, high levels of unemployment, political graft, and labor disorders that were plaguing the city, they wondered? As a result, many Republicans crossed party lines and voted for his opponents. Perhaps that was for the best as far as TR's career was concerned.

The Mayoral Race

Almost all the city's aldermen were under indictment for taking bribes, workers were extremely underpaid for the long hours they toiled—sometimes as many as sixteen hours a day—and labor unions were agitating for power.

ESSENTIAL

Significantly, 207 separate unions, representing 50,000 local employees, banded together as the Central Labor Union and got behind George, as did labor leader Samuel Gompers, who had sparked TR's interest in politics just a few years earlier. TR did not have anywhere near the name recognition George did or empathy for the city's residents, according to his opponents.

Hewitt represented the most powerful political machine in New York—and the United States. He was a seasoned campaigner who had served five terms in the U.S. House of Representatives. (He resigned during his fifth term to take over his mayoral duties.) Strangely enough, he shared some characteristics with TR that George could not emulate.

Hewitt, like TR, was rich and a philanthropist. That helped him, but it worked against TR. Hewitt had worked his way to millionaire status starting with a public school background, whereas TR had been born with the proverbial silver spoon in his mouth. In truth, by 1886 TR's personal wealth was nowhere near Hewitt's.

FACT

There were 219,992 votes cast in the 1886 New York City mayoral election. The breakdown, according to the November 14, 1886, *New York Times*: Hewitt (90,552); George (68,110); Roosevelt (60,435); Wardwell (582). The final tally left 313 votes unaccounted for, but the missing votes were not enough to sway the outcome.

In the long run, Hewitt's age (he was sixty-four years old), government experience, family connections, ties to a political machine, and promise that he was the only candidate who could save New York City from "socialism, communism, anarchism, nihilism, and revolution" were too much for TR to overcome.

TR campaigned enthusiastically, but lost badly in the November 2, 1886, election. He placed a distant third behind runner-up Henry George. There was one consolation: he did not finish last. That honor went to Prohibition Party candidate William T. Wardwell.

TR Takes the Loss in Stride

No doubt the results of the race elicited a sigh of relief from Edith. They did not faze TR. He commented simply, "Well, anyway, I had a bully time." The loss provided him with valuable experience that he would use in later years and freed him to make wedding plans with Edith despite his reservations.

It was understandable, given the social mores of the period, that TR was reluctant to marry a second time, especially so soon after Alice's untimely death. But, Edith Kermit Carow's charms were too alluring for him to ignore.

TR and Edith were married in a small wedding with few guests at St. George's Church, Hanover Square, in London on December 2, 1886. Britain's future ambassador to the United States during World War I, Cecil Spring Rice, was TR's best man. That was the first day of a long and happy marriage for Edith and TR.

In a Fog

Weather conditions on the day of their wedding were far from ideal. Anyone who believed in omens had to wonder if they signaled a cloudy future for the young couple. The fog swirling throughout the church was so thick that the bride and groom had difficulty picking each other out in the crowd.

TR wore a pair of bright orange gloves so Edith could identify him, lest she marry the wrong man. Fog notwithstanding, the ceremony went on and the honeymoon, which lasted for thirty-three years, began. She obviously did not marry the wrong man.

The newlyweds stayed in Europe for their fifteen-week honeymoon. TR, ever the romantic and adventurer, took the opportunity to lead a group to the top of Mont Blanc, the highest mountain in the Alps. The British Royal Society was so impressed with his achievement that it inducted him into its ranks, which was a significant honor.

Honeymoon Adventure

TR was a little careful in where they went, what they did, and who they saw on the honeymoon. He did not want to go places that he and first wife Alice had visited together, since his memories of her were still strong. Nevertheless, they traveled extensively and cavorted with a wide range of people, especially in England.

Cecil Spring Rice, or "Springy," as TR called him, opened doors for the Roosevelts. TR spent large blocks of time at exclusive social clubs like the Athenaeum and St. James, which was noted as a gathering place for traveling diplomats. He socialized with political and literary figures such as the poet Robert Browning; Sir James Bryce, a member of the British Parliament at the time; and George Otto Trevelyan, a noted statesman, historian, and writer.

The social contacts were beneficial to TR, especially in the case of Bryce, who was appointed in 1907 as the British ambassador to the United States during TR's first full term as president. The Roosevelts were often weekend guests at country houses around the nation.

TR and Edith spent the winter months on the Riviera and then traveled to Italy, where they visited Milan, Rome, Venice, and Florence. In Florence, reality struck. It was there that they heard about the terrible blizzards that had devastated the Badlands while they were frolicking in Europe.

The news put a crimp in their honeymoon, since TR realized that the money they were spending might run out due to the destruction of his cattle. He had lost most of his herds in the fierce weather.

A Babysitter for Alice

There existed another vexing problem: what to do about baby Alice. TR wanted to let Bamie raise her. Edith did not. She wanted Alice to be part of their family. They opted to defer any decision on her care until they returned to the United States and talked to his sister Bamie.

As happy as TR and Edith were in Europe, they realized that no honeymoon could last forever. They returned to the United States in the spring of 1887 and settled down eventually at Oyster Bay, Long Island, in a house that he had contracted for in March 1884 with the firm of Joseph Wood & Sons of Lawrence, Long Island.

FACT

Originally, Theodore intended to name the house at Oyster Bay "Leeholm" in honor of Alice's family. He changed it to Sagamore Hill in memory of Sagamore Mohannis, the Indian chief who used the hill as a meeting place and signed his people's rights to the land over to the settlers in the 1660s.

Construction of the house was completed in 1885. Ironically, he had built the house for Alice, but her death precluded any life together for them at Oyster Bay. Nevertheless, Bamie had insisted that he build the house, because young Alice needed a home. Bamie's persistence was sagacious as events turned out.

Edith and TR established a pattern in their home that would persist through their years of marriage. Edith managed the house and the budget well, particularly in light of TR's reduced income due to the loss of his cattle. She did it so well that she managed to buy a house for him without his knowledge once they moved to Washington, D.C., and he became president.

Edith the Money Manager

Many people considered Edith to be a better judge than TR of men and of money. They needed that balance, because of his lack of money management skills and his overall joy of life, which tended to cost him a few dollars here and there. Her money management and social skills served them in good stead as the number of Roosevelts increased at Sagamore Hill and beyond.

The experience Edith gained dealing with limited financial resources came into play after they were married. She and TR had both learned a valuable lesson based on her family's setbacks and the losses he had incurred after the Badlands disaster. They kept tighter reins on their own finances once the honeymoon ended.

Edith was no stranger to dwindling resources. Her own family, although affluent prior to the Civil War, suffered severe financial setbacks afterwards due to inflation and her father's alcoholism. Their fortunes were reversed badly enough by 1867 that the Carows could not afford their own home. They lived with relatives, but their social standing remained intact.

The Family Grows

The couple did not waste any time starting a family. They already had one child. Alice came to live with them shortly after they began their married life. Again, Bamie's steady influence played a role in the decision, as it did so often in TR's life. She helped them resolve their dilemma over what to do about Alice. Bamie turned young Alice over to Edith and TR in May of 1887, although it broke her heart to do so.

Their own first child, Theodore Jr., was born on September 13, 1887, at Sagamore Hill. Kermit followed two years later, on October 10, 1889, also at Sagamore Hill. Their third and final child delivered at the Long Island homestead, Ethel Carow, arrived on August 13, 1891.

In a June 11, 1906, letter to Ethel, TR revealed his feelings for Sagamore Hill: "I am glad that what changes have been made in the house are good, and I look forward . . . to seeing them . . . Fond as I am of the White House . . . there isn't any place in the world like home—like Sagamore Hill, where things are our own, with our own associations, and where it is real country."

As TR accepted new responsibilities and assignments, the family moved to fit their circumstances. Archibald Bulloch was born in Washington, D.C., on April 9, 1894. Quentin followed him on November 19, 1897. He was the couple's final child. They all made TR happy, although they were not without problems.

Edith Carow Roosevelt with Quentin on chair, 1903

Edith had several miscarriages between children. But he and Edith bore up well under the strains of managing a career and raising children, as he averred time and time again in the book, *Theodore Roosevelt's Letters to His Children*. One letter in particular, written on December 26, 1903, to his sister Corinne (Mrs. Douglas Robinson), displayed how emotional he could be about family relationships, as a boy himself and a father:

We had a delightful Christmas yesterday— just such a Christmas thirty or forty years ago we used to have under Father's and Mother's supervision in 20th Street and 57th street . . . I wonder whether there ever can come in life a thrill of greater exaltation and rapture than that which comes to one between the ages of say six and fourteen, when the library door is thrown open and you walk in to see all the gifts, like a materialized fairy land, arrayed on your special table?

TR was happy with his circumstances and his family almost every place they went, even Pine Knot.

Pine Knot

During TR's first full term as president, Edith decided they should have a place away from the White House where he could unwind. She envisioned a rustic cabin where they could indulge in the types of outdoor activities they both liked. Edith was not sure he would go along with her, so she purchased a place in Virginia without telling him. It was about as rural as she could get.

Edith bought a fifteen-acre plot about a four-hour train ride and a ten-mile horseback or carriage ride away from Washington, D.C., (about 60 miles) with a small, fairly new cottage on it, on which construction began in 1903. She paid $280 for the "retreat," including alterations she made.

At the time of purchase, there was 12 feet by 32 feet of space on each of two floors. There were no stove, chimney, well, or toilet facilities, inside or out. Quickly, Edith had a ground floor partition removed, end fireplaces added, and the central stair moved to the side to create a single lodge room.

She named the place Pine Knot, since it was rife with pine trees. One month after she bought the place, Edith sprung her surprise on TR.

The president of the United States soon found himself at a retreat with no plumbing, no running water, and no electricity. They had to go to a spring down the hill from the cabin to fetch water. But, they had plenty of nature to keep them occupied. That was uppermost in Edith's mind when she bought the place.

A pretty wife, a successful hunt, and a cherished son to write to were the ingredients for a happy life for TR, especially in light of the many crises he was juggling simultaneously at the White House. Based on his letters about Pine Knot, it was a great place for him to get away, if only for a few days.

No Home Improvements

Edith may not have gotten her money's worth after all was said and done, but she did achieve a sense of self-satisfaction. TR and Edith did use Pine Knot, although not often. They visited the place at least nine times, mostly around Thanksgiving and Christmas, between 1905 and May 1908, their final "mini-vacation" there.

Sometimes the children would accompany them, but more often than not it was just Edith and TR alone with nature and each other, which suited both of them just fine. Among the children, only Alice never visited the retreat.

The Roosevelts never made any major improvements to the retreat. In July 1911, Edith Roosevelt purchased seventy-five more acres at Pine Knot, anticipating that her husband would run for a second full term as president. The family held on to the property until 1941, when Edith sold it to George

Omohundro, their longtime neighbor and TR's hunting partner. That closed another chapter in the Roosevelt family's life, another one that held fond memories for them.

Turning Two Losses Into a Win

In the final analysis, the two major losses in TR's life between February 14, 1884, and November 2, 1886, turned out to be positive events. As heartbroken as TR was over the death of Alice Hathaway Lee, he rebounded magnificently. His subsequent marriage to Edith Carow turned out to be one of the happiest relationships of his life.

The blow he suffered in losing the 1886 mayoral race contributed to the beginning and enduring strength of that relationship. Moreover, it served as a positive experience for him.

TR learned that losing a political race is no disgrace as long as you treat it as a teachable moment, apply the lessons you learned, and move on. He did just that. Together, he, Edith, and their children moved on and up.

7-1 TR was the twenty-sixth president of the United States. What number first lady was Edith?

A. Twenty-seventh
B. Twenty-sixth
C. Thirty-ninth
D. Fifteenth

7-2 Edith Roosevelt enjoyed fine music. She instituted the tradition of East Room Musicales in the White House. On January 15, 1904, a noted young cellist played for the Roosevelts during his first solo tour of the United States. Who was it?

A. Karl Davydov
B. Pablo Casals
C. Yo-Yo Ma
D. Gaetano Braga

7-3 The Prohibition Party is the oldest "third party" in the United States.

A. True
B. False

7-4 In the presidential campaign of 1932, Edith Carow Roosevelt campaigned for:

A. Herbert Hoover.
B. Franklin Delano Roosevelt.
C. Andrew Jackson.
D. Eugene Debs.

7-5 Even though Robert Browning was not a particularly successful poet, he influenced the works of which well-known twentieth-century poet?

A. T. S. Eliot
B. Ezra Pound
C. Robert Frost
D. All of the above

7-6 Anna ("Bamie") Roosevelt did not marry until she was forty years old.

A. True
B. False

ANSWERS

7-1. A: The numbers of presidents and first ladies do not match. President John Tyler had two official first ladies, since he remarried during his term.

7-2. B: Pablo Casals is considered by some people to be the finest cellist ever. A few weeks later, on March 9, he made his debut at Carnegie Hall in New York.

7-3. True: The Prohibition Party was founded in 1869 and still exists.

7-4. A: She campaigned for the Republican candidate. Franklin Delano Roosevelt was a Democrat.

7-5. D: Browning did not earn a lot of respect as a poet until the late 1860s, well into his career.

7-6. True: She married forty-nine-year-old William Sheffield Cowles in 1895.

CHAPTER 8

Mr. Roosevelt Becomes a "Job Hopper"

"The opposition to reform is generally well led by skilled parliamentarians, and they fight with the vindictiveness natural to men who see a chance of striking at the institution which has baffled their greed. These men have a gift at office-mongering, just as other men have a peculiar knack at picking pockets; and they are joined by all the honest dull men, who vote wrong out of pure ignorance, and by a very few sincere and intelligent, but wholly misguided people."

Losing the mayor's race did not hurt TR. It opened more doors for him. After the election, people in high places began to see his potential and appointed him to positions on the local and national levels that helped him refine his leadership skills. The experiences in the years between the mayoral race in 1886 and the gubernatorial campaign of 1898 provided the seasoning he needed to enter the toughest political arena of all: the presidency of the United States.

New Opportunities

TR did not seem devastated by his loss in the 1886 New York City mayoral race. He was a self-confident man who knew that better opportunities would come along.

For three years after the election, TR dabbled in a number of activities. He remained in New York attending to his duties as trustee of the Orthopaedic Hospital, director of the New York Infant Asylum, and assignments with several other institutions with which he was associated. He also continued writing.

TR had demonstrated his considerable political skills and savvy running against Hewitt and George. Even though he lost the campaign, TR had attracted the attention of Republican Party leaders. Nevertheless, he did not seem to be in a hurry to get involved in politics again.

Between 1887 and 1889, TR published six books. TR remained open to opportunities should they come along—which they did.

Commissioner Roosevelt

The Republicans nominated Benjamin Harrison as their presidential candidate in 1888. TR campaigned vigorously throughout the Midwest for the nominee. Harrison emerged victorious after a hard campaign. He did not forget TR's support.

One of the issues on which Harrison campaigned was civil service reform. He favored the merit system over the patronage system, but his was not a particularly popular position among members of Congress. He wanted someone on the United States Civil Service Commission who would not care particularly what Congress had to say about one side versus the other. He needed a reformer on the Commission, and Theodore Roosevelt was the perfect candidate.

On May 7, 1889, President Harrison appointed TR to the United States Civil Service Commission, along with another reformer, Hugh Smith Thompson, the former governor of South Carolina and assistant secretary of the treasury under Harrison's predecessor, Grover Cleveland. Much to the surprise of the *New York Times*, TR accepted the nomination.

A reporter wrote in the May 7, 1885, edition of the *New York Times*, "It was at first feared that he would not accept the position, as it requires a residence in Washington for a great deal of the time." The rest of the reporter's statement provided an insight into the psyche of Theodore Roosevelt, suggesting that he needed some publicity in his work, even if he had to relocate to get it.

FACT

The United States Civil Service Commission was created on January 16, 1883, as part of the Pendleton Civil Service Reform Act to oversee the federal government's civil service. The law required some applicants to take civil service exams to get designated jobs and prohibited elected officials and political appointees from firing or removing civil servants in some situations.

TR Surprises Everyone

TR not only brought some life to the position, but he retained his post with the Commission for the next six years. He took his duties seriously—so seriously, in fact, that he drew a lot of criticism and unwanted attention for doing a job that many people in government did not take seriously. As usual, he developed unique ways of handling his critics.

TR did an end run to convince congressmen who opposed him to comply with his reforms. He simply got the public involved. He explained:

> *Occasionally we would bring to terms these Senators or Congressmen who fought the Commission by the simple expedient of not holding examinations in their districts. This always brought frantic appeals from their constituents, and we would explain that unfortunately the appropriations had been cut, so that we could not hold examinations in every district, and that obviously we could not neglect the districts of those Congressmen who believed in the reform and therefore in the examinations.*

Those congressmen usually came around to agreeing with TR as he continued his reform efforts.

Spoiling the Spoils System

President Harrison was aware of TR's dislike of political patronage and partisan influence. The new commissioner sank his teeth into the job immediately with his usual zeal for rooting out spoils wherever he saw them.

TR had experience in the civil service reform arena. He had served as a member of the New York Civil Service Reform Association in the early 1880s. As a New York state assemblyman, he worked to pass the first state civil service act in the nation, the New York State Civil Service Act of 1883. He worked just as hard on the national level to create a civil service system that would attract the best people into government.

As commissioner, TR espoused three major principles: the civil service system should create equal opportunities for all citizens, not just those who knew certain politicians; the only people who should be appointed to federal jobs were those who had the right experience; and public servants should not suffer for their political beliefs or gender. (One of his accomplishments in his six years in office was opening civil service positions to women.)

Theodore Roosevelt pulling an elephant's tail in a political cartoon, 1889. The cartoon shows Benjamin Harrison on a Republican Party elephant labeled "Tannerism," which is tearing down civil service rules, as TR, Thompson, and C. Lyman try to restrain the elephant by pulling on its tail. Caption reads "This is the 'pull' that civil service reform has with this administration."

If those principles were met, fraud and political abuse in government would be wiped out, and corrupt government officials would be exposed. The system worked just fine.

TR's reach was far and wide as he strove to implement fairness in the civil service system. He did not tolerate violations of his principles or of the code. Only one week into the job he recommended that examination board members in New York be fired for selling test questions to the public for $50.

QUOTE

TR acknowledged that he made enemies as Civil Service commissioner. He said, "I have made the Commission a living force, and in consequence the outcry among the spoilsmen has become furious. But I answered militantly that as long as I was responsible, the law should be enforced up to the handle everywhere, fearlessly and honestly."

And, to show that he did not play favorites regardless of who appointed him, he ordered Baltimore police to arrest postal employees who were buying votes for the re-election of President Harrison. The practice did not help President Harrison. In a game of presidential ping-pong, he lost the 1892 election to Grover Cleveland, whom he had defeated in 1888. Even though Cleveland was a Democrat, he reappointed TR to the commissioner post.

A Troubling Second Term

There were a couple of incidents in TR's second term as commissioner that made him step back and wonder if he could be doing more elsewhere to fight corruption. Even though there were tangible signs that he was effecting change, he wasn't sure he was doing enough. As he saw it, labor was still driving the economy, and workers were still on the short end of the stick.

When two of the largest employers in the United States, the Philadelphia and Reading Railroad and the National Cordage Company, failed in 1893, it set off a nationwide depression. The stock market tumbled, banks and investment firms called in loans, companies fell into bankruptcy, and unemployment rates reached 25 percent. More than 15,000 companies closed their doors during the crisis.

The deep recession of 1893 affected TR adversely. So did the Pullman Palace Car Company strike of 1894. The ongoing depression of 1893 forced the company to reduce its workforce by 75 percent, rehire some workers, and then cut wages. Through all this, the company refused to lower the rent for workers who lived in company-built houses. Eventually the workers went on strike.

The Pullman strike was the first national strike in U.S. history. For the first time, people were exposed to unsatisfactory labor issues and a hint of socialism because of Eugene Debs's union leadership. TR and other reformers saw an opportunity in the strike to balance the economic differences between labor and capitalism. But another problem surfaced: excessive force by the U.S. government to quell the strike.

Courts invoked the Sherman Act against labor unions, instead of against the company. President Cleveland dispatched federal troops to Chicago to suppress the strikers. Those actions forced TR to step back and analyze the need for balance.

A New Understanding

TR realized "that an even greater fight must be waged to improve economic conditions, and to secure social and industrial justice, justice as between individuals and justice as between classes." And, he "began to see that political effort was largely valuable as it found expression and resulted in such social and industrial betterment."

He wanted new venues to pursue that greater fight. On May 5, 1895, TR resigned from the Civil Service Commission to take a new position: police commissioner of New York City.

Joining the Police Force

TR's next chance to fight graft and corruption came in New York City, with its population of 2 million people. Recently elected Republican Mayor William Strong offered him the opportunity to serve as the head of the street-cleaning department. TR passed that up. He did not feel that he had the experience. But there was an opening on the Board of Police Commissioners, which the mayor offered as an alternative.

One of TR's oldest friends, Henry Cabot Lodge, pressed him to accept the position, which gave him the opportunity to return to his home base and root out corruption. On May 6, 1895, Mayor Strong appointed TR to the four-member board, at a salary of $5,000 per year. His appointment, which was for six years, lasted only two.

Strong appointed three other members: Frederick D. Grant, a Republican and oldest son of former President Ulysses S. Grant; Andrew D. Parker, a Democrat who would eventually become a thorn in TR's side; and John Monks, another Democrat. His co-commissioners elected him as board president. TR left Washington, D.C., that same day to fight City Hall—literally.

FACT

TR should have gotten an inkling of the problems besetting the Board of Police Commissioners right away. Two outgoing members, both Republicans, were asked to resign, but they refused. Therefore, the new mayor, a Republican, ousted them under the Power of Removal Act. Both former commissioners protested their removals vigorously—especially since a member of their own party sent them packing.

The biggest obstacle he faced was the setup of the board. It was designed to make sure nothing could be done to influence the way the police department functioned. The board included two Democrats and two Republicans. That almost assured that the members would not agree on much.

TR promised to be nonpartisan as police commissioner. He wrote, "I was appointed with the distinct understanding that I was to administer the Police Department with entire disregard of partisan politics, and only from the standpoint of a good citizen interested in promoting the welfare of all good citizens."

The commissioners appointed a police chief who they could not remove without a trial subject to review by a court. The chief and a single commissioner could stop anything proposed by the other three commissioners. That had the potential to create permanent deadlocks among the commissioners.

To compound matters, the mayor appointed the commissioners, but he could not remove them unless the governor of New York agreed. That was not likely in most cases due to the machinations of Tammany Hall, the political machine that ran the city and the state. Tammany Hall seemed to be exceeding its own levels of greed and graft where the department was concerned.

Finally, the commissioners could appoint police officers, but they could not fire them without a trial and a subsequent review by the courts. That was a political structure that almost guaranteed that any attempts at reforms would be difficult at best, if not outright impossible. Some men might have thrown up their hands in despair. TR did not.

TR Accepts the Challenge

Just as the Board of Commissioners was almost powerless to change the structure of the police department in the late 1800s, police officers in New York City were all but powerless to change the culture of the wide-open city. Gambling, drinking, prostitution, drugs, and other forms of vice were available to anyone who wanted to participate.

The police were in on the action in many cases. They were taking bribes—from the top down—to turn a blind eye or share in the profits. In turn, the police shared their bribes or payments with the Tammany Hall politicians. TR set out to begin his reforms at once.

TR was not content to work from behind a desk. He became a veritable field training officer who actually worked the streets with the cops on the beat. One person who accompanied him often on his patrols was Jacob Riis, a newspaperman and muckraker extraordinaire.

Jacob Riis was a photojournalist for the *New York Evening Sun*. He specialized in reporting on the plight of the poor people in New York City. Riis was one of the first reporters to use flash powder, which allowed him to take photos of the insides of tenements and show people how depressing the city's slums really were.

In December 1889, *Scribner's Magazine* published Riis's photo essay of New York City slum life. The next year an expanded version came out in book form, titled *How the Other Half Lives*. TR read the book and took action once he became the police commissioner by ordering the police to close the lodging houses they ran—where Riis had often resided in his youth.

TR Takes the Riis Tour

Riis opened TR's eyes to a side of the city that he knew about but did not often experience. Riis had grown up in the tenements of New York City. He knew how hard life was for the people who lived in them and how deep the police department's influence ran.

Riis made sure that TR got to see the city at its worst, which made the commissioner anxious to make it into what it could be at its best. What he learned from his relationship with Riis played a big role in his political leadership as governor of New York state and president of the United States after he left the police department.

Not a Good First Day

TR walked into chaos his first day on the job in the form of a piece of legislation designed to reform the police department and render him practically useless. That was the Ainsworth Bill, sponsored in the New York State Assembly by Danforth E. Ainsworth in his final year as an assemblyman.

FACT

Police Chief Thomas F. Byrnes was known for his brutal tactics when interrogating suspected criminals. He described it as giving them the "third degree," a term attributed to him. He was an effective police officer and chief and a shrewd money manager. Byrnes amassed a fortune of $350,000 on a salary of $2,000 a year, based on "sound advice" from his Wall Street friends.

Among its provisions, the bill changed the title of chief of police to superintendent of police and increased the incumbent's power. It also gave the superintendent the authority to try all cases of charges against members of the force. And, the bill stipulated that the superintendent could be removed from office only if he was deemed to be totally incapable of running the department. In effect, the superintendent would be untouchable.

Not surprisingly, the incumbent Chief of Police Thomas F. Byrnes supported the bill completely. The commissioners did not. They found an ally. Mayor Strong vetoed the bill, which did not pass. That spelled doom for Chief Byrnes.

According to a lengthy May 28, 1895, article in the *New York Times*, Chief Byrnes retired at his own request after thirty-two years of service. He was granted a $3,000 per year pension. Inspector Peter Conlin was named to replace him. The reporter noted that Byrnes's retirement "effectually disposes of the statement which had gained circulation that charges were to have been preferred against the retiring chief."

QUOTE

Two days after Chief Byrnes's departure, Acting Chief Colin laid down the law to his administrators. He said: "The captains and acting captains were warned that there must be no laxity in the enforcement of [the excise laws] on Sundays and during the prohibited hours," and that "courteous, polite treatment of citizens would be insisted upon."

That same day, the board accepted the retirement of several other officers, except for one captain "against whom charges had been filed." TR had been on the job only three weeks and he had already made it clear that reforms had started.

Beer, Telephones, and Walk-Arounds

TR took aim at the street patrolmen as well as administrators. He was the epitome of an equal opportunity enforcer of laws and police procedures. One of his goals was to emulate his Civil Service Commission days and make merit rather than patronage the system for hiring and promoting police officers. One attempt in particular got him into trouble with city residents and caused him to wonder if he really wanted to be the police commissioner.

New York City had a law against drinking on Sundays, which the police conveniently overlooked. He decided to enforce it, mainly because he believed laws had to be obeyed, even if he considered them unfair or impractical. That created a stir in the city.

Residents were forced to find outlets at places like Coney Island to grab a beer. German-Americans in particular were incensed that their beer gardens were closed on Sundays. They held an anti-Roosevelt parade. Some people went so far as to mail bombs to TR. Fortunately, they were defused.

FACT

TR was innovative. Once, when an anti-Semitic speaker from Germany came to New York City to deliver a speech, Jewish citizens asked TR to ban the speech. He told them he could not do that. Instead, he assigned the speaker a bodyguard of approximately forty Jewish policemen in order to make the speaker uncomfortable—and a bit foolish.

Commissioner Roosevelt could not get used to the constant resistance he received to even the best-intentioned moves to upgrade the police department. One of his fellow commissioners in particular, Andrew Parker, began opposing him on issue after issue. A feud developed between the two men that became counterproductive. The resistance perplexed TR.

TR wrote:

[We were] right in excluding politics from promotions . . . It was because of our acting in this manner, resolutely warring on dishonesty . . . and refusing to pay heed to any consideration except the good of the service and the city, and the merits of the men themselves, that we drew down upon our heads the bitter and malignant animosity of the bread-and-butter spoils politicians.

ESSENTIAL

In his brief tenure, TR and his fellow commissioners introduced a bicycle squad and pistol shooting practice, standardized officers' use of pistols, installed telephones in station houses, implemented annual physical exams for officers, and instituted new disciplinary rules. They appointed 1,600 new recruits based on their physical and mental qualifications, rather than on their political affiliations.

TR did some positive things to boost the morale of the police force and improve officers' efficiency. The board made it a point to reward officers for exemplary performance. "During our two years' service we found it necessary over a hundred times to single out men for special mention because of some feat of heroism," he wrote.

The Innovative Hiring Process

TR was aware that the merit approach was not perfect. He stated that competitive examinations were a means to an end. They did not always mean that the people who passed them would turn out to be ideal public servants. But, he explained, the examination system was better than the patronage alternative.

He cited as an example the appointment of 2,000 new police officers in New York City at one time when he was the police commissioner. There were 6,000 to 8,000 candidates for the openings. The commissioners had two choices in selecting the successful applicants: rely on outsiders' recommendations or apply the competitive examination. He preferred the examination route, which the board chose.

Under TR's leadership, all the applicants underwent rigid physical and mental examinations. Those who passed took the written competitive examination, which was not particularly rigorous. As TR described the test, it required "only the knowledge that any good primary common school education would meet—that is, a test of ordinary intelligence and simple mental training."

As he said, the tests were not foolproof. Sometimes potentially good recruits failed and men who turned out to be bad cops passed. Generally, he said, "As a rule, the men with intelligence sufficient to enable them to answer the questions were of a type very distinctly above that of those who failed."

In any event, the new competitive examination system marked an innovative step forward in the New York City police department's hiring process—and a success for TR.

The list of accomplishments was impressive, but it was not all TR wanted to get done. Despite his good intentions, the job wore him down. He was ready for a new, less taxing job. President William McKinley came to his rescue and appointed him assistant secretary of the navy. It was back to Washington, D.C., for the Roosevelt family.

QUIZ

8-1 Grover Cleveland won the 1888 presidential election popular vote by 90,000 votes. Yet Benjamin Harrison became the president.

A. True
B. False

8-2 TR transferred thousands of jobs from patronage-related to civil service positions during his six years as a Civil Service commissioner. How many?

A. 100,000
B. 1,014
C. 26,000
D. 47,000

8-3 The principal author of the 1890 Sherman Anti-Trust Act, the first federal statute designed to limit the actions of cartels and monopolies, was:

A. former Union army general William T. Sherman.
B. Sherman Truman.
C. singer Bobby Sherman.
D. U.S. Senator John Sherman (R-Ohio).

8-4 Before George Mortimer Pullman invented the railroad sleeping car, he built:

A. coffins.
B. sewer covers.
C. cabooses.
D. reputations.

8-5 Hugh Smith Thompson, the former governor of South Carolina who served with TR as a United States Civil Service commissioner, died in New York City on November 20, 1904, from complications due to a malady that affected TR during his lifetime. It was:

A. malaria.
B. gun shot.
C. asthma.
D. polio.

ANSWERS

8-5. C
8-4. A
8-3. D
8-2. C
8-1. A: *True. Harrison won the electoral college vote by a wide margin, 233–168.*

CHAPTER 9

TR Tacks and Sails in a Different Direction

"As for the political effect of my actions, in the first place, I never can get on in politics, and in the second, I would rather have led that charge and earned my colonelcy than served three terms in the US Senate. It makes me feel as though I could now leave something to my children which will serve as an apology for my having existed."

TR's fascination with naval affairs got a boost in 1897 when President McKinley appointed him as assistant secretary of the navy. The president might as well have put him in charge. His navy "career" did not last long. When the Spanish-American War began in 1898, TR jumped ship and joined the army. Colonel Roosevelt led a famous unit named the "Rough Riders" in the war. For his efforts he earned the nation's highest award for bravery, the Medal of Honor, although it took 103 years before he received it.

TR the "War Hawk"

President McKinley had taken notice of TR's performance as the commissioner of police in New York City. He needed a man with TR's energy and efficiency to run the civilian wing of the U.S. Navy, which was in need of an upgrade. Some of TR's most reliable friends, most notably Henry Cabot Lodge, urged the president to appoint the brash young man as assistant secretary of the navy. He heeded their advice.

On April 19, 1897, President McKinley named TR to the position. TR may have been an assistant technically, but he turned himself into the de facto commander of the navy and gave Washington, D.C., a taste of what was to come when he became president. That was something no one envisioned at the time.

FACT

The title of assistant secretary of the navy was created in 1861, during the Civil War. The incumbent's job was to oversee the navy's civilian personnel and administer its shore facilities. The government did away with the position in 1869 after the war ended but reinstated it in 1890. It was discontinued for good in 1954.

TR assumed his navy duties at a time when the organization was in a state of disarray and war with Spain was on the horizon. The navy was woefully unprepared for a war. President McKinley knew that. He did not want the United States to get involved in it unless there was no diplomatic way to avoid it. In that, he and TR disagreed. His new assistant secretary of the navy began at once to prepare the service for the war he was sure could not be averted and which a lot of people did not want.

In his autobiography, TR noted that he was in the minority at the time in preparing for the war. He said that "The big financiers and the men generally who were susceptible to touch on the money nerve, and who cared nothing for National honor if it conflicted even temporarily with business prosperity, were against the war." So were philanthropists, newspapers, and most of the Congress.

"Most of the Congressmen were content to follow the worst of all possible courses, that is, to pass resolutions which made war more likely, and yet to decline to take measures which would enable us to meet the war if it did come," TR proclaimed. He planned to proceed with his preparation, despite the opposition he faced. And he did it as if he were running the show.

Running the Navy

Many of the navy's ships were unseaworthy, and it was lacking in auxiliary vessels to support the large warships. Worse, the public was not in favor of building new ships. The navy resorted to subterfuge to tell citizens what it was building.

ESSENTIAL

The primary issue between the United States and Spain in the 1890s was the overbearing conduct of the Spanish governor in Cuba. The United States was also worried that Spain was exerting too much power in the Caribbean, contrary to the Monroe Doctrine. Cuban revolutionaries' activities against the Spanish were increasing. The instability and political unrest in the region rattled U.S. authorities.

Traditionally, most Americans, including political leaders, believed their navy should operate solely to protect commerce and the U.S. coast. They did not believe big warships were needed to do that. TR disagreed. He believed that a large navy with powerful warships was essential to fight wars and keep the peace. TR insisted that he abhorred war. But, he said, "I advocate preparation for war in order to avert war; and I should never advocate war unless it were the only alternative to dishonor." Nevertheless, he did in the case of the Spanish-American war.

A New Name for Warships

TR pushed for large, technologically advanced battleships—even if they had to be called something else. For a while, to get around the label "battleships," the navy started calling its new warships armored cruisers. Then it switched the terminology to satisfy the people who believed only in the "coast and commerce" role for the navy.

The new ships became "coast defense battleships." The ships that fell into that category lacked seaworthiness and coal capacity. So the navy started building bigger and better ships labeled "sea-going coast defense battleships."

At the start of the Spanish-American War, the navy had on its active list six battleships, two armored cruisers, thirteen protected cruisers, six steel monitors, eight old iron monitors, thirty-three unprotected cruisers and gunboats, six torpedo boats, and twelve tugs. There were no auxiliary vessels other than the tugs to support them.

As a result of the name changing and inability to focus on the right ship for the right purpose, the navy entered the Spanish-American War with a motley collection of warships that TR alleged could not win a battle. He vowed to change that.

TR's First Year in Office

One of the first things TR did in his first year was what he did best: identify the right people with whom to work. He socialized and communicated with naval historian Alfred Thayer Mahan and naval strategists Commodore George Dewey and Captain Robley D. Evans, and developed plans for fighting what he considered an inevitable war with Spain. Then, he appointed Dewey to command the Asiatic Squadron. The latter accomplishment was just the type of move that drove some of TR's critics—and supporters—to distraction.

Alfred Thayer Mahan began his U.S. Navy career as an officer in the American Civil War. He believed naval power was the key to strong foreign policy, which he stressed in his 1890 book, *The Influence of Sea Power upon History, 1660–1783*. The book, which TR reviewed for the *Atlantic Monthly* in 1890, influenced the navy as it strengthened its forces and developed new strategies.

Even though he was the "assistant secretary," TR had a penchant for setting policy on his own initiative, especially when the secretary of the navy, John Davis Long, was out of office, which was often. Long had a penchant for taking extended lunches, breaks, and vacations to his native New England for long periods to escape the hot Washington, D.C., summer weather.

Additionally, Long was not interested in the mundane day-to-day details of navy administration. He left those to TR, which he later regretted. TR did try to keep Long apprised of what he was doing. He wrote detailed letters to the secretary to update him on his activities, but Long mostly ignored them at his own risk.

The Newspapers Keep Tabs

Long may not have known what TR was up to a large part of the time, but the newspapers did. The *New York Sun* said in an article that "the liveliest spot in Washington . . . is the Navy Department. The decks are cleared for action. Acting Secretary Roosevelt . . . has the whole Navy bordering on a war footing. It remains only to sand down the decks and pipe to quarters to action."

FACT

John Davis Long was born in Maine in 1838. He served as a congressman from Massachusetts and the state's governor before becoming Secretary of the Navy in 1897. Long is credited with laying the groundwork for the "new navy" developed under President Theodore Roosevelt—Long's former assistant, who actually did a lot of the work.

While Long was visiting New England, TR was socializing at the Metropolitan Club in Washington with the president of the Naval Board of Inspection and Survey, the attending surgeon to President McKinley, and assorted navy leaders. That gave him the opportunity to identify people he could trust and who agreed with his views on naval affairs.

He also spent a lot of time sailing aboard the battleship *Iowa*, commanded by Rear Admiral William T. Sampson, who led the navy's significant victory in the Battle of Santiago de Cuba during the war.

Socializing with the "right" people worked to TR's advantage, but it diminished Long's effectiveness as the secretary of the navy. In his absence, his "assistant" was prone to make decisions that rightly were Long's to make. When TR was not making decisions, he was studying how he could improve the navy.

In a strange twist of events, TR retained Long as secretary of the Navy for the first eight months of his presidency. However, Long was uncomfortable with serving as a subordinate to his former assistant, so he resigned from the position on April 30, 1902, and returned to private life in Massachusetts.

Hitting the Target

One agenda item that TR attacked almost immediately was correcting a glaring deficiency among navy gunners: their marksmanship. It was a problem similar to one he had addressed with the New York City police department, to which he had introduced uniform weapons regulations and firing ranges.

The navy was using bigger guns, but the principle was the same: the purpose in shooting at something was to hit it. He conducted a study to see how big a problem the navy faced.

TR learned that while the navy was building bigger ships with advanced weaponry for its time, it was not conducting marksmanship drills that matched the upgrades. It was applying Civil War tactics to twentieth-century technology, which was a drawback in naval combat.

Sims Sees the Problem

He discovered that the gunners realized a small proportion of hits to shots fired. Worse, he found, even the navy did not realize it had a problem in that respect. Fortunately, at least one navy officer, William S. Sims, understood the problem, but he was not in a position to remedy it since he was posted in Paris up to and during the Spanish-American War.

TR recognized that the war would start before he could resolve the marksmanship situation. But he took notice of Sims and was determined to use his expertise in the future. TR tabled action on the problem until he was in a better position to address it, which he did when he became president. And Sims became his naval aide for two-and-a-half years, from 1907–1909.

As the Spanish-American War turned out, the navy's poor gunnery skills did not matter, nor did Sims's warnings. The Spanish navy proved to be no match for the Americans. The work TR had done to prepare the navy for the war and the appointments he had made when the secretary of the navy was "Long" gone contributed heavily to the Americans' victory. The navy's performance proved the truth in TR's words regarding gunnery: "The shots that hit are the shots that count."

FACT

Navy officer William S. Sims wrote several letters to navy administrators to voice his concerns about sailors' poor marksmanship. They ignored Sims and branded him as an alarmist. Practically the only supporters he had were TR and Richard Wainwright, the executive officer of the battleship *Maine*, the catalyst for the war that blew up in Havana harbor.

Pushing for War

TR's talent for identifying and appointing the right people for the right purpose came to the fore in the Spanish-American War. Where he could not appoint people directly, he influenced the people who could. It was due largely to his influence that Admiral George Dewey, the commander at the decisive Battle of Manila, which started the war, received his position, although there were officers senior to him. It was TR who ordered Dewey to sail for Manila in the Philippines to take up a position to fight the Spanish navy. He sent the order when Long was out of the office!

ESSENTIAL

Ten days after the *Maine* sank, Long took a day off to relieve the stress of being on a war footing. He told TR emphatically not to do anything that would impact the navy—or the country. That was like telling him not to attack graft wherever he encountered it.

TR began at once to move ships, people, ammunition, and materiel into place for the war he was sure was about to begin. In effect, he promoted himself to acting, rather than assistant, secretary of the navy.

He sent a cablegram to Dewey on February 25, 1898, with specific instructions:

Dewey, Hong Kong: Order the squadron, except the Monocacy, to Hong Kong. Keep full of coal. In the event of declaration of war Spain, your duty will be to see that the Spanish squadron does not leave the Asiatic coast, and then offensive operations in Philippine Islands. Keep Olympia until further orders.

—ROOSEVELT.

TR knew that *Monocacy* was unfit for war or anything else. The thirty-two-year-old ship had been built during the Civil War. It was emblematic of the mixed collection of "something old, something new, something borrowed" fleet the navy maintained. And the *Olympia* had been ordered to return to the United States. Based on TR's orders, it stayed in the Pacific and led the U.S. armada in the Battle of Manila Bay.

Long was not pleased with Roosevelt, which was nothing new. He considered TR a "bull in a china shop." But he seldom did anything to stop his assistant's rash behavior. According to the papers Long wrote after he left office, despite occasional differences of opinion, the conservative small-navy secretary got on well with the impetuous large-navy assistant and was sorry to see him go off to war in 1898. Off he went, though, as a lieutenant colonel in the United States Army.

From Navy to Army

Even though TR had put a lot of time and effort into preparing the navy for war, he could not participate with it since he was not a member. He was itching to get involved actively in the fighting. On May 10, 1898, he resigned from the navy and "joined" the army, even though he had no military experience to speak of.

TR had a serious desire to test his mettle in war—any war. He believed that young men—and he considered himself one of them, even though he was forty years old at the time—should always be prepared to serve their country as a way to prove their strength and courage. He gave himself the opportunity to follow his own advice.

According to TR, "The young men of the country should realize that it is the duty of every one of them to prepare himself so that in time of need he may speedily become an efficient soldier—a duty now generally forgotten, but which should be recognized as one of the vitally essential parts of every man's training."

At the onset of the Spanish-American War, the army was in worse shape than the navy. It did not have enough troops to conduct a skirmish, let alone a war. Consequently, President McKinley called for 125,000 volunteers to supplement the army. More than a million men responded—including TR, as a recruiter and a soldier.

Portrait of Colonel Theodore Roosevelt, 1898

One of TR's considerable strengths was his ability to organize. That asset came to the fore as he and his old friend Leonard Wood raised a regiment of volunteer cavalry called the "Rough Riders." Their official name was the First U.S. Volunteer Cavalry.

The regiment consisted of a unique group of rugged Westerners, most of them from the Southwest territories of the United States. TR became their leader. "Colonel" Roosevelt went off to war. Surprisingly, Long wondered if his former assistant had lost his sanity.

Long gave credit where credit was due. In his journal, he admitted that TR "has been of great use; a man of unbounded energy and force, and thoroughly honest, which is the main thing." But, he opined, "He has lost his head in this unutterable folly of deserting the post where he is of most service and running off to ride a horse and, probably, brush mosquitoes from his neck on the Florida sands."

TR pulled a few strings to get his commission. One of his champions was Secretary of War Russell A. Alger. Alger, a Civil War veteran, was fond of TR and a patient of Leonard Wood. He offered TR command of one of the National Volunteer Cavalry regiments being raised. Later, Alger would try to block TR's Medal of Honor recommendation.

In that last statement, he was wrong. TR went a lot farther than Florida, geographically and accomplishment wise.

The secretary also provided insight into TR's character. "His heart is right, and he means well, but it is one of those cases of aberration—desertion—vain glory; of which he is utterly unaware. He thinks he is following his highest ideal, whereas, in fact, as without exception, he is acting like a fool."

The most significant comment Long included was a prediction that came true. "And yet," he wrote, "how absurd all this will sound if, by some turn of fortune, he should accomplish some great thing and strike a very high mark." TR did "accomplish some great thing," but that did not diminish the acumen Long displayed in his remarks.

Leading the Rough Riders

Roosevelt was in charge of a group of approximately 1,000 Rough Riders, of whom he knew little, since Wood had recruited most of them. He suspected that they were good horsemen because most of them came from the Southwest. As he wrote about them later, "In all the world there could be no better material for soldiers than that afforded by these grim hunters of the mountains, these wild rough riders of the plains."

Beyond the fact that they were sturdy men, TR did not know much of anything about their training, when—or if—they would be called to action, or how the army planned to utilize them. He learned that the army did not have a clue, either.

QUOTE

TR's problem was not recruiting men. He wrote, "Within a day or two after it was announced that we were to raise the regiment, we were literally deluged with applications from every quarter of the Union. Without the slightest trouble, so far as men went, we could have raised a brigade or even a division. The difficulty lay in arming, equipping, mounting, and disciplining the men we selected."

TR recalled that while he was still assistant secretary of the navy he had tried to find out what the Department of War's strategy for fighting the war

Theodore Roosevelt and Rough Riders atop San Juan Hill, 1898

was. He said tersely, "They had no plans. Even during the final months before the outbreak of hostilities very little was done in the way of efficient preparation." Nevertheless, he and Wood began training their troops.

The Rough Riders were a diverse group. The 1,000 members were ranchers, cowboys, gamblers, and a few outlaws. The Easterners in the unit were primarily college dropouts and young men from the "upper crust" of society who were looking for a little adventure in their lives. They shared one basic asset: all of them were ready to fight.

Wood and TR set up a training camp at San Antonio, Texas, to equip and prepare their unit for combat. They did so knowing that their chances of getting into battle were slim. Even though the army had attracted large numbers of recruits, not all of the units to which they were assigned were fit for battle. The Rough Riders had an advantage: Wood was an experienced war-fighter and a Medal of Honor recipient. That medal added a bit of luster to the Rough Riders' reputation.

By the end of May 1898 the Rough Riders were as ready for battle as they were ever going to be. They shipped off to Tampa, Florida, and left from there for Santiago de Cuba on June 13, minus a critical element of their cavalry equipment: their horses.

No Horsing Around

The War Department was in such haste to get troops to Cuba that it did not pay enough attention to the logistical side of the operation. The only way the horses could have gotten to Cuba was by swimming. So the Rough Riders arrived in the battle zone without their horses, which reduced them from a cavalry unit to an infantry regiment. That did not matter once they got into combat, as long as their leader had a mount.

TR was the only Rough Rider who had a horse when the unit reached Cuba. But he did not have a dress uniform, which he did not need for combat purposes anyway. He had only his service uniform—the only uniform he had in his short stint in the army.

The Rough Riders may have been better off without their horses. Their steeds were not heavy enough for cavalry use, and many were unbroken. Half the horses bucked when riders mounted them or, according to TR, "possessed some other of the amiable weaknesses incident to horse life on the great ranches." Some of the animals were unmanageable, even for Rough Riders.

The Battle of Las Guasimas

Once the Rough Riders arrived in Cuba, they joined the Fifth Corps, a well-trained and well-equipped unit comprised of a combination of volunteers and regular army soldiers. It was not long before they were pressed into battle at Las Guasimas, a village not too far from Santiago. That was a prelude to the Battle of San Juan Hill.

The battle at Las Guasimas exposed a weakness in TR's unit. The men were not used to walking or to the hot, sultry Cuban weather. As a result, only 500 Rough Riders participated in the fighting.

TR remained cool under hostile fire. He was finally getting the chance to test his mettle in a war, one that he had agitated for so vociferously. He was not entirely sure of what he should do at times as the fighting raged.

"I was still very much in the dark as to where the main body of the Spanish forces were, or exactly what lines the battle was following, and was very uncertain what I ought to do," he recalled. "But I knew it could not be wrong to go forward, and I thought I would find Wood and then see what he wished me to do." TR recognized that some advice was needed.

What happened at the Battle of Las Guasimas?
The American forces sustained several casualties at the Battle of Las Guasimas. Eight Rough Riders were killed; thirty-four were wounded. The number of wounded did not include two or three whose wounds were so minor that they were not reported. Altogether, of the 964 American soldiers in the battle, sixteen were killed and fifty-two wounded.

"I was in a mood to cordially welcome guidance, for it was most bewildering to fight an enemy whom one so rarely saw," he concluded. With the help of Colonel Wood and his able officers, TR got through the battle, which allowed the Americans to continue toward Santiago. In the field, Wood was promoted to Brigadier General and TR was made Colonel of the Rough Riders. More fighting—and a bit of glory for TR—lay ahead.

Battle of Santiago

At first the strategy of the American forces at the Battle of Santiago was to drive their Spanish opposition off the high ground by firing at them from fairly static positions along a line below the hills. TR saw the folly in that and advocated a charge up the hills.

He ordered the Rough Riders to attack. Other troops joined them. The Battle of Santiago intensified as they rushed up toward the enemy positions.

FACT

The Battle of San Juan Hill is somewhat of a misnomer. TR refers to his part as a battle at Kettle Hill, and historians sometimes call it the Battle of San Juan Heights. Collectively, the fight there is known as the Battle of San Juan Hill.

TR led the charge on his horse, Little Texas. Since he was the only man there on horseback, he reached the crest of Kettle Hill before the infantry soldiers. There, he nearly ran into a wire fence, at which point he dismounted and parted with Little Texas. He did not expect to see his horse again—or anything else. A couple of bullets had scraped Little Texas, and one had grazed TR in the elbow.

The charge up the hill had turned into a contest among members of the Rough Riders and other units to see who could reach the top first. The issue was never truly settled. What mattered was who won the battle. That was indisputably the Americans.

TR noted:

The first guidons planted [on the hill] were those of the three New Mexican troops, G, E, and F, of my regiment . . . On the extreme right of the hill, at the opposite end from where we struck it . . . men of the Ninth were first up. Each of the five captains was firm in the belief that his troop was first up.

The chaos of battle continued. TR noted, "It is astonishing what a limited area of vision and experience one has in the hurly-burly of a battle." At one point he led a charge on Spanish positions only to learn that he was virtually alone. His men had not heard his order. He returned to his troops, chided them for not following, reissued his order, and led the charge once again.

More Troops to Lead

TR was no longer commanding only Rough Riders as the fighting continued. During the confusion of battle, unit integrity faded. Members of individual units broke up and merged with one another. TR was leading an amalgamation of troops; all followed him in pursuit of the Spanish troops.

The Rough Riders regiment employed 490 men at the Battle of San Juan Hill. Eighty-nine were killed or wounded. That was the highest number suffered by any U.S. cavalry regiment engaged in the battle. The fighting was more intense than it had been at Las Guasimas, which resulted in the Rough Riders' high casualty count.

Gradually, the fighting ended and the Americans won a significant victory at the San Juan hills. Once again, they paid a steep price for their effort.

The Aftermath of the Battle

Two controversies arose after the Battle of San Juan Hill ended. One involved returning the Rough Riders to the United States immediately. The other was a Medal of Honor recommendation for Roosevelt.

On August 3, 1898, the commander of the U.S. troops in Cuba, Major General William R. Shafter, held a meeting with the medical and commanding officers of the Fifth Corps at Santiago. Shafter read a letter from Secretary of War Alger ordering him to move the troops to the interior of Cuba. The order ran contrary to the officers' wishes. They wanted their troops returned to the United States to alleviate the risk of tropical diseases such as malaria and yellow fever.

TR expressed his concerns to General Shafter in a letter explaining why the troops should be sent home. In the letter, TR wrote, "I write only because I cannot see our men, who have fought so bravely and who have endured extreme hardship and danger so uncomplainingly, go to destruction without striving so far as lies in me to avert a doom as fearful as it is unnecessary and undeserved."

QUOTE

TR called malaria the "Cuban fever." It affected him long after his return to the United States. He mentioned in a May 2, 1905, letter to his son Kermit that, while on a hunting trip in Colorado, "I have been a little knocked out by the Cuban fever. Up to that time I was simply in splendid shape." He may have left Cuba, but Cuba never left him.

Shafter handed the letter to a correspondent for the Associated Press. The resulting publicity upset Secretary Alger and may have played a role in the subsequent denial of TR's Medal of Honor recommendation. Once the troops returned to the United States, action on approving the Medal of Honor languished—for the next 103 years.

TR's Medal of Honor Controversy

Even though Alger had a soft spot in his heart for TR, he was not keen on authorizing the Medal of Honor for the Colonel. The bad publicity that resulted from the news in the press discouraged him and President McKinley from pursuing the matter.

After McKinley was assassinated in September 1901, TR took over as president. He did not feel that it was right for him to authorize his own Medal of Honor. (Alger had been dismissed for incompetence by that time.) After TR left office in 1909, the matter remained in limbo.

After Congress eliminated the statute of limitations on Medal of Honor awards, Roosevelt family members, congressional representatives, and other supporters pressed for the authorization of TR's award. The army continued to resist their pleas.

Some army historians felt that he had not really earned the medal. They argued that other soldiers had done as many brave things at the Battle of San Juan Hill as the Colonel had, and they were equally deserving of Medals of Honor.

FACT

Until 1996, there was a statute of limitations for awarding a Medal of Honor. The recommendation had to be submitted within two years of the action. The subsequent review process could take eighteen to twenty-four months. In 1996, Congress repealed the statute of limitations on military decorations. That cleared the way for a reexamination of TR's award.

TR Receives His Medal

Eventually, due to pressure from TR's supporters, the army relented. In a White House ceremony on January 16, 2001, President Bill Clinton presented TR's Medal of Honor to Tweed Roosevelt, TR's great-grandson. The award was a long time coming, but it was welcome to the Roosevelt family.

The award of the Medal of Honor to TR closed a memorable chapter in his life. He returned to the United States with a trace of malaria, a lot of bittersweet memories, and renewed ambition to pursue his political career. His successes in previous government positions and the acclamations he received for his service in Cuba opened new possibilities for him—in New York.

QUIZ

9-1 Most of the navy's ships were powered by coal in 1898 when the Spanish-American War began. They were refueled by ships known as colliers. How many colliers did the navy have in its fleet at the time?

A. 0
B. 20
C. 54
D. 113

9-2 The battleship *Maine* blew up in Havana Harbor on February 15, 1898. That was the incident that led to the Spanish-American War. Ultimately, investigators determined that the cause of the explosion was:

A. a faulty tailpipe.
B. Cuban dissidents.
C. Spanish sailors operating from a submarine.
D. unknown initially.

9-3 Leonard Wood is the only member of the U.S. Army to hold this distinction:

A. the only medical officer to ever hold the position of chief of staff of the army
B. the only medical officer to attain the rank of major general
C. the only major general in the army born in New Hampshire
D. the only medical officer in the army in 1910 named Leonard

9-4 The Rough Riders included a large number of American Indians.

A. True
B. False

9-5 How many Spanish soldiers did TR take credit for killing during the Battle of San Juan Hill?

A. just enough to qualify for the Medal of Honor
B. none
C. so many he could not count them
D. one

9-6 Only two father-son teams have ever earned the Medal of Honor. One was Theodore Roosevelt and Theodore Roosevelt Jr. The other was:

A. Carl and Rob Reiner.
B. Arthur and Douglas MacArthur.
C. John Adams and John Quincy Adams.
D. Dwight and John Eisenhower.

9-1. A: The navy purchased 20 colliers in March and April 1898 to supply the 86 ships it had in its fleet at the time. The only auxiliary ships available were 12 tugboats. The rest were warships, some of which were left over from the Civil War.

9-2. D

9-3. A: He was named chief of staff of the army in 1910; no other medical officer has been named to the post since.

9-4. True: The unit included Cherokees, Chickasaws, Choctaws, and Creeks. TR described them thusly: "Only a few were of pure blood. The others shaded off until they were absolutely indistinguishable from their white comrades; with whom, it may be mentioned, they all lived on terms of complete equality."

9-5. D: One. He was running up the hill when two Spanish soldiers jumped up about ten yards away from TR. They ran away, but he fired twice at them. He missed one but shot the second soldier fatally.

9-6. B: Arthur MacArthur earned his for valor at the Battle of Missionary Ridge, Tennessee, November 25, 1863. It was awarded on June 30, 1890. Douglas received his on April 1, 1942, "For conspicuous leadership in preparing the Philippine Islands to resist conquest, for gallantry and intrepidity above and beyond the call of duty in action against invading Japanese forces, and for the heroic conduct of defensive and offensive operations on the Bataan Peninsula."

CHAPTER 10

From Governor to Vice President to President

"The course I followed, of regarding the Executive as subject only to the people, and, under the Constitution, bound to serve the people affirmatively in cases where the Constitution does not explicitly forbid him to render the service, was substantially the course followed by both Andrew Jackson and Abraham Lincoln."

After TR returned to New York in 1898, events in his life moved quickly. Within the space of three years he progressed from governor of New York to vice president of the United States to president of the United States. He achieved some remarkable successes as governor, but incurred a few enemies along the way. They connived to get him nominated to the vice president's position, which he did not particularly covet. Fate took care of the rest in the form of a national tragedy: the assassination of President William McKinley.

Looking for New Fields to Conquer

After earning the public's respect for his exploits in Cuba, TR looked for new fields to conquer. The next logical step from a political standpoint was the governorship of his home state of New York.

He had already made his mark at the state level as an assemblyman. TR knew that simply dropping his hat into the proverbial ring would not guarantee his election. He had finished second in the ring at Harvard during the intramural championships. He had no intention of finishing as a runner-up again.

FACT

TR continued his hobby of boxing at Harvard. He admitted that he was not good at the sport. But he entered one tournament at the school in which he did pretty well. He reached the semifinals or finals (he could not remember which). TR considered that a major achievement, even though he admitted that it was one of his rare athletic accomplishments.

New York state politics were rough-and-tumble in the late nineteenth century. The state government was rife with corruption, and political bosses ruled the roost. Some of those bosses were less than happy when they learned that TR was contemplating a run for governor. He had been anti-machine and anti-corruption as an assemblyman. There was no reason for them to believe that he would be any different as governor. Their fears that he would attempt radical reforms were justified.

TR was a bit of an enigma from a party standpoint in New York. The Democrats ruled the political landscape for the most part in New York City and at the state government level. TR, as a Republican, was pretty much an interloper. Even his own party members did not always trust him completely, since he was not their model of a "machine" Republican. After all, he showed anti-business tendencies at times and even worked with Democrats on occasion for what he perceived as the common good.

When the gubernatorial campaign began in 1898, neither party knew what to expect from TR. He gave them an idea in the way he wrangled the Republican nomination.

TR Finagles the Nomination

The Republicans believed that TR intended to attack corruption in their party if he won the governor's office. The Democrats were sure that he was going to launch a statewide anti-corruption campaign against both parties. Republicans were a bit reluctant to nominate him, then.

ESSENTIAL

TR did an end run around the party bosses to secure the nomination, even though he made it sound like a fait accompli in his autobiography: "In September, 1898, the First Volunteer Cavalry, in company with most of the Fifth Army Corps, was disbanded, and a few days later, I was nominated for Governor of New York by the Republican party." Those words disguised the political chicanery to which he resorted to get the party's nod—and at which he was adept.

TR took advantage of a new political group, the Citizens Union, to ensure Republican support. He approached Citizens Union leaders and suggested that they form a ticket to run against both major parties. The group's executive committee thought that was a swell idea and assumed that TR was going to head the ticket. He didn't do anything to dissuade them from the notion.

The committee launched a petition campaign to get the party on the ballot and collected 6,000 signatures. Naturally, the signers believed TR was heading the ticket. So did the Republicans, who feared that the new party might have a chance to win the election with TR as their candidate.

That created a quandary for them, since the incumbent governor, Frank S. Black, was a Republican. But his administration had been plagued by corruption and scandals. Their solution was simple. Dump Black and nominate Roosevelt—at their peril.

No "Platt"-itudes for TR

Republican Party boss U.S. Senator Thomas C. Platt was not particularly keen on Roosevelt as a candidate. He and his colleagues viewed TR as a maverick who was more than likely to do things his way, rather than the way the party machine wanted them done.

Platt needed assurances from TR that he would toe the party line—or at least make it appear that he was working with them. They set up a meeting at Platt's hotel residence in New York City to hammer out an agreement.

FACT

New York State Republican Party boss Thomas C. Platt served in the U.S. Senate briefly in 1881 and from 1897–1909. His chief claim to fame occurred on January 21, 1897, when his photograph in the *New York Tribune* became the first halftone reproduction to appear in a mass circulation daily paper.

Part of Platt's reluctance to endorse TR had to do with the young man's character. Some people, Platt among them, perceived TR as an overzealous, myopic reformer who could not or would not be flexible in his attempts to root out corruption or seek social justice. That characterization haunted Platt.

He feared that neither Republicans nor independents would vote for TR because of his intransigence on reform issues. In truth, Roosevelt was not as inflexible as some people thought.

TR was interested in results, and he realized that the only way to get them was by working with a range of people who shared his goals. He was a man of action, but not one who acted just to do something. He listened to people who had good ideas, and he was willing to accomplish his goals in small steps, rather than all at once.

Not everybody believed TR could compromise to get things done. Poet Edgar Lee Masters wrote in 1904, "One of Mr. Roosevelt's apologists has said that he compromised with his ideals in order to get power to carry some of them into effect. But this never has and never can be done. The man who thus sophisticates with his own mind has surrendered his power."

TR knew the meaning of compromise—and the limitations of power. That is what Platt wanted to hear.

TR Runs as a Republican

To prove that he understood the meaning of compromise, TR promised Platt that he would consult with him on appointments to office and important policy matters. That was good enough for Platt. He agreed to support TR for the governor's office. A few months later, he couldn't wait to get rid of TR.

Once Platt gave TR his blessing, the now-Republican candidate notified the Citizens Union group that he could not accept its nomination. He ran as a Republican. The Citizens Union replaced Roosevelt with Theodore Bacon.

TR ran his campaign in a low-key fashion, based more on his popularity than any specific platform. He promised the voters he would run a "clean" administration without outlining anything specific. That was enough for them, although his election was far from a landslide.

In the gubernatorial election of 1898, TR attracted 661,707 votes. His Democratic foe, Augustus Van Wyck, had 643,921. Bacon received 2,103 votes. New York state had a new governor: Theodore Roosevelt. His tenure was short-lived.

Corruption Becomes a Target

TR assumed office on January 1, 1899. He quickly justified the Republicans' and Democrats' fears that he would attempt reforms, this time statewide instead of only in New York City. Governor Roosevelt pushed for—and got passed—some progressive legislation. And, he did not waste any time showing Platt that "consultation" had many definitions as the two men became embroiled in an Erie Canal debate.

FACT

Governor Roosevelt made the resumption of the state's canal system a top priority in 1899. He appointed the Committee on Canals to study the system and make recommendations for action. Based on their recommendations and TR's intercession, the Barge Canal System emerged.

One of the most scandal-ridden departments in Black's administration had been the state canal system office, where there was a need for a new administrator. The entire canal system was in danger of collapsing in 1898 due to insufficient funds. Work stopped suddenly on the partially completed "Nine Million Dollar Improvement," as it was called. The new governor would not allow that to happen.

Platt promised the job of canal director to a Syracuse crony, Francis J. Hendricks. TR objected to the appointment and offered his own list of candidates.

TR did not select a particular person; he simply told Platt to pick one from the list. From that point on, that was the method by which most administrative positions were filled. Platt got his desired role in the process, but TR maintained his independence, which he also exercised in the lawmaking process. Moreover, he saved the state money.

From March 1889 to October 1889, it cost the state $450,000 to operate its canals, compared to $590,000 for the same period the previous year, a savings of about 25 percent. The comparative costs are somewhat misleading, since there was more activity on the canals in the 1889 fiscal year. That was TR's goal as governor: higher productivity for less cost.

Canal restoration was one of several issues TR addressed in his first year in office. He supported laws to advance civil service reform law in New York and the United States, improve conditions in tenement sweatshops in New York City, strengthen factory inspection procedures, limit work hours for public employees and women and children to eight hours a day, improve the public education system, and conserve resources.

ESSENTIAL

Equal taxation was a cornerstone of TR's governorship. He noted in his first annual message, "Absolute equality, absolute justice in matters of taxation will probably never be realized; but we can approximate it much more closely than at present." His attempts to achieve equality and justice in taxation created a rift with Republican Party leaders.

He advocated a minimum wage for New York City schoolteachers, sought legislation to allow the state Supreme Court to inspect corporations' books, and backed anti-monopoly laws. One effort in particular incensed Platt and the party leaders: TR pushed through a new tax on public franchises. In the process, he was biting the hand that fed Platt and his cronies.

Taxing Public Franchises and Platt's Patience

Large corporations in New York provided Republican Party leaders with hefty monetary donations. Platt did not want to see those funds dry up. TR wasn't averse to political contributions; he was concerned that many of the corporations that provided the funding were not paying their fair shares of taxes. The two men locked horns over the issue.

QUOTE

TR was puzzled about why people opposed the franchise tax. He wrote, "I came to the conclusion that it was a matter of plain decency and honesty that these companies should pay a tax on their franchises, inasmuch as they did nothing that could be considered as service rendered the public in lieu of a tax." That settled the matter in his mind.

Many of the corporations that supported Platt and the party financially operated public franchises that supplied services such as water and gas. These franchises were not taxed. Neither they nor the political bosses wanted them to be. The governor did. He forced a franchise tax through the state legislature.

TR's justification for the franchise tax was clear. He said, "A change should never be shirked on the ground of its being radical, when the abuse has become flagrant and no other remedy appears possible. This was the case with the taxation of local franchises in this State." He won the argument and initiated a political falling out with Platt.

The governor's successful implementation of the franchise tax accomplished two things: it added money to the state's coffers and angered Platt, whose minions grew concerned that the boss could not control TR. Even worse from Platt's standpoint, Roosevelt was winning the public relations campaign and would have been a shoo-in for re-election, which the party boss did not want.

The Power of Public Relations

The new governor was not content to simply oversee the passage of laws. He enlisted the aid of the press corps to make sure the citizens of the state knew that he was working incessantly on their behalf and defying the machine. He knew the value of good public relations and newspapers.

FACT

TR met twice daily with the Capitol press corps when he was in Albany to answer questions and provide rumors, gossip, and anecdotes about various topics. There was a price for his "show." If press corps members published anything other than official news, they would be banned from his press conferences. Not many of them were willing to pay that price.

TR also gained favor with the public as he traveled tirelessly around the state making speeches and presiding over ceremonial affairs. The people did not care much what he had to say. They were just happy that their governor made it clear he was on their side and that he was pursuing their interests despite opposition from legislators and party bosses. As a result, legislators and bosses alike grew somewhat reluctant to challenge TR.

A Rift Develops Between Platt and TR

Another area in which the governor was making sometimes unwelcome inroads was the relationship between the state and corporate wealth. Platt and his supporters were not pleased that TR was seeking to balance corporate profits with the needs of the general public. This was an old battle for TR, but it created another wedge between him and the party bosses.

"Nothing needs closer attention, nothing deserves to be treated with more courage, caution and sanity, than the relations of the State to corporate wealth, and indeed to vast individual wealth," he proclaimed.

TR was exhibiting his political acumen in pointing out that new government and business relationships were needed to deal with the upcoming twentieth-century revolution in industrial and societal conditions. He intended as governor to usher in some of those changes.

There were some areas in which TR governed that did not upset the Republican Party. One of them was conservation, long a favorite issue of his. He advocated the improvement of laws governing fisheries, forests, and game, including an increase in the number of game wardens and a reorganization of the Fisheries, Forest and Game Commission.

His purposes were to manage the state's forests and wildlife as efficiently and cost effectively as possible, improve the related laws and administration, and provide recreational outlets for the public.

FACT

TR had strict criteria for the game wardens he wanted hired. They had to be fit men who were hired and retained based on their "zeal, ability and efficiency with which they perform their duties." They also had to be woodsmen whose only job was to work in the forests. They were to have no outside business.

Republican Party leaders had no quarrel with TR and his efforts to protect the state's resources—as long as they did not impinge on their business interests. Yet, there was growing tension between Platt and TR regarding many of his activities as governor, which made the party leaders wonder if they wanted him in office for a second term, which TR wanted but they did not. They sensed a power struggle looming between themselves and TR that favored him.

Friction Grows

It did not appear to the party leaders that the governor was wearing himself out in office. He was administrating the state's affairs so effortlessly that he had managed to complete two books while in Albany: *The Rough Riders* and *Oliver Cromwell*. But he was wearing them out. They simply were not seeing eye-to-eye.

Platt increased his efforts to get TR out of the governor's chair—and New York state, if possible. TR continued to govern, despite opposition from his own party leaders in many areas of his administration. That set up a conflict between the two men that spilled over into the entire Republican Party as different factions sought to find the right position for him.

One of the things that kept TR going in New York was his ability to take a punch and keep on fighting. He said, "I no more expected special consideration in politics than I would have expected it in the boxing ring. I wished to act squarely to others, and I wished to be able to show that I could hold my own as against others." He proved as governor that he could do both.

Some of TR's opponents wanted to bury him in a job where he could not harm them. His supporters wanted just the opposite; they sought a position that would give him some exposure to the voting public as a steppingstone to the presidency. After a great deal of infighting, the two factions arrived at a compromise: the vice presidency of the United States.

Next Stop: Vice President of the United States

The perfect opportunity for Platt to move TR up—and out—of the state came quickly. Roosevelt had been in office for only a year and people were beginning to tout him as an ideal presidential candidate. TR did nothing to discourage such talk, even though he really did not want the job. Even Platt saw that TR had presidential potential.

One of TR's most ardent supporters for vice president was his old Western buddy "Buffalo Bill" Cody. At one campaign stop in Kansas, Cody made an eloquent speech on his behalf. He ended it with a few quaint words: "A cyclone from the West had come; no wonder the rats hunted their cellars!" McKinley and TR won Kansas by a wide margin.

The party leader started making inquiries about TR's chances for the 1900 presidential election. Platt had the same problem that had hindered his choice of candidates for governor of New York in 1898: there was a Republican incumbent in place. That had not deterred Platt in 1898; it didn't in 1900, either.

Incumbent and highly popular U.S. President William McKinley was almost a lock for re-election in 1900. He had done well in his first term, and there was no reason to believe that he would not continue to retain his effectiveness. But he did not have a vice president as the election approached.

Governor Theodore Roosevelt after nomination as VP in 1900

Vice President Garrett Hobart died of heart failure on November 21, 1889, and the party did not replace him. Platt suggested discreetly that Theodore Roosevelt would be an ideal vice president. He placed Roosevelt's name into the mix. The idea captivated most high-ranking Republicans—including President McKinley.

Roosevelt raised strenuous objections to becoming vice president, claiming that he could not afford to pay his expenses in Washington, D.C., and that his supporters in New York state wanted him to remain as governor. Both arguments had merit.

The national clamor for him to be McKinley's running mate won the day, however. He threw himself into the campaign.

On March 4, 1901, TR became the vice president of the United States. He did not hold the position long.

Vice President Theodore Roosevelt

Even though TR got caught up in a political fight not of his own choosing at the 1900 Republican Convention, he benefited ultimately from the outcome. He had some doubts about his duties as vice president for the few months he was in office.

TR did not exactly set the Senate on fire with his March 4, 1901, inaugural speech. It was short at only 411 words. And it was tepid. He closed by saying,

But there is also every reason for facing [these duties] with highhearted resolution and eager and confident faith in our capacity to do them aright . . . Most deeply do I appreciate the privilege of my position; for high, indeed, is the honor of presiding over the American Senate at the outset of the twentieth century.

His words outweighed his actions in the coming months.

One problem TR faced as vice president was his inability to shape and implement his own policies. He had to follow the party line, which had never been his preference. And his duties were limited. His primary role was to preside over the Senate, which did not enthrall him. Regardless, he threw himself into the role even though he found it boring at best.

The fact that he had a limited knowledge of parliamentary procedures did not help him carry out his role—or impress the senators over whom he was presiding. Somehow, as TR always did, he muddled through until the Senate adjourned.

Back to Oyster Bay

During the summer of 1901, TR returned to his retreat at Oyster Bay. He accepted speaking engagements and focused on foreign affairs. TR stuck to topics with which he was familiar: building the navy and alerting his audiences to the growing power of certain nations such as Germany and Japan. He and President McKinley were in agreement on many of TR's ideas, but they did not work together to develop them.

TR also began developing a base of support for a possible presidential campaign in 1904. The Republican nomination would be open, since McKinley would have completed two terms already. And TR realized that the popularity he had enjoyed after the Spanish-American War was fading, so 1904 might represent his best chance for running for president.

As TR laid the groundwork for his presidential campaign and honed his foreign relations expertise and skills, fate stepped in. An assassin named Leon Czolgosz shot President McKinley on September 6, 1901. McKinley died several days later, in the early morning of September 14.

President of the United States

TR took the oath of office the same day President McKinley died. In his typical courageous manner, he did not give a second thought to the danger that the position involved.

The twenty-sixth president of the United States, Theodore Roosevelt, told Congress in his first annual message on December 3, 1901:

> *No man will ever be restrained from becoming President by any fear as to his personal safety. If the risk to the President's life became great, it would mean that the office would more and more come to be filled by men of a spirit which would make them resolute and merciless in dealing with every friend of disorder.*

FACT

Strangely enough, even though three of the past seven presidents elected since 1860 had been assassinated, TR finished his first term without a vice president. And his vice president from 1905–1909, Charles W. Fairbanks, served in a capacity similar to the one TR had envisioned in his: one of relative anonymity.

TR proved to be as resolute as the man he described in his speech. The continuity in the office of the president of the United States stayed in place uninterrupted as Theodore Roosevelt stepped into the White House.

QUIZ

10-1   President William McKinley was assassinated in September 1901. How many other U.S. presidents had been assassinated up to that point?

A. Seven
B. Three
C. Two
D. None

10-2   "Buffalo Bill" Cody, one of TR's old friends, got his nickname from:

A. his birthplace of Buffalo, Wyoming.
B. his ability to "buffalo" people.
C. his skills at shooting bison.
D. his experience as mayor of Buffalo, Wyoming.

10-3   Who told the *New York Tribune* in February 1900 that "under no circumstances could I, or would I, accept the nomination for the vice presidency?"

A. Roosevelt Grier
B. Franklin D. Roosevelt
C. Thomas C. Platt
D. Theodore Roosevelt

10-4   Edgar Lee Masters, who was not a fan of TR, was:

A. the man after whom a famous golf tournament in Augusta, Georgia, is named.
B. a poet who is best known for his *Spoon River Anthology*.
C. TR's first vice president.
D. one of the Rough Riders wounded at the Battle of Santiago.

10-5   Leon Czolgosz was executed for assassinating President McKinley less than two months after his crime.

A. True
B. False

ANSWERS

10-5. *True: Czolgosz assassinated McKinley on September 6, 1901. He was executed on October 29, 1901.*

10-4. *B*

10-3. *D*

10-2. *C: Cody earned a living by providing bison meat to Kansas Pacific Railroad workers. At one point, he killed 4,280 bison during an eight-month period in 1867–1868.*

10-1. *C: Abraham Lincoln (April 14, 1865) and James Garfield (July 2, 1881)*

CHAPTER 11

TR's First Term

"We demand that big business give the people a square deal; in return
we must insist that when anyone engaged in big business honestly
endeavors to do right he shall himself be given a square deal."
(Letter to Sir Edward Grey, November 15, 1913)

TR did not enter the White House with a specific agenda. He intended to follow McKinley's policies and retain his personnel. His primary goal initially was to exercise his right and duty to do anything that "the needs of the nation demanded unless such action was forbidden by the Constitution or by the laws." He did not waste time causing "to be done many things not previously done by the President and the heads of the departments"—some of which might not have been expected from a Republican president.

Newlands Act

Reclamation and forestry were two of TR's first priorities when he assumed the presidency. He had gained an appreciation for reclamation and conservation in his days in the Badlands and as the governor of New York. The White House gave him the influence he needed to push conservation on a national scale.

One of the lessons he had learned was that the western part of the United States was never going to grow if it did not have adequate water. That had been made abundantly clear by John Wesley Powell when he began exploring the West shortly after the Civil War ended. He noted that after the winter snow melted and the spring rains ended, the region went into a dry period. That was an impediment to farming, ranching, and increasing the population.

FACT

John Wesley Powell, like TR, was a self-trained naturalist. Although he lost an arm while fighting for the Union during the Civil War, he embarked on rugged field trips throughout the West, including one expedition to explore the Grand Canyon in 1869. His findings were invaluable in mapping the West—and supplying its need for water.

Powell suggested that an extensive irrigation system was needed to provide the badly needed water, and he mapped locations for dams and irrigation projects. A lot of people agreed with him, especially after a series of droughts hit the West in the 1890s. But nobody acted to do anything about the situation until TR stepped in.

After McKinley's death and before TR moved into the White House, two of the men with whom he had worked on conservation projects in New York state—Gifford Pinchot and Frederick Haynes Newell—presented him with plans for a national irrigation system in the West and the consolidation of the forest work of the government in the Bureau of Forestry. The plans intrigued the president, but he recognized that implementing them would be difficult.

Natural resources were not the focal point of the federal government at the turn of the twentieth century. Every project suggested was tied up in legalistic red tape. President Roosevelt was not a great fan of bureaucracy, so he looked for ways to do an end run around the people in charge of natural resources.

As he described the situation:

The relation of the conservation of natural resources to the problems of National welfare and National efficiency had not yet dawned on the public mind. The reclamation of arid public lands in the West was still a matter for private enterprise alone; and our magnificent river system, with its superb possibilities for public usefulness, was dealt with by the National Government not as a unit, but as a disconnected series of pork-barrel problems . . .

He set out to change that situation.

Talking to Congress

TR actively participated in drafting the reclamation bill to control what went into it and to prevent opponents from wrecking it by insisting on individual states' rights over national interests. In the process, he signaled lawmakers and the rest of America that he was a "hands-on" president, and that he would become involved personally in issues near and dear to his heart.

TR's first step was to tell Congress how vital the irrigation issue was in national interests. He did that in his first message to Congress on December 3, 1901. That same day several Western senators and congressmen formed a committee to draft a reclamation bill. The chief architect was Francis G. Newlands of Nevada, after whom the eventual bill was named.

It did not take long for Congress to pass a bill. On June 17, 1902, Congress passed "An Act Appropriating the receipts from the sale and disposal of public lands in certain States and Territories to the construction of irrigation works for the reclamation of arid lands." (The official name explains why the bill became known as the Newlands Reclamation Act.)

The act set aside the proceeds of the disposal of public lands for the purpose of reclaiming waste areas of the West through irrigation and building new homes upon the land. The settlers were responsible for repaying the money the government appropriated for the projects.

The repayments could be reused as a revolving fund that was available continuously for any work done. Work began immediately.

Without the Newlands Act and the water it made available, much of the West could not have been settled. Only ten months into his presidency, TR had accomplished a major piece of legislation that had significant repercussions for the entire country, not just localized sections. That was a major departure from ordinary federal government operations.

FACT

Twenty-eight irrigation projects attributed to the Newlands Act began between 1902 and 1906. They involved more than 3 million acres and more than 30,000 farms. Many of the dams built were higher than any constructed previously across the globe. The dams fed main-line canals over 7,000 miles in total length and involved the construction of tens of thousands of culverts and bridges.

New Services and Names

Five years after the initial passage of the act, the secretary of the interior created the United States Reclamation Service within the United States Geological Survey to administer the program. That same year, the service was renamed the United States Bureau of Reclamation.

Not everybody was happy with TR's reclamation project. Opponents argued that he had acted illegally and hastily without regard to costs or constitutionality of the law. Such criticisms would become as common during the rest of TR's presidency as the rivers and creeks that irrigated the arid West at the turn of the century.

Mostly, though, opponents were upset that TR could turn bureaucratic red tape into legislation quickly. That was his style as president, and the Newlands Act was the first—but not the last—time he would do it.

TR Is Taken for a Ride

It was not often that anyone could take Theodore Roosevelt for a ride. But on August 22, 1902, he rode in a purple-lined Columbia Electric Victoria during a parade in Hartford, Connecticut. Twenty carriages followed behind.

Theodore Roosevelt delivers speech in Hannibal, Missouri, 1903

Normally, the carriage—or simply a horse—would have been TR's preferred mode of travel. But he always used a horse and carriage for official government purposes.

FACT

Technically, TR was not the first U.S. president to ride in an automobile. President McKinley rode in cars a couple times while in office, but never in public. Also, he was transported to a hospital in an electric ambulance after being shot. But TR holds the distinction of being the first U.S. president to ride in a car in public—and to own one as well.

Cars were just becoming part of the U.S. government's travel fleet during TR's second term in office. In 1907, the Secret Service started using two White Company steamers it borrowed from the army to transport visitors to and from the railroad station in Oyster Bay, where TR spent time in the summer.

There was no official appropriation for the use of these cars, but he did use them occasionally. Consequently, he became the first president to ride in a U.S. government automobile.

TR was more interested in enacting significant legislation and acting in the best interests of the American people than he was in establishing "firsts" as a president. That work continued.

The First Bird Reservation

Many of TR's opponents believed his ideas and actions were for the proverbial birds. They were right to some extent. He was a great supporter of the preservation of birds and took steps as president to make sure they were protected.

TR believed that birds should be saved for utilitarian reasons, none of which had to do with money. He lamented the passage of birds like the passenger pigeon, which had been driven to extinction by habitat loss and overhunting. So he acted to make sure that they were protected. His efforts to do so were nothing new for him.

ESSENTIAL

When TR was governor of New York, making clothes and other articles of apparel with bird feathers was a common practice in the state. He expressed revulsion to the technique. As he emphasized, "Birds in the trees and on the beaches were much more beautiful than on women's hats." Since plume hunters were extremely busy in Florida, he decided to start his bird preservation activities there.

Ornithologists were concerned with the devastation hunters were causing among pelicans, herons, egrets, and other birds that featured commercially attractive plumage. They were beginning to reduce the numbers of those birds to the point that extinction was possible.

Many of the birds gathered at tiny Pelican Island, about four acres in size, located in the Indian River Lagoon on the east coast of central Florida. The ornithologists decided that was a good place to make a stand. Paul Kroegel, a local resident concerned with the pelicans on the island; the Florida Audubon Society; and the American Ornithologists' Union petitioned President Roosevelt directly for relief.

The president was all too glad to accede to the request. In typical fashion he did not want to waste time going through Congress or battling red tape. He asked his advisors if there was any law that would prevent him from declaring Pelican Island a federal bird reservation. None, they said.

Without fanfare, on March 14, 1903, he signed a proclamation stating simply, "It is hereby ordered that Pelican Island in Indian River in section nine, township thirty-one south, range thirty-nine east, State of Florida, be, and it is hereby reserved and set apart for the use of the Department of Agriculture as a preserve and breeding ground for native birds."

The first of the fifty-one bird refuges he created became a reality—and he did it without ruffling many feathers.

Striking Down a Strike

TR had been in office for about eight months when his first major crisis arose. Anthracite coal miners in eastern Pennsylvania went on strike in early May 1902 for higher wages and better working conditions. Normally, a local strike would not draw the attention of the president of the United States. This one was different.

Almost every American relied on coal for energy purposes at this point in history, and a lot of people panicked over the thought of disrupted supplies with winter approaching. The United Mine Workers, led by John Mitchell, and the owner of the mine, George Baer, who also owned the Philadelphia and Reading Railroad company, drew their lines in the sand. The scene was set for a battle involving TR.

Neither the union nor the mine owner budged as the strike began. Union leader John Mitchell took the initiative and asked the president to establish an independent arbitration committee to resolve the impasse.

TR asked his commissioner of labor, Carroll D. Wright, to look into the causes of the strike. Wright formulated a report that acknowledged each side's position and proposed reforms, including a recommended nine-hour workday on an experimental basis, instead of the standard ten-hour workday in place at the time, and limited collective bargaining.

TR held back Wright's report, lest he appear to be pro-union. And, even though Mitchell had proposed the committee, the miners refused to go along with arbitration. So did Baer. Eventually, TR set up a fact-finding group to study the issues and proposed his own solution.

No Settlement in Sight

Negotiations dragged on, and the president chafed to get fully involved. His attorney general, Philander Knox, cautioned him that he did not have the authority to intervene.

Lack of authority did not bother TR. Under pressure from the union, the owner, his own party, and the public, he threatened to replace the workers with army troops, by force if necessary. His goal was to mine coal, regardless of who was doing the work.

TR figured that the negotiators could work toward a settlement while the soldiers dug. The fact that they were not trained in the art of coal mining did not bother TR. His plan raised a few eyebrows among politicians, citizens, and everyone else who had a vested interest in settling the strike.

Secretary of War Elihu Root came to TR's rescue. He worked with banker J. P. Morgan, who had financial interests in Baer's railroad, to convince the miners that independent arbitration was in their best interests. Finally, they agreed. In mid-October 1902, President Roosevelt announced that an agreement to end the strike had been reached. The 163-day strike ended on October 23.

Everyone Wins a Little

As a result of the solution to the strike, each side got a little of what they asked for. The miners received a 10 percent pay increase instead of the 20 percent they had demanded. Their workday was cut from ten to nine hours; they had asked for an eight-hour workday. They had also demanded recognition for their union by the mine owners.

The owners refused to recognize the UMW, but they were forced to accept a six-person arbitration board composed of equal numbers of labor and management representatives to settle subsequent labor disputes. As far as Mitchell was concerned, that was a de facto recognition of the UMW. The biggest winner, though, was TR.

The public credited TR with ending the strike, even though Wright, Root, Morgan, and former President Grover Cleveland had done yeoman's work to resolve the issues involved. His popularity continued to grow, especially as he attacked the trusts that were so prominent in the country.

Trustbuster Extraordinaire

One of the aspects of TR's presidency that might have caught people off guard a bit was his approach to big business. Anyone who looked at his history should not have been surprised.

TR had come down hard against big businesses when he was an alderman and governor, which was antithetical to traditional Republican Party policy. But, TR was not a typical Republican. He continued his "trustbusting" practices as president by urging Congress to control large corporations by whatever means possible.

ESSENTIAL

TR felt that a first step regarding big business's influence in the United States was to convince the public that government should curb its power. Americans were leery of large trusts, but they were also skeptical of government regulation. He vowed to change public opinion about government's role in business and establish controls acceptable to citizens, business operators, and politicians.

TR did not want to eliminate big business's power completely; he wanted to mitigate it through practical regulation. The challenge required a balancing act. He started with a new Department of Commerce and Labor.

There were antitrust laws in place, most notably the Sherman Act of 1890, but TR did not think they had enough teeth and were not being enforced adequately. So in 1903 he convinced Congress that the country needed a department to oversee interstate commerce and labor relations.

In response, Congress created the Department of Commerce and Labor, the first new entity at that level the government had created since the Civil War. Businesses lobbied heavily against the creation, but they lost their battle. The department included a Bureau of Corporations, whose charge was to uncover violations of current antitrust laws.

Next, he ordered Attorney General Knox to start filing lawsuits against large monopolistic companies, including J. P. Morgan's Northern Securities Company, John D. Rockefeller's Standard Oil Trust, and James B. Duke's tobacco trust. Government attorneys launched the first of the forty-five such suits that were introduced during TR's administration. The fallout was almost immediate.

Not a Popular Person

On February 19, 1902, TR ordered the first antitrust suit under the Sherman Act. His aim was to dissolve Northern Securities Company, a holding company formed in 1901 by business financier J. P. Morgan and railroad entrepreneurs James J. Hill and Edward H. Harriman to dominate railroad traffic in the West. The company controlled the stock of the Great Northern, Northern Pacific, and the Chicago, Burlington and Quincy railroads.

TR alleged that NSC was monopolizing railroad traffic between Chicago and the northwestern part of the country, which did not fit into his concept of fair business practices. When Knox filed the lawsuit on the basis of restraint of trade, Morgan and Republican Senator Mark Hanna from Ohio pleaded personally with TR to stop the lawsuit, but the president refused. Off to court they went.

FACT

NSC's attorneys argued that the company did not engage in interstate commerce; it was merely a stockholder. The case reached the U.S. Supreme Court. By a margin of 5-4, the justices agreed with the government and ordered the company's breakup. That was a major victory for the president.

The government's victory heightened TR's popularity with the people. More important, it put a halt to railroad operators' efforts to consolidate the nation's railroads into a monopoly and lessened business giants' zeal for creating holding companies.

Finally, it put the Morgans, Hills, and Harrimans of the business world on notice that they were not safe from anti-monopoly lawsuits or legislation. TR had already proved that to unions. Now he showed business owners that he was willing to regulate them as well.

The NSC victory was only the first for TR. Later, other trusts, such as Standard Oil, suffered the same fate. President Roosevelt proved that he was an equal opportunity arbiter when it came to creating as stable a business environment as possible for U.S. companies—and for the people they served.

Building the Panama Canal

By 1870, American trade with the rest of the world was expanding. That meant merchants would need more ships to transport their goods and shorter routes to accommodate them. The U.S. government turned to a project that had intrigued people ever since 1513, when the Spanish explorer Vasco Núñez de Balboa crossed the Isthmus of Panama: building a canal between the Atlantic and Pacific oceans.

ESSENTIAL

Many people considered the isthmus ideal for a canal to shorten the trip between the eastern and western hemispheres. The U.S. Navy inherited the task of finding such a route. After examining a number of possibilities, the navy and the government settled on the Isthmus of Panama as the best place, even though it was farther from trade routes and narrower than alternate sites.

An international company formed in 1876 to build a canal received a concession from Colombia, of which Panama was a part. That attempt failed. Next, a French company led by Ferdinand Marie de Lesseps, the builder of the Suez Canal, stepped in. The company began construction in 1880. That project also failed, due primarily to the staggering cost in lives and accidents such as landslides. Almost 22,000 workers died, mainly from malaria and yellow fever.

Efforts to build the passage languished until 1889, when the U.S. Congress created an Isthmian Canal Commission to analyze the feasibility of a Central American canal and recommend a route.

Initially, the commission recommended a route through Nicaragua. Then it changed its decision. There the matter rested until the French company offered the United States its assets for $40 million. That revived American interest in the project. All it took was Theodore Roosevelt to get it going. First, though, he had some minor problems to resolve, such as turning Panama into a free country.

TR Takes Charge

Panama joined Colombia in 1821 after a Central American revolt against Spain. Colombia posed a problem for TR during negotiations for rights to build the Panama Canal, since its government believed that he was bullying them into making a deal.

On the other hand, the president believed that politically unstable Panama owed something to the United States, which had intervened in its internal affairs thirteen times between 1850 and 1900.

QUOTE

TR was not convinced he had to deal with Colombia. He wrote in his autobiography, "Since 1846 we had a treaty with . . . New Granada, the predecessor of . . . Colombia . . . [and] Panama, by which . . . the United States was guaranteed . . . right of way across the Isthmus of Panama by any mode of communication that might be constructed . . . in return our Government guaranteed the . . . neutrality of the Isthmus with a view to the preservation of free transit."

In the final fifty years of the nineteenth century, Panama had been ruled by forty administrations and suffered through fifty riots and five attempted secessions. When Panama declared its independence in 1903, the U.S. government supported it. That had as much to do with Colombia's intransigence in dealing with the Roosevelt administration over canal rights as it did with Panama's independence.

TR saw the Panama Canal as a necessary passage for expediting U.S. military forces around the globe. Consequently, he vowed to build the canal, which he said in his autobiography was the most important action he took during his presidency. Neither Colombia nor an effete U.S. Congress was going to get in his way.

On January 22, 1903, TR's secretary of state John Hay signed the Hay-Herran Treaty between the United States and Colombia. According to the terms, Colombia would grant a lease in perpetuity to the United States on a six-mile-wide strip across the Isthmus of Panama in exchange for $10 million and an annual payment of $250,000.

The U.S. Senate ratified the treaty on March 14, 1903, but the Colombian Senate did not follow suit. The Colombians held out for $25 million, which infuriated TR. He thought that was extortion. He looked for another way to gain access to the coveted canal ground.

Yet Another Revolution

If nothing else, President Roosevelt knew how to take advantage of an opportunity to accomplish something he wanted badly. News reached Washington that yet another revolution was beginning in Panama. The word was that the Panamanians would be happy to turn over canal rights to the United States under the same terms Colombia had rejected.

That gave TR an idea. After all, the United States had intervened in Panama's politics before. Why not now, when the United States had something valuable to gain?

TR did not openly support the revolution in Panama, but he did let folks know through back channels that he would not oppose it. And, if a U.S. warship or two should show up in Panama by coincidence to support the rumored coup, so much the better. That is exactly what happened.

On November 2, 1903, the U.S. Navy's gunboat *Nashville* arrived in Colon, Panama, with a contingent of marines. That was "barely on time," according to TR. Another ten U.S. warships settled offshore. The day after *Nashville* arrived, the coup occurred. The coincidence was remarkable.

The Colombian troops there might have put down the coup, but they were reluctant to do so in the presence of *Nashville*, the U.S. Marines, and the warships offshore that inhibited any attempts to reinforce them. Years later, TR claimed that the Colombian troops had actually supported the revolution.

Immediately after the coup ended, Panama declared its independence, which the United States and several Latin American countries recognized. Within two weeks, the Hay-Bunau-Varilla Treaty, negotiated by Secretary of State Hay and French citizen Phillipe Bunau-Varilla, an official of the French canal company, emerged.

The Hay-Bunau-Varilla Treaty

The agreement allowed the United States to build a canal through a ten-mile-wide, perpetually leased section of central Panama, to use more land if needed, and to intervene militarily in Panama, which it had already done. It required the United States to guarantee Panama's independence and pay $10 million, plus $250,000 annually. Events moved quickly after that.

Panama ratified the treaty on December 4, 1903. The U.S. Senate did the same—or at least advised that it be ratified—on February 23, 1904. President Roosevelt signed it officially two days later.

The two countries exchanged ratifications on February 26, 1904, and proclaimed it official. That was record time for two governments to negotiate, draw up, and ratify a treaty of significant proportions. That was TR's intention from the get-go, and he could get things accomplished when he saw an opportunity.

QUOTE

TR explained years later in a speech what he did: "The Panama Canal would not have started if I had not taken hold of it . . . The beginning of work on the canal would be fifty years in the future. Fortunately [the opportunity] came at a period when I could act unhampered. Accordingly I took the Isthmus, started the canal and then left Congress not to debate the canal, but to debate me."

TR was sure he had acted correctly. He wrote, "From the beginning to the end our course was . . . in absolute accord with the highest of standards of international morality. Criticism of it can come only from misinformation, or . . . a sentimentality which represents both mental weakness and a moral twist. To have acted otherwise . . . would have been on my part betrayal of the interests of the United States." Critics decried what he had done.

The *New York Times* Disagrees

The *New York Times*, often a thorn in TR's side, proclaimed loudly that Roosevelt's coup was an "act of sordid conquest." Later, in a December 10, 1908, article, it admitted that "Roosevelt's Panama Canal Account Holds Up."

The Democrats had intimated that Roosevelt's deal with the Panamanians was a scheme to help his brother-in-law Douglas Robinson and President-elect William H. Taft's brother Charles make money.

They also alleged that "the whole Panama affair, including the shift from the Nicaraguan route to the lower Isthmus, was contrived by [American attorney William Nelson] Cromwell, as the representative, not of the French Company, but of the American syndicate, and that the President in his eagerness to get at the work of building a canal, was an easy victim." The newspaper refuted those claims and printed its proof in a lead article.

A *New York Times* reporter stated:

All the papers in Washington bearing on the purchase of the canal property have been overhauled and submitted to the correspondent of the New York Times. In them was nothing to indicate that the Government officials connected with the purchase had any knowledge of the ownership of the stock in the company which owned the property or that any Americans were interested in the matter.

Arguments over the affair continued long after the deal was completed. That was no surprise; TR's Panama Canal triumph may have been the most controversial action of his presidency. While the arguments raged, construction went on, with TR right there.

TR Grabs a Shovel

TR was so excited about the project that he visited Panama in November 1906. That made him the first American president to visit a foreign country while in office.

Theodore Roosevelt operates an American steam shovel at Culebra Cut, Panama Canal

His usual energy frustrated the Secret Service agents and trip arrangers. He made unscheduled visits to workers and hospitals and demanded to see places, people, and things that were not on the itinerary, such as work sites, black workers, military personnel, and steam shovels. By the time he left, people were glad to see him go so work could continue without his incessant interruptions.

QUOTE

TR noted in his autobiography, "A finer body of men has never been gathered by any nation than the men who have done the work of building the Panama Canal . . . they have all felt an eager pride in their work; and they have made not only America but the whole world their debtors by what they have accomplished."

The Panama Canal opened officially on August 15, 1914. It was a proud moment for the United States and Theodore Roosevelt, who, despite the controversy surrounding the project, saw it through to completion.

Elected on His Own Record

TR was pleased with his accomplishment in his three years in office. So were the Republican Party and the American people. The party nominated him unanimously for a full term to continue what he had started. His platform was simple: maintain the protective tariff, increase foreign trade, uphold the gold standard, expand the merchant marine, promote a strong navy, and support the president's foreign and domestic policies.

The Democrats nominated Alton B. Parker, the chief judge of the New York Court of Appeals, who had served on the state's Supreme Court when Roosevelt was governor. He was not much competition.

Parker tried to convince the voters that electing him would put an end to a "rule of individual caprice" and "usurpation of authority." They disagreed. On November 8, 1904, they elected TR by a wide majority.

He was poised to continue his policies and presidential style for at least another four years. Once elected for his first full term, he jumped into it prepared to accomplish great things.

11-1   What is an isthmus?

A. A narrow strip of land connecting two larger masses of land
B. a religious holiday celebrated in December
C. a body of water separating two countries
D. a measure of liquid in Central America

11-2   The Panama Canal saved sailors how many miles on a voyage between New York and San Francisco?

A. 10,000
B. 7,872
C. 5,289
D. 3,601

11-3   Eventually, the United States paid Colombia its original asking price for the Panama Canal.

A. True
B. False

11-4   How many federal bird reservations did Theodore Roosevelt create as president?

A. 3,417
B. 94
C. 51
D. 612

11-5   When did the last passenger pigeon in the United States die?

A. 1914
B. 1900
C. 2010
D. 1847

ANSWERS

11-1. A: There are two other definitions, both having to do with anatomy. An isthmus can be a narrow strip of tissue joining two larger organs or parts of an organ, or a narrow passage connecting two larger cavities.
11-2. B: If the Panama Canal had not been built, they would have had to sail around Cape Horn, South America, instead—a rather long journey.
11-3. True: In 1921, the United States paid Colombia $25 million for its loss of Panama.
11-4. C
11-5. A: It is believed that the last passenger pigeon in the United States, Martha, died on September 1, 1914, at the Cincinnati Zoo.

CHAPTER 12

His Second Act Is Better than His First

"I am glad to be elected President in my own right."

TR had a lot to be proud of after his first term. He had no intention of sitting on his laurels. He wanted to lead the United States into the twentieth century as a world power, knowing that all the turmoil across the globe would eventually involve the country. He also had ambitious plans for his domestic conservation and reform efforts. The president pursued his foreign and domestic agenda with a great deal of fervor and achieved notable results on both fronts.

1905 Is a Busy Year

1905 got off to a favorable start for TR long before his Inauguration Day. The first piece of good news came on January 30, when the Supreme Court ruled unanimously for the United States in its "trustbusting" case against the meat packing firm of Swift & Company.

The Swift & Company decision affected interstate commerce and expanded federal power under the commerce clause of the U.S. Constitution by ruling that locally operated businesses that made products sold in interstate markets could be subject to federal regulation. The decision set a positive tone for the rest of the year—and his administration.

Two days after the Swift & Company news, TR accomplished another milestone by establishing the National Forest Service. Four months later he made the Wichita Forest in Oklahoma the first federal game preserve. He established three more before his term ended: the Grand Canyon (1908); Fire Island, Alaska (1909); and National Bison Range, Montana (1909).

FACT

By 1900 there were 550 living bison in the United States. In 1905, the American Bison Society and the New York Zoological Society donated fifteen bison to the Wichita National Forest and Game Preserve in Oklahoma. Congress contributed $15,000 to support the move and TR set aside the land as a federal reserve. Bison were on their way to recovery.

TR's most pressing issue that year was negotiating peace between Japan and Russia, which were involved in a mutually destructive war over territorial dominance.

We Have Responsibilities

In his inauguration speech on March 4, 1905, TR set the tone for his first full term in office. He told Americans that their country's international role was expanding out of necessity.

"We have become a great nation, forced by the fact of its greatness into relations with the other nations of the earth, and we must behave as beseems a people with such responsibilities," he said. "Much has been given us, and much will rightfully be expected from us."

TR stressed his usual message of "duties to others and duties to ourselves, and we can shirk neither." As events turned out, he took those words seriously.

TR also hinted at his domestic policy. He noted that industrial development had changed society tremendously, and not always for the better.

"The conditions which have told for our marvelous material well-being, which have developed to a very high degree our energy, self-reliance, and individual initiative, have also brought the care and anxiety inseparable from the accumulation of great wealth in industrial centers," he observed. His meaning was clear.

TR was going to address the "accumulation of great wealth" in the interests of righteousness and social justice. For him, the words he uttered were more than empty rhetoric. He intended to act. The ride began immediately.

Ode to Mothers

TR delivered a speech to the National Congress of Mothers in Washington, D.C., on March 13, 1905, that showed another side of him. It was no secret that he was sympathetic to the status of women and children in society. As he wrote in a later book, *The Conservation of Womanhood and Childhood*, published in 1912, "We must work then for each partial remedy that may alleviate something of the misery of mankind, that may cause a measurable betterment in the condition of children, women and men."

The book was actually an expanded version of a speech he delivered in 1911 to the Civic Forum and the Child's Welfare League. One promotional piece for the book stated:

> *Conservation has been long a favorite theme with the ex-President, and no phase of it has interested him more than that applying to Womanhood and Childhood. It is here presented as revised and extended by him during the activities of his summer campaign of 1912.*

TR was looking ahead for issues to address in his presidential campaign that year. By 1912, the plight of womanhood and childhood had become familiar themes for TR—and suitable issues for a presidential campaign. First, he had to end a war.

Peace Between Russia and Japan

Russia and Japan went to war in February 1904 over the issue of who had dominance in Korea and Manchuria. The war was short, but costly, for both countries. By 1905, it was beginning to affect the rest of the world.

TR and his counterparts around the globe did not see any end in sight to the war, even though Japan was gaining the upper hand. They sought a way to stop the fighting before other countries became involved. TR stepped in to settle a dispute, as many people expected him to do. After all, he had settled the coal strike a couple of years earlier. Why not end a war as well?

FACT

John Hay, TR's secretary of state, had been one of President Lincoln's secretaries. He and TR's father had also been friends. Even though TR wanted to conduct the Russo-Japanese War peace talks himself, it would have been too delicate for him to remove Hay. Fate stepped in. Hay died in July 1905, which allowed the president to lead the negotiations.

In June 1905, TR volunteered to meet with delegates from the two countries to settle their differences aboard his presidential yacht, *Mayflower*, which was moored at Oyster Bay. Both sides agreed. He stayed there while the negotiators moved to the naval base at Portsmouth, New Hampshire, in August 1905 to hammer out the details of the peace talks.

Delegates shuttled back and forth between Portsmouth and Oyster Bay. It took a few weeks to negotiate a solution satisfactory to both sides, but Russia and Japan finally signed a peace treaty at Kittery, Maine, on September 5.

According to the terms, Russia recognized Japan as the dominant power in Korea and turned over its naval leases of Port Arthur, Manchuria and the

Liaotung Peninsula, as well as the southern half of Sakhalin Island, to Japan. Both countries consented to restore power in Manchuria to China. The settlement was a political coup for President Roosevelt, but he had no illusions about its impact on peace around the world.

TR recognized that the growing power of Eastern countries and their opposition to interference from their Western counterparts was a powder keg waiting for a match. The fact that Japan had emerged victorious in a war against a traditional Western power—a first-time event for any Eastern country—was a signal to him that the United States must heed.

QUOTE

TR wrote in a September 8, 1905, letter to his political opponent and disarmament advocate, Carl Schurz, "Until people get it firmly fixed in their minds that peace is valuable chiefly as a means to righteousness, and that it can only be considered as an end when it also coincides with righteousness, we can do only a limited amount to advance its coming on this earth."

He did not believe peace was a viable option anywhere around the globe. The United States needed to flex its muscles in preparation. Before he could arrange for that, he received a pleasant reward for his efforts at Portsmouth.

Streamlining the Executive Office

On June 2, 1905, TR created a Commission on Department Methods to look into ways to streamline the "conduct of the executive business of the Government in all its branches on the most effective basis in the light of the best modern business practice." He believed the system in place was ineffective and costly. And, TR boasted, the commission's work would be performed "wholly without cost to the government."

The effort paid off. The commission recommended changes in the way the Executive Branch operated that saved the government hundreds of thousands of dollars.

The biggest outcome of the study and the ultimate implementation of the recommendations created a new view among workers in the public sector regarding the importance of their work for the public. TR was always looking for ways to improve processes and save money for the citizens. He gave them a direct example of how to use money for the public good after he won the Nobel Peace Prize.

TR saved the country money. He noted, "One thing is worth pointing out: During the seven and a half years of my Administration we . . . reduced the burden of the taxpayers; for we reduced the interest-bearing debt by more than $90,000,000. To achieve a marked increase in efficiency and at the same time an increase in economy is not an easy feat; but we performed it."

Winning the Nobel Prize

The Nobel Prize Committee singled out TR for his prowess in negotiating peace between Japan and Russia. On December 10, 1906, it awarded him

the Nobel Peace Prize. It was the first time in its five-year history that the Nobel Prize had been awarded to an American. It was also the first half of the singular Nobel Prize and Medal of Honor combination awarded to TR, who became the only U.S. president to earn both.

TR tried to downplay the significance of the award, which included a large gold medal, a diploma in a fancy case, and a cash stipend. He was

Santa brings Theodore Roosevelt the Nobel Prize in a newspaper cartoon between 1906–1907. The caption reads: "The Christmas Surprise Teddy—wonder if old Santa Claus could have made any mistake?" The Norwegian Parliament is dressed as Santa Claus delivering the Nobel Prize in a Christmas stocking to TR, who's shown in a child's body.

more interested in the intangible rewards: knowing that he had ended at least one war and the prestige that went along with the prize. He vowed to donate the money to various charities. TR advised the committee accordingly in his acceptance speech, which he did not deliver personally. That honor went to Herbert H. D. Peirce, who gave it in Oslo, Norway, on December 10, 1906.

FACT

Herbert H. D. Peirce, TR's third assistant secretary of state, was responsible for arranging the deliberations of the Russo-Japanese War at Portsmouth, New Hampshire. He was also the first person outside the negotiating rooms there to learn that a settlement had been reached. Peirce was the U.S. minister to Norway from August 13, 1906, to May 30, 1911.

In his speech he said simply that if he had not been president of the United States, he would not have been involved in the peace process. Therefore, he advised the money truly belonged to the people of the United States.

TR, in his typical altruistic fashion, proposed to use it as seed money for a "foundation to forward the cause of industrial peace . . . of righteousness and justice, the only kind of peace worth having." The foundation was never established. Instead, he donated the money to World War I relief projects.

ESSENTIAL

Ed Renehan, Jr. mentioned in his book, *The Lion's Pride*, that TR made twenty-eight war donations. He explained: "A few of the gifts included $6,900 to the Red Cross; $5,000 to Eleanor for her Y.M.C.A. project; an additional $4,000 to the YMCA National War Work Council; and $1,000 to Edith's sister, Emily Carow, a volunteer with the Italian Red Cross at Porto Maurizo, Italy."

TR was in no rush to pick up the money or the Nobel Prize. He waited until 1910, when he just happened to be in the area of Norway. He visited Christiana (renamed Oslo in 1925) to receive both. True to his word, TR turned the medal over to the White House, where it still resides.

Immigration Restriction Act of 1907

There was one unfinished piece of business for TR regarding Japan after he oversaw the Russo-Japanese War treaty. The Japanese had never been completely satisfied with the outcome of the negotiations. They were upset that he had blocked reparations they felt were due from the Russians.

The Japanese had another item that rankled them, which was not related to the treaty. They did not like the way Americans were treating their countrymen who had moved to the West Coast, specifically California. They believed that American farmers and laborers were mistreating Japanese immigrants.

In 1905, Japan annexed Korea, and its growing dominance in Manchuria—in defiance of China—continued. And the American public was becoming increasingly uncomfortable with Japan. By 1907, people in both countries felt that war might be imminent between Japan and the United States. TR sought to improve diplomatic relations between the two countries to avert it.

TR believed that Californians had a legitimate concern about Japanese immigration. He noted, "The people of California were right in insisting that the Japanese should not come thither in mass, that there should be no influx of laborers, of agricultural workers, or small tradesmen—in short, no mass settlement or immigration."

Immigration complaints and dissatisfaction over the terms of the Russo-Japanese Treaty were Japanese concerns in TR's viewpoint. He had a secondary issue to consider: the United States had established bases in the Philippines, which were closer to Japan than to the United States. He wanted to protect those bases as the United States expanded its foothold in the Eastern hemisphere, which would be difficult in the event of Japanese aggression. The president instructed Secretary of State Elihu Root to sit down with the Japanese to reach an accord.

The "Root" of the Problem

There was a small breakthrough in 1907 when the two countries reached a "gentleman's agreement" on immigration numbers. The Japanese agreed to limit the number of people coming to the United States, while the Americans promised to recognize the presence of the Japanese already living in the United States; to permit entry to their wives, children, and parents; and to avoid legal discrimination against Japanese children in California schools. That promise did not stop some Americans from discriminating against Japanese immigrants, however.

As a follow-up to the 1907 agreement, Root struck a deal with the Japanese ambassador to the United States, Kogoro Takahira, which really did not address the core issues. In the pact signed on November 3, 1908, the United States and Japan pledged to maintain the status quo in the Far East, recognize China's independence and territorial integrity, support an "open door" policy in China, and consult one another if further crises erupted in the Far East.

The mutual "hands-off" agreement was a temporary fix, but the clamor for and fear of war between the two countries abated after Root and Takahira arrived at their accord. Should it flare up again, TR was ready.

The "Great White Fleet"

One of the president's primary motivators for the American Navy's 1907–1909 grand global tour was to let the Japanese know that the United States had modern, technologically advanced ships and that he could—and would—employ them anywhere in the world if necessary. That was the underlying reason for what would become known later on as the voyage of the "Great White Fleet."

QUOTE

TR said, "At that time, as I happen to know, neither the English nor the German authorities believed it possible to take a fleet of great battleships round the world. They did not believe that their own fleets could perform the feat, and still less did they believe that the American fleet could. I made up my mind that it was time to have a show down in the matter."

As commander in chief of the armed forces, President Roosevelt was proud of "his" new navy, especially the battleships that had been added to the fleet—and which he had played a part in building. He wanted to let the rest of the world share in his pride and announce that the United States was strengthening its navy in anticipation of taking its foreign duties seriously.

In 1907, he saw a chance to showcase his innovative battleships and alert other countries to the existence of the new player in the international community. No other country had ever completed such a large undertaking satisfactorily.

TR had always believed that strong military forces were essential to keeping the peace, however oxymoronic that sounded. He wrote in his autobiography, "There would have been no war in 1812 if, in the previous decade, America, instead of announcing that 'peace was her passion,' instead of acting on the theory that unpreparedness averts war, had been willing to go to the expense of providing a fleet of a score of ships of the line."

As he noted, "This is no new thing. Americans learn only from catastrophes and not from experience."

New Ships Growing Old

TR knew that other nations were building bigger and better ships to protect their maritime resources around the globe. He had seen what the Japanese Navy had done in the Russo-Japanese War in 1905 and realized the potential of the British ship, H.M.S. *Dreadnought*, the first of the modern "all-big-gun" battleships, which had been launched in 1906. As modern as the "Great White Fleet" was to TR, it was in danger of becoming obsolete.

FACT

The armada TR dispatched was not known originally as the "Great White Fleet." That nickname came into being long after the fleet completed its voyage. The name derived from the white paint on the ships' exterior, which was the navy's peacetime color. The bow of each vessel was decorated with gilded scrollwork and a red, white, and blue banner.

Navies were also experimenting with submarines, airplanes, and other modern weapons. The president felt that it was time for the United States to display its naval prowess. Despite opposition from several quarters, he dispatched a U.S. Navy fleet on a voyage around the world. There was a bit of chicanery in his plan.

Some of the president's opponents, notably Senator Eugene Hale (D-Maine), chairman of the Naval Appropriations Committee, tried to thwart TR's grandiose plan by withholding funds for the endeavor. TR met his threat. He informed Hale that he already had the money, and he challenged Congress to try and get it back. That ended the threat, and the ships sailed as scheduled.

A Fleet in Sheep's Clothing

There was a great deal of ceremony as the ships left Hampton Roads, Virginia, on December 16, 1907, en route to their first stop, Port of Spain, Trinidad. TR watched from the yacht *Mayflower* as the fleet under the command of Rear Admiral Robley D. Evans, aboard the battleship *Connecticut*, sailed away. As impressive as the sight was, there was an undercurrent of deception involved in the undertaking. All was not as it seemed.

On the outside, the ships were gleaming. The interiors were a different matter. Some of the ships had malfunctioning engines. Two, *Alabama* and *Maine*, had to drop out along the route. They were replaced by *Wisconsin* and *Nebraska*; if any more had been unable to continue, there would have been no substitutes.

The navy sent every battleship it had on the cruise, except for two that were not seaworthy. Even the fleet commander had to be replaced when the fleet reached San Francisco. The ailing Admiral Evans turned command over to Rear Admiral Charles S. Sperry.

Ships and Sailors Battle the Elements

The fleet was composed of sixteen steel-clad, steam-powered battleships, all built after the Spanish-American War, and numerous auxiliary support vessels crewed by 14,000 sailors and marines. Destroyers and other ships dropped in and out along the way as the goodwill tour progressed, with a few diversions.

Ships of the fleet were diverted to Sicily to lend a hand to earthquake victims there. Crewmembers of *Illinois* recovered the bodies of the American consul and his wife among the ruins. In October 1908 the fleet sailed into a typhoon off Formosa. Several ships sustained minor damage; one sailor was lost at sea.

Mishaps, triumphs, and the trials and travails of twenty port stops on six continents ensured that the fleet returned to the United States a bit less white than it had been when it left in 1907. As the ships sailed into Hampton Roads on February 22, 1909, there was TR, aboard *Mayflower*, to greet them, just as he had seen them off.

FACT

The cruise was by no means uneventful for the sailors, especially in Brazil. A bar brawl erupted in Rio de Janeiro between sailors from the *Louisiana* and local longshoremen that threatened to create an international incident. But representatives from the navy and Brazil ironed out the misunderstanding and the fleet moved on.

It was one of his final acts as president. The fleet returned just three weeks before TR was scheduled to leave office.

After Action Report

When President Roosevelt sent the Great White Fleet on its worldwide tour, he had several goals in mind: he wanted to test the navy's readiness, promote international goodwill, and make sure the countries around the globe understood that the United States was a naval power. TR had stated before he dispatched the fleet that he wanted "all failures, blunders and shortcomings to be made apparent in time of peace and not in time of war." In that respect, the cruise was a success.

The navy learned some lessons and uncovered some glitches and weaknesses in its equipment, strategies, and seaworthiness, which it addressed in due course. The ships' return answered any doubts TR might have had about the navy's ability to function under stress. It could—and it would prove it again in the near future.

End of Presidency

TR's role as U.S. president ended in 1909, but that was not the end of his political career. He made a promise that he would not run for a third term.

True to his word, he honored that promise, but insisted on picking a nominee as his replacement.

QUOTE

"I regarded the custom [of not running for a third term] as applying practically . . . to a President who had been seven and a half years in office as to one who had been eight years in office . . . in the teeth of a practically unanimous demand . . . that I accept another nomination, and the reasonable certainty that the nomination would be ratified at the polls . . . the substance of the custom applied to me in 1908."

He persuaded the Republicans to nominate his secretary of war, William Howard Taft, for president. Taft won the election easily over his Democrat opponent, William Jennings Bryan. As of March 4, 1909, TR was out of the White House—but not out of politics. He did not rule out another term eventually, since he believed that "the third term tradition has no value whatever except as it applies to a third consecutive term."

TR proved the truth in that statement after he saw what happened to the United States once he left office. He eventually considered that third term.

12-1 October 11 is a little-known holiday in the bison community. What event do they celebrate on that day?

A. Christopher Columbus saw bison for the first time.
B. The first bison farm was founded.
C. Buffalo, New York, celebrates its anniversary.
D. A herd of bison arrived at an Oklahoma game preserve.

12-2 TR had six locks of Abraham Lincoln's hair in a ring he wore on his Inauguration Day. Where did he get the ring?

A. at a Washington, D.C., pawn shop
B. as a birthday gift from Abraham Lincoln
C. from John Hay
D. his father left it to him

12-3 The "Great White Fleet" sailed around the world between December 1907 and February 1909. How many miles did it cover during its voyage?

A. 1,492
B. 113,642
C. 75,000
D. 43,347

12-4 Ironically, the Nobel Peace prize is named after the inventor of:

A. noble gases
B. dynamite
C. the Nobel cannon
D. the atomic bomb

ANSWERS

12-4. B: Dynamite is often used for some decidedly nonpeaceful purposes.

12-3. D: The trip was broken into three legs: Hampton Roads, Virginia, to San Francisco (14,556 miles); San Francisco to Manila, Philippine Islands (16,336 miles); Manila to Hampton Roads (12,455).

12-2. C: John Hay purchased the hairs removed from President Lincoln at his autopsy for $100 and placed them into the ring.

12-1. D: On October 11, 1907, a healthy herd of bison comprising six bulls and nine cows shipped by rail from the New York Zoological Park to Oklahoma arrived and took up residence in the plains and mountains of Wichita National Forest and Game Preserve.

CHAPTER 13

Conserving Natural Resources

---

*"What the Reclamation Act [of 1902] has done for the country
is by no means limited to its material accomplishment.
This Act and the results flowing from it have helped powerfully
to prove to the Nation that it can handle its own resources and
exercise direct and business-like control over them."*

TR was an ardent conservationist. He collaborated with whatever individuals and organizations were willing to work to protect the nation's natural resources for their own and future generations. TR was especially active in his seven and a half years as president, during which he confronted opponents of conservation, such as business people and Congress, with steely resolve. He and his collaborators saved millions of acres and protected wildlife for the American people. His conservation legacy is still being felt today, and no doubt will be for generations to come.

A "Bully Pulpit"

TR told Congress in his seventh annual message on December 3, 1907, that "The conservation of our natural resources and their proper use constitute the fundamental problem which underlies almost every other problem of our national life." He had a perfect platform from which to deliver that message.

The White House provided the pulpit; he delivered the sermons. But he did more than sermonize. TR practiced what he preached. He began by coining the phrase "bully pulpit."

QUOTE

TR first used the term "bully pulpit" to describe the presidency. He said, "I suppose my critics will call that preaching, but I have got such a bully pulpit!" "Bully" had been one of his favorite words for years. He used it to describe something great. All he did was combine it with pulpit and a new phrase was born.

Conservation was not a new issue for TR when he assumed the presidency in 1901. He had been pushing it for years. As a child, TR had learned the need to treat animals with respect and maintain a balance of nature to conserve their numbers for the benefit of hunters and society. It was a natural extension of that belief to press for conservation of natural resources.

His egalitarian motives for conservation were evident in this passage from "Wilderness Reserves; The Yellowstone Park":

> *It is entirely in our power as a nation to preserve large tracts of wilderness, which are valueless for agricultural purposes and unfit for settlement, as playgrounds for rich and poor alike, and to preserve the game so that it shall continue to exist for the benefit of all lovers of nature, and to give reasonable opportunities for the exercise of the skill of the hunter, whether he is or is not a man of means.*

TR began his conservation efforts long before entering the White House, albeit in a limited fashion. As a member of the New York State Assembly, he was too involved in fighting graft and corruption to address conservation issues. But TR did donate a large part of his Roosevelt Museum of Natural History to the Smithsonian Institution.

TR learned early in life that hunters needed to be conservationists. After all, needlessly slaughtering animals was counterproductive to their hunting activities. TR saw the need for a code of ethics among hunters as a step to ensuring a steady supply of wildlife. As usual, when he saw a need for something, he acted.

Early Efforts

His experiences in the Badlands reinforced in TR's mind a need for conservation, especially in the West, where weather conditions were harsher than in the East, water was at a premium, and some animals, such as the buffalo, were being hunted to extinction for commercial purposes. Alleviating these conditions became a primary goal for TR. He began to push for conservation shortly after his return from the Badlands.

In 1887, Roosevelt and a large group of concerned conservationists founded the Boone and Crockett Club to implement such a code. They established other goals: to work for the elimination of industrial hunting, the creation of wildlife reserves, and a conservation-oriented regulation of hunting.

FACT

The Boone and Crockett Club is still in existence—and still working at the same goals as when TR and his group established it. Part of its mission statement sums up TR's philosophy about hunting and conservation in general: to "support the use and enjoyment of our wildlife heritage to the fullest extent by this and future generations."

The founders of the Boone and Crockett Club included approximately twenty to twenty-five scientists, military leaders, politicians, explorers, writers, and industrialists. The group was typical of Roosevelt's alliances: eclectic and action-oriented.

Governor and Conservationist

It wasn't until TR became governor of New York state that he found the perfect "bully pulpit" he needed to push for conservation. He admitted in his autobiography:

All that later I strove for in the Nation in connection with Conservation was foreshadowed by what I strove to obtain for New York State when I was Governor; and I was already working in connection with Gifford Pinchot and Newell.

As governor, he worked closely with prominent New Yorkers and New Jerseyites to create the Palisades Interstate Park to conserve a significant historic and national landscape. He urged the legislature, among other things, to push forest conservation, outlaw the use of feathers as adornments, and set aside land for public use.

On November 28, 1899, TR wrote:

The State should not permit within its limits factories to make bird skins or bird feathers into articles of ornament or wearing apparel. Ordinary birds, and especially song birds, should be rigidly protected. Game birds should never be shot to a greater extent than will offset the natural rate of increase.

TR learned from the creation of the PIP that when government officials and members of the public worked together they could accomplish significant milestones in the area of conservation despite heavy opposition. He also learned more about the power of women.

The PIP

In the late 1890s, large companies were destroying the Palisades Cliffs along the New Jersey side of the Hudson River to acquire gravel for roadbeds and broken stone for concrete. The quarries were not only eyesores but were creating irreparable damage to the environment. People living across the river in New York were upset about the destruction, too. Folks sought ways to stop the quarrying activities before the Palisades fell into the river.

The American Scenic and Historic Preservation Society, incorporated in 1895, was one of the leading opponents of the quarrying in the Palisades. The group was composed of many prominent socialites in the New York area who were determined to stop the destruction and save the Palisades and the Hudson River. TR knew many of them, since he traveled in the same social circles.

Clubs, newspapers, lawmakers, and other individuals and organizations joined the battle against the quarrying companies. They tried everything they could think of to shut them down. They even tried to get the army to establish a military base along the cliffs. The army was not interested. The businesses were too strong and withstood the lobbying—until women's suffrage stepped in.

Palisades quarries employed hundreds of workers. They shipped the stone as far away as New Orleans for $1 a ton. Workers blasted the stone, crushed it, loaded it onto barges, and shipped it. Not using expensive overland transportation made possible huge profits. It is no wonder the quarries did not want to close without a fight.

Astute politicians such as TR could see the handwriting on the wall. He had always promoted women's suffrage. The Palisades situation gave him a chance to work with them to accomplish something meaningful.

Members of the Englewood (New Jersey) Women's Club accepted the responsibility for ending the quarrying. They banded together with similar women's groups across the state to save the Palisades. They generated enough pressure and negative public opinion to attract the attention of lawmakers in New Jersey and New York.

Legislators in New York and New Jersey passed laws to form an Interstate Commission to purchase and manage land along the Palisades. Private individuals added money to facilitate the buying process. One of them was J. P. Morgan, who would later lock horns with TR during his antitrust campaign.

Finally, in 1900, TR and his counterpart in New Jersey, Governor Foster Vorhees, signed legislation that made possible the solution to the problem. The Interstate Commission bought out the quarries and the Palisades were saved. The efforts enhanced TR's reputation as a conservation-minded politician, which he used as leverage when he reached the White House. That was where he truly stood out as a conservationist.

A Slow Start

TR was not particularly active in pursuing conservation efforts in his first term as president. He appointed only one commission during those years, the Public Lands Commission. Its charge was to study public land policy and laws. He became more aggressive in his second term, much to Congress's chagrin.

FACT

TR waited two years to appoint his first conservation commission. He established the Public Lands Commission on October 22, 1903, to study public land policy and laws. The commission's findings contributed to new government regulations overseeing the use of open range and federal lands. It was almost four years until he appointed his next one.

For a while, world events such as seeking re-election, finding a solution to the Russo-Japanese War, and overseeing the building of the Panama Canal pushed conservation issues into a corner.

But they were always foremost in his mind. When TR pushed conservation into the forefront, he did it with a vengeance.

Too Many Commissions

Starting in 1907, TR appointed five more commissions. The first was the Inland Waterways Commission, which he appointed on March 14 to study the river systems of the United States, the development of water power, flood control, and land reclamation.

TR believed that the country's inland waterways had to be developed. The process involved many other important water problems, and he wanted them all considered before the development began. The Inland Waterways Commission began a flood of similar appointments. Before the flood began, TR issued a call to the governors of the nation's states and territories to gather in Washington, D.C., to determine what conservation issues had to be addressed. The crowd expanded beyond the governors. The attendees also included the members of the Supreme Court and the Cabinet and a collection of scientists and national leaders.

FACT

TR appointed so many conservation commissions between March 1907 and August 1908 that Congress ordered him to cease and desist. In 1909, it ordered him to stop appointing additional commissions without its authorization, even though he only had a couple more months to serve as president. Altogether, he appointed six commissions while he was president.

TR and his friend Gifford Pinchot set up the May 13–15, 1908, Governor's Conference to promote a national effort to create agencies responsible for conserving the country's natural resources. The governors adopted a declaration supporting conservation. The conference led to the appointment of thirty-eight state conservation commissions. The meeting was the forerunner of the annual governor's conference in Washington, D.C.

Originally, the conference was intended to cover only water issues. But conservationist William John ("WJ") McGee convinced TR to expand it to cover more topics. Based on McGee's credentials, TR could not turn him down. The conference went on as planned—with a widely expanded agenda.

A New Commission

TR did not wait long to act on the results of the conference. On June 8, 1908, he appointed the National Conservation Commission to prepare the first inventory of the natural resources of the United States.

The commission was composed of four sections: water, forests, lands, and minerals. Each section had a chairman. Gifford Pinchot, who was the chairman of the executive committee, declared that the conference was the turning point in the conservation movement in American history.

TR was proud of the fact that his commissions were all volunteer in nature. The members were not paid, and the government did not contribute to their funding. That was a throwback to his years as governor of New York state, when he created the commission to resolve the Palisades situation.

Pinchot wrote in his autobiography, *Breaking New Ground*, that the conference "Spread far and wide the new proposition that the purpose of Conservation is the greatest good of the greatest number for the longest time. It asserted that the conservation of natural resources is the one most fundamentally important material problem of all." Moreover, he asserted, it "put Conservation in a firm place in the knowledge and thinking of the people. From that moment it became an inseparable part of the national policy of the United States."

Congress Balks

Later in 1908, TR created the Country Life Commission. He appointed Liberty Hyde Bailey, director of the College of Agriculture at Cornell University in New York, as chairman. The commission's assignment was to study the status of rural life and make suggestions on how to integrate the lesser populated areas of the United States into mainstream America.

By that time, Congress was getting testy about TR's commissions. It refused to pay the printing costs for Bailey's final report, which advocated creating a large agricultural society in the United States. That did not impact the publication.

The Spokane, Washington, Chamber of Commerce published the report. TR forged ahead, undeterred by Congress's reluctance to pay for his commission's report or threats to put the brakes on his creation of others.

The National Conservation Committee completed its work quickly. Its extensive report filled three volumes. Twenty governors, representatives from twenty-two state conservation commissions, and other interested parties assembled in Washington, D.C., in December 1908 to hear the report.

FACT

One of the reasons Congress was growing more concerned about TR's ever-widening focus on conservation was his attempt to make it a worldwide effort. The members were right. At the North American Conservation Conference in 1909 he called for an international session. His call was ignored.

The ramifications of the commission's work were far reaching and long lasting. The report provided by the National Conservation Committee encouraged TR to expand his conservation efforts. Even though the end of his presidency was nearing, he accelerated his attempts to push his agenda. TR convened the North American Conservation Conference in the White House on February 18, 1909.

Ending Exploitation

In the final analysis, TR accomplished quite a bit from a conservation standpoint in his seven years as president. One of his most significant contributions was in public relations. He raised the nation's awareness of the need for conservation and put "Big Business" on notice that it had to start paying attention to saving natural resources, even if he had to take them out of its hands—which he did.

TR's conservation efforts included withdrawing coal, mineral, oil, phosphate, and water-power site lands from private exploitation. In the process, he relied on his old trick of enlisting allies who were best equipped to help him.

He worked with a consortium of industrialists, business moguls, and prominent naturalists such as John Muir and John Burroughs to accomplish his conservation goals. TR was relentless, and he traveled far and wide to promote his interests.

John Muir

TR visited with John Muir in California in 1903 to discuss adding Yosemite Valley and the Mariposa sequoia grove to Yosemite National Park. That was not necessarily what TR had in mind when he went out there on a camping trip. Nevertheless, that is what he did. He did not always agree with Muir, but expanding Yosemite National Park seemed like a good idea.

FACT

The credit for founding the Sierra Club goes to TR. He suggested to John Muir that such an organization would be a great asset for conservationists. Accordingly, Muir organized the club in 1892. He was its first president, and he served in that capacity until his death in 1914.

After Muir died, TR wrote a glowing tribute to him in the January 16, 1915, edition of *Outlook* magazine. He said:

Muir talked even better than he wrote. His greatest influence was always upon those who were brought into personal contact with him. But he wrote well, and while his books have not the peculiar charm that a very, very few other writers on similar subjects have had, they will nevertheless last long. Our generation owes much to John Muir.

In retrospect, the same could be said about TR.

John Burroughs

Another conservationist with whom TR worked was John Burroughs. The two shared special mutual interests: a love of nature and a desire to preserve it. Burroughs wrote about nature while TR acted legislatively to preserve it. Together, they were effective in providing Americans with an appreciation for conservation.

John Burroughs was one of TR's favorite authors and a longtime friend. Burroughs called TR "a rare combination of sportsman and naturalist." In return, TR wrote about Burroughs's writing: "Every lover of outdoor life must feel a sense of affectionate obligation to you." As a gesture of respect,

TR dedicated his book, *Outdoor Pleasures of an American Outdoorsman*, to Burroughs.

In reference to the two-week camping trip the two took in Yellowstone National Park in 1903, TR continued, "You were with me on one of the trips described in this volume, and I trust that to look it over will recall the pleasant days we spent together." Their writings are enjoyed by sportsmen, conservationists, and lovers of literature nearly 100 years after their deaths—a fact that would please them both to no end.

Signs of Success

By the time TR left the White House, conservation was a significant issue among politicians and the public. He happily reported those signs in his conservation initiatives as proponents became more active in their efforts.

Theodore Roosevelt camping with John Burroughs at Yellowstone Park, 1903

After a 1901 hunting trip to Colorado, he wrote in *Outdoor Pleasures of an American Outdoorsman*:

This high country is the summer home of the Colorado elk, now woefully diminished in numbers, and of the Colorado blacktail deer, which are still very plentiful, but which, unless better protected, will follow the elk in the next few decades. I am happy to say that there are now signs to show that the State is waking up to the need of protecting both elk and deer; the few remaining mountain sheep in Colorado are so successfully protected that they are said to be increasing in numbers.

That single paragraph summed up his conservation concerns: diminishing numbers, the need for better protection, people's awakenings regarding the need for protecting natural resources, and successful results. It was a tribute to his conservation efforts as well.

Enemies of Conservation

TR and his conservation-minded friends, some of who almost made saving resources a religion, had created a movement that picked up speed—and enemies. Once business leaders figured out that conservation was going to cost them money, they began to fight attempts to promote it. Even Congress fought against the conservation of natural resources at times.

Fighting with Congress and business people over the value and costs of conservation was one thing TR would not miss after he left office. Neither would he give up his own campaign to protect the nation's resources. TR redirected his efforts to private ventures, while his supporters carried on the fight in their own arenas. Together, they set a trend for future, never-ending battles over conservation issues.

FACT

Together, TR and Pinchot helped preserve more than 170 million acres of land by designating them as national parks and monuments. One of the president's last acts was to designate Mount Olympus in Washington state as a national monument—only two days before he left office in 1909.

The Aftermath

TR's influence and efforts to push conservation lasted long after he left office. His actions in the area led to the formation of the National Park Service, which was established on August 25, 1916. That was only part of his legacy.

FACT

> According to some estimates, TR placed approximately 230 million acres of natural resources under federal protection during his tenure as president. That included parks, forests, game and bird preserves, and other unique natural resources. Congress, business people, and other critics may have opposed him at times, but he succeeded in conserving huge amounts of resources for all the people of the United States.

One of TR's most enduring pieces of legislation was the Antiquities Act of 1906, which he signed on June 8 that year. It made possible the preservation of historic, scientific, commemorative, and cultural values of the archaeological and historic sites and structures on public land. Most importantly, it obligated—and continues to obligate—the federal agencies that manage that land to act in the best interests of present and future generations.

"Present and future . . ." That highlighted TR's attitude about conversation. Not only was it intended to save natural resources for everybody, but for those of future generations. That was typical of TR when it came to conservation—and almost everything else in which he had an interest. He was always looking ahead.

13-1 The multitalented scientist "WJ" McGee never earned a formal college degree.

A. True
B. False

13-2 TR appointed Liberty Hyde Bailey as chairman of the National Commission on Country Life because he was:

A. the best car salesman in a small town in upstate New York.
B. distantly related to the Roosevelts.
C. experienced as a botanist and horticulturalist.
D. the former president of Cornell College in Iowa.

13-3 John Burroughs was:

A. the author of the Tarzan books.
B. author Edgar Rice Burroughs's twin brother.
C. a nature writer and essayist in the 1800s and 1900s.
D. opposed to fishing for sport.

13-4 The Antiquities Act passed by Congress in 1906 was designed to:

A. protect the elderly.
B. set fixed prices at antiques shops in the Western United States.
C. make sure that no person over age sixty-six could be elected as president of the United States.
D. establish that archeological sites on public lands are important public resources.

13-5 Which of these activities was TR not fond of?

A. fishing
B. hunting
C. horseback riding
D. writing letters to his children

ANSWERS

13-1. *True: Although McGee was well versed in numerous scientific fields, the only college degree he had was an honorary degree from Cornell College in 1901.*

13-2. C

13-3. C

13-4. D

13-5. A: *John Burroughs said that one of the differences between him and TR was that Burroughs enjoyed fishing, while TR did not.*

CHAPTER 14

The Nonpolitical Years

"This country will not be a good place for any of us to live in if it is not a reasonably good place for all of us to live in . . . Laws are enacted for the benefit of the whole people, and must not be construed as permitting discrimination against some of the people."

TR hit the ground running after he left the White House in 1909. He led an eleven-month safari to East Africa and followed that with a three-month sojourn through Europe. TR visited a few countries with no specific agenda, except for picking up his Nobel Peace Prize in Norway. Once he returned to the United States, he limited his activities to a few speeches, writing, and relaxing with his family. It was a restful period, especially for someone as energetic as TR. His hibernation was the calm before the storm.

Leading a Safari

TR was out of office with no particular plans. Sitting idle was never one of his favorite pastimes. He needed something meaningful to do. The Smithsonian Institution came to the rescue and asked him to lead a scientific expedition to British East Africa, which lasted from April 21, 1909, to March 14, 1910.

FACT

The cost of the expedition was $100,000 (about $2.5 million in 2010 terms), or about $8.77 per specimen collected. (The number of specimens collected was 11,397.) The Smithsonian paid half, which it generated from requests for donations. TR added $25,000, as did Andrew Carnegie. The party included two guides, two zoologists, a physician, a photographer (Kermit), and a "bwana," or boss (TR).

Technically, TR was the leader, but in name only. The true leader was R. J. Cunninghame (alternately spelled Cunningham), a guide from the expedition's outfitter, Newland & Tarlton. But TR was the star of the trip. Without him, the safari might have been just one more expedition to Africa. Because it was him and he was still riding a wave of post-presidency popularity, his trip started a rash of safaris among adventurers who could afford the hefty cost.

TR was grateful for the opportunity. It gave him the chance to further his knowledge of natural history, hunt big game, and spend quality time with his son Kermit.

While in Africa, TR started coming face-to-face with his own mortality and the passing of the torch. Again, while talking about Kermit, this time in a letter to Ethel, he wrote about their last hunt together. They were successful.

Between them, they shot three giant eland. "We worked hard," TR wrote. "Kermit of course worked hardest, for he is really a first-class walker and runner; I had to go slowly, but I kept at it all day and every day." He still had the will. Some of his famed energy was lacking.

Theodore Roosevelt and his big bull rhino

FACT

TR and Kermit combined killed 512 animals during their safari, including seventeen lions, eleven elephants, and twenty rhinoceroses. Once, while TR was standing over a freshly killed eland, a guide told him about a rhinoceros standing nearby. He rushed over and shot it, too. That was how hunters gathered "specimens" in those days.

TR had always wanted to take a safari such as this one. But it provided more proof to some of his detractors that he wanted to shoot wildlife, not catalog it. He told the audience at his November 18, 1910, presentation to the National Geographic Society:

Really, I would be ashamed of myself sometimes, for I felt as if I had all the fun. I would kill the rhinoceros or whatever it was, and then [the scientists] would go out and do the solid, hard work of preparing it. They would spend a day or two preserving the specimens, while I would go and get something else.

In TR's final report to the Smithsonian, he gives the credit for the safari to the other members: "The invertebrates were collected carefully by Dr. Mearns, with some assistance from Messrs. Cunningham and Kermit Roosevelt . . . Anthropological materials were gathered by Dr. Mearns with some assistance from others; a collection was contributed by Major Ross, an American in the government service at Nairobi," etc. His report made it sound as if he did not do any of the work, which was rarely the case with TR.

Homesick

As much as TR was enjoying himself, he was tiring of the safari by the end of the year, especially as Christmas arrived. He told Ethel in a letter written two days before Christmas that, "I am so eagerly looking forward to the end, when I shall see darling, pretty Mother, my own sweetheart, and the very nicest of all nice daughters—you blessed girlie." He did not have much longer to wait.

Eventually, TR had to leave and find some other projects to attack. The safari ended in March 1910; he was left with a lot of time on his hands and nothing to do with it.

QUOTE

The safari piqued TR's curiosity. He wrote: "I wish field naturalists would observe the relation of zebras and wild dogs . . . It seemed to us that zebras did not share the fear felt by the other game for the dogs." There were questions he wanted answers to, but he could not answer himself. The same curiosity he exhibited as a child came to the fore in Africa.

TR allowed that he had never passed a more interesting eleven months than those he spent in Africa, especially from the standpoint of a scientist. However, it was time for a new adventure. Europe seemed like a good place to find one—especially since Edith was going to meet him there.

No Rush to Get Home

TR did not return to the United States immediately. He traveled around Europe for a few months, giving speeches, collecting honoraria, and representing the country at King Edward VII of Great Britain's funeral.

QUOTE

President Taft asked TR to represent the United States at the funeral of Great Britain's King Edward VII, who died on May 6, 1910. TR announced to France's ambassador to Great Britain, Paul Cambon, that he would do so "dressed in khaki and boots with a Buffalo Bill hat and armed with a saber and pistols." Edith nixed that idea. He rode in a carriage at the funeral and wore a top hat and tails.

He took a side trip to Denmark and Norway in early May to pick up his Nobel Peace Prize, since he was in the area. During his May 5 acceptance speech, the man who had urged the United States to go to war against Spain in 1898 and who would push for its entry into World War I in Europe, declared that, "Peace is generally good in itself, but it is never the highest good unless it comes as the handmaid of righteousness; and it becomes a very evil thing if it serves merely as a mask for cowardice and sloth, or as an instrument to further the ends of despotism or anarchy."

Three weeks later, he received an honorary membership in the Cambridge Union, Cambridge University's debating society. TR was in his glory during those days in Europe.

FACT

On May 26, 1910, TR gave a speech at the Cambridge Union. Just prior to it, *Punch* magazine printed a cartoon depicting the lions guarding the Nelson Monument at Trafalgar Square in London. The statue, surrounded by policemen, featured a sign that read, "These lions are not to be shot," an obvious reference to the large number of animals TR had killed in Africa in the interest of science.

One speech in particular caught people's attention: his April 23, 1910, presentation at the Sorbonne in Paris.

In his "Citizenship in a Republic" talk, TR lauded people of action, not those who sit by idly and let others do the work:

It is not the critic who counts: not the man who points out how the strong man stumbles or where the doer of deeds could have done better. The credit belongs to the man who is actually in the arena, whose face is marred by dust and sweat and blood, who strives valiantly, who errs and comes up short again and again, because there is no effort without error or shortcoming, but who knows the great enthusiasms, the great devotions, who spends himself for a worthy cause; who, at the best, knows, in the end, the triumph of high achievement, and who, at the worst, if he fails, at least he fails while daring greatly, so that his place shall never be with those cold and timid souls who know neither victory nor defeat.

That passage caught the world's attention, and gave the listeners an insight into TR's philosophy of life.

Side Trip to France

While he was in France, TR received an invitation to review French troops and maneuvers at the Château de Vincennes, a medieval castle and dungeon used for military schools. He got to watch the maneuvers and a practice battle staged for him. The party included Robert Bacon, the American ambassador to France, Jules Jusserand, the French ambassador to the United States, and General Jean B. Dalstein, the military governor of Paris.

There was a comical side to the day at the military school. TR was dressed formally in striped trousers. The French had to adjust the horse's stirrups and place leggings over TR's trousers to accommodate his clothing. Nevertheless, he rode with dignity as he passed on horseback through the more appropriately dressed French cavalry units. It was quite a day for TR.

Stirring Up Controversy

A few weeks after his "Citizenship in a Republic" speech, TR spoke at the Guildhall in London. He elaborated a bit on his Sorbonne remarks, with a few words that reflected his directness: "I wish to say a few words because they are true, without regard to whether or not they are pleasant."

He generated a bit of a controversy in his speech when he spoke about Britain's role in Egypt.

FACT

The Corporation of the City of London, the oldest corporation in the world, presented TR with the "Freedom of the City" on May 31, 1910. He used the occasion to present a speech on "British Rule in Africa," a subject about which he had learned a lot in his recent safari.

TR was brutally direct in his choice of words. He told his audience that someone had to rule Egypt to restore order out of chaos, but they had better do it right. He advised that, "If you stay in Egypt it is your first duty to keep order, and above all things also to punish murder and to bring to justice all who directly or indirectly invite others to commit murder or condone the crime when it is committed."

ESSENTIAL

The *New York Times* published the full-text transcript of the speech TR gave at the Guildhall on June 5, 1910. That is believed to be the first time the *Times* reproduced a speech of any kind word for word. It also carried a lengthy analysis about the speech in its June 4, 1910, issue.

Some detractors construed his meaning as an invitation to apply violence and injustice against the "fanatical" Egyptians. They also charged that he referenced the Egyptians' attempts at self-government as "farcical." "Fanatical" and "farcical" were not words he used. Regardless of his exact words, he created a worldwide firestorm.

TR's comments drew derision and criticism from people on all sides of the political spectrum, especially in London, where liberals accused him of basing his comments on a single safari to Africa rather than on any real knowledge of Egypt or Britain's role in ruling it. As TR said, truth trumped pleasantness. Per usual, truth lay in the eyes of the beholder, and the controversy he created was something to behold.

Not everything he said at Guildhall was controversial. He also said, "The people at home, whether in Europe or America, who live softly, often fail fully to realize what is being done for them by the men who are actually engaged in the pioneer work of civilization abroad." That had been true in his forays into Cuba and the Philippines. He saw it as true when he was updating the British on the status of their rule in Egypt.

Prescreening

Contrary to popular belief, TR did not make his comments out of the blue. He had submitted his speech to high-ranking British government officers prior to delivering it. They had approved his remarks. He was on solid ground in what he said. Critics had never daunted him before. They did not this time, either.

Historian William Roscoe Thayer theorized in his 1919 book, *Theodore Roosevelt: An Intimate Biography,* that the British government wanted someone to warn people that it could not let the Egyptians' problems remain unaddressed. They were happy that TR was willing to be their spokesperson, since he was respected worldwide and did not have a personal interest in the issue.

TR was stirring up the people of France and England. He also stirred up some of the people in Italy—specifically Pope Pius X.

Putting Off the Pope

As TR's Guildhall speech demonstrated, his post-safari trip to Europe was not without controversy. An incident regarding a proposed visit to see Pope Pius X in Rome drew a lot of negative publicity for him. Some people labeled him anti-Catholic. The argument showed that TR could generate controversy wherever he went, even when he was just trying to enjoy himself.

TR had asked the U.S. ambassador to Italy, John G. A. Leishman Sr. to arrange an audience with the pope—if it was mutually convenient. The pope agreed to an April 5 meeting. TR wrote in a March 25 cable that if the pope did not receive him, "I shall not for a moment question the propriety of his action."

ESSENTIAL

A few months prior to TR's proposed audience, his former vice president, Charles Fairbanks, had refused to promise papal representatives that he would not speak to a meeting of the Methodist Episcopal Church in Rome on his visit there. Consequently, the pope's representatives refused to grant Fairbanks an audience with the pope. That incident fueled the fire when TR arrived.

The negotiations dragged on—but never directly between the pope and TR. Eventually, the meeting fell through. Catholics believed that TR had snubbed the pope. The issue took on a larger-than-it-had-to-be life.

The *New York Times* declared flat out in an April 4, 1910, headline that "Roosevelt refuses to visit Pope." In another article, Archbishop William H. O'Connell of Boston proclaimed in the *New York Times* that TR's failure to visit the pope was "insulting and a violation of Mr. Roosevelt's principle of a 'Square Deal.'" Critics weighed in on both sides of the issue, which became an international incident.

Getting TR's Side

TR explained his side in the *Outlook*, for which he became an editor. He wrote:

Bitter comment and criticism, acrimonious attack and defense, are not only profitless but harmful, and to seize upon such an incident as this as an occasion for controversy would be wholly indefensible and should be frowned upon by Catholics and Protestants alike.

Gradually, the issue went away—and so did TR. He left Italy and returned to the friendlier confines of other European countries.

Back Home

After some months in Europe, TR returned to the United States. He arrived in New York City on June 18, 1910, aboard the ocean liner *Kaiserin Auguste Victoria*. The city staged an elaborate homecoming that attracted 1 million people. TR transferred to two revenue cutters and sailed up the Hudson River, followed by a flotilla of nearly 100 vessels of all shapes and sizes. The mayor of New York City, William J. Gaynor, and TR both gave the obligatory speeches followed by a parade up Broadway and Fifth Avenue.

The "Welcome Home" parade for TR included nearly 2,000 veterans of the Spanish-American War. Among them were his Rough Riders, First United States Volunteer Cavalry, who preceded his open carriage. The war had been over for twelve years, but the troops' adulation for TR was still evident. And the bands played on.

Once the furor over his return abated, TR took it easy. He completed and published *African Game Trails* and gave speeches. He could not forget, though, the fact that his successor as president of the United States, William Howard Taft, was not living up to his expectations. It was only a matter of time before he addressed his dissatisfaction.

The "New Nationalism"

An August 31, 1910, address on "New Nationalism" at Osawatomie, Kansas, signaled that he was getting restless. TR continued to speak out for everyone as part of the "New Nationalism"—and as a prelude to his return to politics.

In August 1910, the state of Kansas dedicated the John Brown Memorial Park in Osawatomie in honor of the famous abolitionist and his fight against Missouri pro-slavery forces. The highlight of the two-day event was TR's speech to the 30,000 people in attendance, which gained national attention.

In his speech, TR summed up the essence of his philosophy:

At many stages in the advance of humanity, this conflict between the men who possess more than they have earned and the men who have earned more than they possess is the central condition of progress. In our day it appears as the struggle of freemen to gain and hold the right of self-government as against the special interests, who twist the methods of free government into machinery for defeating the popular will. At every stage, and under all circumstances, the essence of the struggle is to equalize opportunity, destroy privilege, and give to the life and citizenship of every individual the highest possible value both to himself and to the commonwealth.

The "Square Deal"

TR had fought for equality since his young days as a New York state assemblyman. There was no doubt that he would continue the struggle. In his Osawatomie speech he introduced a new phrase that resonated with his audience—and America. It was the first time he used the phrase "square deal," which became the mantra of progressive politicians from that point on.

"I stand for the square deal," he announced. "But when I say that I am for the square deal, I mean not merely that I stand for fair play under the present rules of the game, but that I stand for having those rules changed so as to work for a more substantial equality of opportunity and of reward for equally good service."

Who better to change them than TR? He had other places to go and projects to complete first.

Riding an Airplane

On October 11, 1910, TR became the first sitting or former U.S. president to fly in an airplane when he took a flight with Arch Hoxsey in St. Louis, Missouri. He was attending the Missouri State Republican Party's convention when Hoxsey invited him to take a ride in his biplane. TR took him up on the offer, somewhat reluctantly.

In keeping with his flamboyant character, TR arrived at the Kinloch aviation field in a motorcade replete with local dignitaries. They included the governor of Missouri, Herbert S. Hadley, the mayor of St. Louis, Henry W. Kiel, and Sheriff Louis Nolte. He watched as Hoxsey inspected the plane. Then they climbed aboard and took off.

Hoxsey had just completed a record flight of 104 miles from Springfield, Illinois, to St. Louis. His flight with TR took considerably less time. Hoxsey got the plane as high as fifty feet off the ground, circled the field twice, and stayed in the air for only four minutes. TR said later that he wished he could have flown for an hour.

Once the short flight ended, TR stepped off the plane, mingled with the crowd, got into his automobile, and drove away. It was an anti-climactic moment for him and another presidential or past-presidential first.

FACT

Taking TR for a short flight got Hoxsey in trouble with the Wright brothers. Hoxsey, who had been trained by Orville Wright, was flying as part of their exhibition team. The Wrights almost fired him because they thought flying celebrities such as TR was too dangerous. They did not want to be responsible if anything went wrong.

While Hoxsey kept his head in the clouds, TR kept his feet planted firmly on the ground and looked for new causes to espouse, but not right away.

Really Resting

For once in his life, TR took a breather from politics. He spent time with his family and caught up on his writing projects. There was one problem gnawing at him, though: he was disenchanted with the policies of President Taft.

When Taft assumed office in 1909, TR was sure he would follow a progressive agenda. By mid-1910 it was clear that he would not. Worse than not following the agenda, he appeared to be trying to rid the Republican Party of its progressive wing. That was anathema to TR's thinking.

TR had enjoyed his time off in the second half of 1910 and took full advantage of the opportunity to reconnect with his family, from which he had been alienated for over a year while traveling through Africa and Europe.

ESSENTIAL

During the 1910 Republican Party primaries, Taft took steps to eliminate progressives from the party. He was afraid that they would challenge his programs and policies if they were elected. For the most part—and uncharacteristically—TR stayed out of the political maneuvering. All Taft succeeded in doing was splitting the party and alienating voters.

The year 1911 would be more of the same, as TR assumed his duties with *Outlook*. His time away from politics ended after that—and TR was back into the race for president of the United States.

14-1   Which famous nineteenth-century writer urged TR to run for president in 1916, even though the two men were reported at times to be enemies?

A. Jack London
B. Mark Twain
C. Booth Tarkington
D. Victor Hugo

14-2   "Bwana" is the respectful Swahili word for:

A. boss.
B. father.
C. president.
D. king.

14-3   Theodore Roosevelt threatened to go to war with England in 1903 if the two countries could not settle the Alaska Boundary dispute.

A. True
B. False

14-4   Osawatomie, Kansas, is best known as:

A. the birthplace of the American clarinet maestro Osawatomie Smith.
B. the place where the buffalo burger was invented.

C. the town where abolitionist John Brown lost a battle against Missouri pro-slavery forces, which resulted in the burning of the town.
D. a Sioux expression for "it's a good day to hunt buffalo."

14-5   The John Brown Memorial Park at Osawatomie, Kansas, was donated to the state by:

A. former National Football League and Kansas City Chiefs quarterback Len Dawson.
B. Ulysses S. Grant.
C. John Burroughs.
D. the women's auxiliary of the Grand Army of the Republic, the Women's Relief Corps.

14-6   Arch Hoxsey, the pilot with whom TR flew in October 1910, died in a plane crash later that year.

A. True
B. False

ANSWERS

14-6. True. He died in a plane crash in Los Angeles on December 31, 1910.

14-5. D: The Grand Army of the Republic was the veterans group comprising Civil War veterans from the Union army.

14-4. C

14-3. True. The matter was resolved peacefully through the decision of a joint commission. It was the final point of disagreement between the two countries dating back to the 1800s. The agreement set the tone for the friendly United States–Great Britain relationship that has endured for over a century.

14-2. A

14-1. A: The New York World newspaper reported that London said that even though he supported TR, no one would vote for him, "because he exalts the cowardice and peace-lovingness of the worshipers of fat."

CHAPTER 15

TR Starts His Own Political Party

"Behind the ostensible government sits enthroned an invisible government, owing no allegiance and acknowledging no responsibility to the people. To destroy this invisible government, to dissolve the unholy alliance between corrupt business and corrupt politics is the first task of the statesmanship of the day."

TR grew disillusioned with the Republican Party once President Taft succeeded him in office. By 1912, TR believed he could do a better job at leading the country than either Taft or the Democrat Party candidate, Woodrow Wilson. So he and some of his supporters formed their own political party to challenge Taft and Wilson. By the time the presidential election was over, all TR had to show for it was a bullet in the chest and a second-place finish. Nevertheless, he prompted some significant changes in the American political system.

Disenchantment with Republicans

1911 was a rare year for TR. He did not publish any books, and the number of speeches he gave dwindled. That gave him more time to follow politics and fret about President Taft's swing away from TR's idea of what he should be doing. That did not bode well for Taft or the Republican Party.

The schism between Taft and the progressives in the Republican Party developed over several key issues, primarily conservation, tariff reform, and foreign policy. TR took some of Taft's changes personally, which could only mean a confrontation between his and the president's supporters. TR may have been out of office, but he preferred to see his policies remain intact.

FACT

One controversy erupted after a *Collier's* magazine article in November 1910 accused Department of the Interior head Richard Ballinger of making available public lands for rich business operators to exploit for monetary gain. That began an open battle between Ballinger and Gifford Pinchot. Subsequent investigations revealed that Ballinger was technically within his rights to do so.

TR decided to run for president again in 1912. He and Taft had gone their separate ways, and TR saw a need to get the United States back on track. He believed he was the right man to correct what he perceived as needing correction. TR went from private citizen to presidential candidate once again.

Taft's approach to foreign affairs left something to be desired among the progressives in the Republican Party. He favored diplomacy more than threats to settle international disputes. TR had not been averse to resolving international issues through arbitration, but he also believed that carrying a "big stick" helped speed negotiations along.

The tariff issue was somewhat perplexing from the TR standpoint. He had ignored it during his presidency. Taft included tariff reform in his campaign platform in 1908, then took no action on it after he was elected. Progressives felt that he really was not serious about changing the structure.

The Payne-Aldrich Tariff constituted Taft's reform. It lowered the general tariff rate from 46 to 41 percent, but raised rates on certain items such as animal hides, iron ore, and coal. Altogether, the legislation lowered 650 tariff items, raised 220, and left 1,150 untouched. It was a compromise that did not make many people happy, progressive or otherwise.

The differences between the progressive and conservative factions of the Republican Party regarding tariffs, conservation, foreign affairs, and other policies created a schism. The door was open for a challenger to Taft for the presidency in the 1912 election or a third-party candidate. Taft still had a lot of support within the party. So was born the "Bull Moose" Party.

The Primary Elections of 1912

Once TR made it known that he was willing to run for president, supporters flocked to his side. There were new developments in the ensuing presidential election that led to major changes in the political landscape after 1912, particularly the inclusion of women in party politics and the expansion of the primary system. The Bull Moose Party may have lost the election, but it altered the face of national politics.

FACT

TR won nine of the twelve primaries: California, Illinois, Maryland, Nebraska, Oregon, South Dakota, Ohio, Pennsylvania, and New Jersey. Taft narrowly won Massachusetts, and LaFollette won North Dakota and Wisconsin, which was uncontested. The delegate count, was 278 for TR, 48 for Taft, and 36 for LaFollette. TR was off to a strong start.

There were three major Republican Party presidential candidates in 1912: the incumbent, William Howard Taft, TR, and U.S. Senator Robert LaFollette of Wisconsin. LaFollette was about as conservative as a politician could get. He ran because he thought both Taft and TR were too liberal!

Until 1912, there were no presidential primaries. The primaries that did exist were at the state level. So this was a year of major electoral upheaval. Not all states held primaries, but in the twelve that held direct presidential contests, TR did well. The results showed that Taft had something to worry about, at least from TR.

Even though TR had a commanding lead in the delegate count, the numbers were misleading. The national party leaders actually had the last say in whose delegates got seated at the convention. As a result, there were 254 delegate seats contested prior to the convention. The Republican National Committee awarded 235 of them to Taft and 19 to TR. The primary results that had looked so promising went up in smoke.

Birth of a New Party

The biggest blow to TR was that the number of disputed votes awarded to Taft all but guaranteed that the incumbent would win the nomination on the first ballot at the National Convention in Chicago in June. LaFollette's chances of winning the nomination were nil. TR's were hardly better. Nevertheless, TR went to Chicago.

Until TR entered the presidential race in 1912, LaFollette was the acknowledged leader of the Progressive Party. Most of his followers switched their support to TR, however. The embittered LaFollette became an independent. He suffered an apparent nervous breakdown during one speech in Philadelphia, dropped out of the race, and backed Wilson.

When it became evident that Taft was going to win the nomination, TR and the bulk of his delegates walked away from the convention. They formed their own party and urged TR to head it. He agreed.

The defectors named their new faction the Progressive Party, met in Chicago for their own convention in August 1912, and named TR as their presidential candidate, with Governor Hiram W. Johnson of California, a co-founder of the Progressive Party, as his vice president. When someone asked TR if he was healthy enough to run for president, he retorted that he was "fit as a bull moose." TR put his stamp on the new party, which became known from that point on as the "Bull Moose" Party.

The "Bull Moose" Roars

TR's supporters rallied to his side as the campaign began. He had a penchant for affiliating with people who would be helpful to him when their support was needed. The presidential race of 1912 was one of those times. Some surprising people allied with him, and he found a new cause or two to espouse.

On the other hand, some surprising people turned away from TR. Among them was his son-in-law, Nicholas Longworth. TR's daughter Alice sided with her father. That strained the Longworth's marriage, which had never been that strong to begin with. TR was grateful for his daughter's support.

One of the surprising elements of the 1912 presidential campaign was the role women played in it. TR had always been supportive of women and children, starting with his sisters and continuing through his political career. Therefore, it should not have surprised anyone that women received a voice in the Bull Moose Party's campaign.

There were several women in attendance at the Bull Moose convention in Chicago. They included doctors, lawyers, college professors, social workers, and other professionals. The women played a large role. Prior to 1912, women had not played a significant role in national politics. If TR had not included them in the Bull Moose Party's campaign in 1912, that trend would have continued. Neither President Taft nor the Democrat candidate, Woodrow Wilson, supported women's suffrage nationally. Only women in a few Western states even had the right to vote, let alone participate in political campaigns. TR changed that.

Jane Addams seconded TR's nomination for president. That was the first time a female had ever spoken at a large political party's national convention.

Jane Addams was an innovative social reformer who attempted to bring people at different economic, ethnic, and social levels closer together in interdependent communities that featured settlement houses. The best known was Hull House, founded in Chicago in 1889 by Jane Addams and Ellen Gates Starr. Addams was also the first woman to win the Nobel Peace Prize, in 1931.

In another step toward progress, the Bull Moose Party mandated four women as members-at-large on the Progressive National Committee. That was another first in the fight for women's suffrage. It ensured that females would be represented at the top of the party's leadership structure. That was a politically popular move among the progressives and drew some significant support for TR.

Books and the Campaign

With extraordinary timing, TR produced two books in 1912. One was *The Conservation of Womanhood and Childhood*, which was a compilation of his thoughts on women's and children's suffrage over the years. His ideas were folded into his campaign platform.

TR noted in the book, "We must work then for each partial remedy that may alleviate something of the misery of mankind, that may cause a measurable betterment in the condition of children, women and men."

Whether by intent or not, TR placed "men" last in the equation. He was, after all, campaigning for everybody's votes in an effort to better conditions for women and children.

The second book was *Realizable Ideals*, a collection of five speeches he delivered in the spring of 1911 at the Pacific Theological Seminary in Berkeley, California. In his presentations he warned, "All our extraordinary material development, our wonderful industrial growth will go for nothing unless with that growth goes hand in hand the moral, the spiritual growth that will enable us to use aright the other as an instrument." That theme, too, tied in nicely with his campaign of 1912.

Everything was in place for TR as the campaign got into full swing in 1912. He approached it with his usual energy and a great deal of hope. The results were not what he hoped for.

FACT

The "chapters" in *Realizable Ideals* featured TR's views on religion and reform. They included "Realizable Ideals," "The Home and the Child," "The Bible and the Life of the People," "The Public Servant and the Eighth Commandment," and "The Shaping of Public Opinion and the Ninth Commandment." They made ideal campaign material for TR in 1912, without the overt religious references.

On the Campaign Trail

Initially, there were five candidates in the 1912 presidential race: the incumbent, William Howard Taft (Republican), Woodrow Wilson (Democrat),

Theodore Roosevelt (Bull Moose), Eugene Debs (Socialist), and Eugene Chafin (Prohibition). Debs and Chafin were never a factor. So, it boiled down to the first three candidates. Each had a solid shot at winning the election.

ESSENTIAL

The presidential election of 1912 drew a lot of interest because of several unique factors. There was a viable third-party candidate, the personal attacks were unusually vicious, sound recordings of campaign addresses became more widely available, and people could watch film footage of the candidates for the first time. The campaign was short—but riveting for the voters.

TR came out swinging. He established himself as the most pro-labor candidate in a speech, "The Liberty of the People." In it, he accused Wilson of siding with the business operators who wanted to oppress workers.

TR noted:

We propose, on the contrary, to extend governmental power in order to secure the liberty of the wage workers, of the men and women who toil in industry, to save the liberty of the oppressed from the oppressor. Mr. Wilson stands for the liberty of the oppressor to oppress. We stand for the limitation of his liberty not to oppress those who are weaker than himself.

There existed a problem with TR's focus, however. Three of the major campaign issues centered around the best way to deal with trusts, whether to give women the right to vote, and whether tariffs should be used to protect trade. Based on his history, TR did not have to explain his approach to trustbusting, he favored the right to vote for women, and he had ignored tariffs while he was president.

Instead of confronting the real and contemporary issues, he ran a campaign based mostly on what had been important when he was running the country. That had only been four years earlier, but times were changing quickly. TR was not quick enough. The voters were not willing to take a step back, especially when some of the issues of the day were in need of resolution and more government regulation did not seem to be the answer.

FACT

TR recorded four speeches for the Edison Company in 1912 and five for the Victor Talking Machine Company. Woodrow Wilson and William Howard Taft also recorded some of their speeches. The speeches TR recorded were the only sound recordings he ever made for commercial release.

Right from the Bull Moose Playbook

TR became the champion of a variety of constituents during the campaign. In one speech, "The Farmer and the Business Man," he solicited support for farmers and suggested that one of his old commissions be resurrected:

> *There is no body of our people whose interests are more inextricably interwoven with the interests of all the people than is the case with the farmers. The Country Life Commission should be revived with greatly increased powers; its abandonment was a severe blow to the interests of our people.*

He hammered at old themes. In his "Social and Industrial Justice" speech, he railed against the courts and their interference with the advancement of social reform:

> *We do not question the general honesty of the courts. But in applying to present-day social conditions the general prohibitions that were intended originally as safeguards to the citizen against the arbitrary power of government in the hands of caste and privilege, these prohibitions have been turned by the courts from safeguards against political and social privilege into barriers against political and social justice and advancement.*

FACT

TR made it clear to the nation that the Republican Party of old was a mere shadow of what it had been when he was at its head. He went so far as to call some of them dishonest.

He said:

Six weeks ago, here in Chicago, I spoke to the honest representatives of a convention which was not dominated by honest men; a convention wherein sat, alas! a majority of men who, with sneering indifference to every principle of right, so acted as to bring to a shameful end a party which had been founded over half a century ago by men in whose souls burned the fire of lofty endeavor.

TR was in fine fettle—even after he was shot.

Attempted Assassination

TR had always believed in going right after a challenger. Even though LaFollette had dropped out of the presidential race, TR went right into his backyard to try to win Wisconsin. He scheduled a speech in Milwaukee three weeks before the election.

On the night of his Milwaukee speech, a deranged man named John Schrank shot TR. Roosevelt's response was terse—and typical. He said that he did not really care if he was shot and continued with his speech.

TR was dining at the Hotel Gilpatrick in Milwaukee on the eve of October 14. He left the hotel at about 8 P.M. to head via automobile for the Milwaukee Auditorium, the site of his scheduled oration. TR stood on the floorboard of the vehicle, waving to the crowd, as he headed for the auditorium.

Events moved fast and in a confused fashion. Schrank, who was merely carrying out his duty as he told the police later, raised his pistol and aimed it at TR. A bystander, Adam Bittner, saw what was happening. He hit Schrank's arm as the gun went off. The deflected bullet tore into TR. The crowd tore into Schrank.

FACT

The Bavarian-born John Schrank was an itinerant ex-tavern keeper from New York City. He allegedly shot TR to deliver a message to U.S. presidents that they should not serve three terms. Schrank was never tried for shooting TR. Doctors pronounced him insane. Schrank was held for thirty years in mental hospitals in Wisconsin until he died in 1943.

Members of the crowd started pummeling Schrank rather brutally, and there were cries to hang him on the spot. Some people even headed for nearby stores to find ropes. TR came to Schrank's rescue. "Don't hurt the poor creature," he implored the crowd. Some of them were stunned that TR was able to talk, let alone stand and speak. But, they acceded to his wishes and let the man alone.

QUOTE

TR did not have much of a comment after the incident. He did say later, "I did not care a rap for being shot." He added that, "It is a trade risk, which every prominent public man ought to accept as a matter of course."

The Show Must Go On

TR completed his journey to the auditorium and delivered his scheduled speech to the 10,000 people assembled there. They knew nothing about the assassination attempt.

He mentioned it to them with a terse statement:

Friends, I shall ask you to be as quiet as possible. I don't know whether you fully understand that I have just been shot; but it takes more than that to kill a Bull Moose. But fortunately I had my manuscript, so you see I was going to make a long speech, and there is a bullet—there is where the bullet went through—and it probably saved me from it going into my heart. The bullet is in me now, so that I cannot make a very long speech, but I will try my best.

Then he spoke for ninety minutes!

FACT

The bullet Schrank fired almost point-blank hit TR's steel eyeglass case, traveled through the fifty-page manuscript of his speech, and entered his chest near the right nipple. Doctors opted not to remove it, since surgery was risky and could cause more damage than the actual shot. It was still in his chest when he died a little over six years later.

TR's Milwaukee speech effectively ended his campaign. He was admitted to a hospital for treatment, where he stayed for a week. Out of respect, Taft and Wilson stopped campaigning, too.

They resumed when TR was released from the hospital. TR did not. Except for one appearance at Madison Square Garden in New York City on October 30, all he could do was sit back and await the election results, which were disappointing.

Another First in Defeat

TR had established a lot of firsts in his career. He set another one in the 1912 presidential election, but it was not a particularly satisfying first for him. Woodrow Wilson won the election, but TR finished second. As a result, he became the first—and only—third-party candidate in U.S. political history to place second in a presidential election.

It was a dubious distinction, but TR was also the first major third-party candidate to become the victim of an assassination attempt. Schrank told police after he shot TR, "Any man looking for a third term ought to be shot." At first, that was all he had to say, and he repeated his statement several times before he gave a full confession.

FACT

Wilson won the 1912 presidential election in a landslide. He earned 6,296,284 votes (41.84 percent), compared to TR's 4,122,721 (27.4 percent) and Taft's 3,486,242 (23.2 percent). In the all-important Electoral College voting, Wilson won 435 votes; TR had eighty-eight. The incumbent, Taft, received the remaining eight. The TR-Taft split gave Wilson the victory. For TR, second place just was not good enough.

Luck may have played a part in TR's second place finish. Taft's vice-presidential running mate, James Sherman, had died a week before the election. That may or may not have had a bearing on the outcome. Johnson did give TR a little help, but not enough.

Results

The Roosevelt-Johnson ticket won only six states: Washington, California, South Dakota, Minnesota, Michigan, and Pennsylvania. They won California by the narrowest of margins—174 votes. TR had 283,610 to Wilson's 283,436. That was due to Johnson's popularity in the state and possibly the ticket's support for women's suffrage, not necessarily because Californians liked TR.

And Wisconsin? Wilson collected 164,230 votes, Taft got 130,596, and TR gathered a paltry 62,448. The people of the state where he had literally been shot figuratively shot him down.

Numbers of votes aside, TR had done quite well for a third-party candidate.

The End of the Progressive Party

Once the 1912 presidential election ended, TR's version of the Progressive Party disappeared. Progressivism itself did not. TR returned to the

Republican Party, but his foray into "Bull Moose" territory was not in vain. Once again, he initiated responses in the political life of the United States with his call for a "New Nationalism."

Significant outcomes of the Bull Moose Party included a new push for federal regulation in a variety of areas. Another was the birth of the primary system. TR and his progressive cronies had demonstrated that presidential hopefuls who did not adhere to the platforms of the two major parties had access to a new system of choosing candidates—or at least the opportunity to have their voices heard.

One important and long-lasting result of TR's candidacy was its effect on women. Their participation in the Progressive Party movement gave them a new voice in American politics, and thrust some females into national prominence. Ostensibly, TR's focus on women's suffrage helped him carry California and Washington. At least one woman, Helen Scott, of Washington, cast a vote for him in the Electoral College that year.

ESSENTIAL

Historians debate whether Helen Scott was actually the first woman in U.S. history to cast an Electoral College vote. It is possible, but unsubstantiated, that some women in California were Progressive Party electors in the 1912 presidential election. Either way, females did cast Electoral College votes in 1912, which was a major step forward for women's suffrage—thanks to TR.

The Bull Moose Party went out of business almost as quickly as it had entered the American political scene. It lasted for only four years, but its short life was not in vain. Thanks to TR and his charismatic leadership, the party left a legacy that progressives could build on. Once again he had influenced the country, even in defeat.

TR lost an election but gained more respect from his fellow Americans— at least some of them. But, as far as presidential elections go, second or third place finishes are meaningless to the runners-up. Neither one is first. TR was still out of a job after the 1912 presidential election ended, but not for long.

QUIZ

15-1 *Collier's* magazine was printed for what audience?

A. coal shovelers aboard U.S. Navy refueling boats
B. owners of dogs that specialized in herding sheep
C. a general audience
D. leaders of the Democrat Party

15-2 Jane Addams was known for her:

A. inspiring fashion sense.
B. innovations in the White House as the first lady when she was married to John Quincy Adams.
C. opinions against women's suffrage.
D. work at Hull House in Chicago.

15-3 Socialist Eugene Debs ran for U.S. president five times. The last time was in 1920. From where did he run his campaign that year?

A. Chicago, Illinois
B. a jail cell
C. Terre Haute, Indiana, his hometown
D. the campus of the Electoral College

15-4 John Schrank checked into a hotel under an assumed name on the day he shot TR. The name was:

A. Albert Ross.
B. Samuel Mudd.
C. James Garfield.
D. Archduke Ferdinand.

15-5 After TR died, Hiram Johnson became the head of the Progressive Party and ran for president in 1920. However, he ran under a different party's banner.

A. True
B. False

15-6 The two Eugenes, Debs and Chafin, received what combined percentage of the vote in the 1912 presidential election?

A. 4
B. 51
C. 14
D. 7.4

ANSWERS

CHAPTER 16

The Final Chapter

" . . . the man who really counts in the world is the doer,
not the mere critic—the man who actually does the work,
even if roughly and imperfectly, not the man who only
talks or writes about how it ought to be done."

TR took his election defeat in stride. As always, he found something to fill his time. He visited South America in 1913 to explore hitherto uncharted regions, where he encountered more adventure than he had anticipated—or wanted. Once TR returned home, he threw himself into politics again, working behind the scenes. He did not lose his sense of adventure, though. When the United States entered World War I, TR volunteered for military duty and started a new run for president. Sadly, he died before his campaign got started.

Staying Active

Once again TR was without a job or a plan. He had put a lot of effort into the 1912 presidential campaign, and it had taken a lot out of him. But, opportunity always knew where to find TR. It found its way to his door once again via his friend, Father John Augustus Zahm, a University of Notre Dame-educated Roman Catholic priest.

In 1908, while TR was still president, Father Zahm suggested that they explore South America together. TR shelved the South America idea temporarily in favor of his safari to Africa. After the Argentinean and Brazilian governments and the American Museum of Natural History invited TR on a speaking tour in 1913, they resurrected the plan.

Kermit was living and working in South America at the time, and the chance to explore with him once again intrigued TR. He accepted the invitation—and contributed $5,000 to help underwrite the venture.

ESSENTIAL

The original purpose of the *Expedicao Scientifica Roosevelt-Rondon*, as the Brazilian government called it, was to conduct mammalogy and ornithology studies for the American Museum of Natural History. (Candido Rondon was Brazil's most famous explorer at the time.) It assumed a geographic nature as well due to the involvement of the Brazilian government, which provided generous financial assistance.

As things turned out, the trip became more than he had bargained for. The expedition lasted for eight months, from October 4, 1913, to May 19, 1914—and may have contributed to shortening TR's life.

Exploring in Brazil

What began as a speaking tour for TR morphed into an exploration of the Rio da Dúvida (River of Doubt) in the Amazon region of Brazil, so named by an explorer who discovered its headwaters but had no idea of where it flowed—and no desire to find out. The expedition included Father Zahm, naturalists George K. Cherrie and Leo E. Miller, Kermit Roosevelt, Rondon, and porters and helpers. (Miller was the nominal leader of the expedition.)

Theodore Roosevelt pointing at a map of South America

Cherrie's specialty was ornithology; Miller's was mammalogy. They were both capable of crossing over into one another's field of expertise. For Cherrie, it was his twenty-eighth tropical exploration trip.

FACT

George K. Cherrie brought back approximately 3,000 bird and animal skins from the River of Doubt expedition to add to the American Museum of Natural History's collection. He also supplied 1,500 photographs. That was a change for a TR exploration trip. The explorers could shoot wildlife with a camera instead of a gun.

The trip was harrowing for TR and his companions. The events would have been the basis for a good adventure movie.

Six Weeks of Hell

The explorers spent six weeks traveling down the River of Doubt, encountering a never-ending series of rapids and waterfalls. They lost five of their seven canoes and three members of the expedition during the trip (four, counting Rondon's dog) and had to build new canoes. One member drowned accidentally in rapids. His body was never recovered. Two others were lost due to a murder.

The porters and other workers were not reliable. One porter stopped working and started stealing his co-worker's food. When a boss tried to discipline the miscreant, the offender murdered him and ran off into the jungle. A posse of Brazilians, including Rondon, tracked him with dogs, but did not find him. The murdered boss was buried at the site of the murder.

During one stretch of forty-eight days they did not see another human being. That was probably a good thing, since the area was populated by tribes of violent natives who were not above killing strangers in their land.

FACT

TR laid out the details of the exploration trip in a May 1, 1914, letter to the Brazilian minister of foreign affairs, H. E. Lauro Muller. He closed the letter with, "My dear Sir, I thank you from my heart for the chance to take part in this great work of exploration." With his typical humility, not once did he mention the injuries, illness, or resulting severe depression that afflicted him during the expedition.

Some natives killed Rondon's dog. That was actually good news. The dog's death alerted its master to the natives' presence and possibly spared his life. The personal price TR paid was even more harrowing.

Sick of the Whole Thing

TR contracted malaria during the expedition, the old "Cuban fever" that had affected him in 1898. To make matters worse, he had cut his leg during the trip. The wound had not healed properly, and the infection led to severe bleeding, swelling, and a temperature of 105 degrees. The combination of malaria and infection drove TR to despair—and to thoughts of suicide.

Some reports claim that for one of the rare times in his life TR had lost hope completely. He was so despondent that he contemplated suicide. TR carried with him a dose of lethal morphine that could kill him. He was at such a low point that he told Kermit and Cherrie to go on without him.

At the height of his illness, the expedition stopped at a series of waterfalls that seemed impassable to the leaders. TR was of no value to them. He was laid up in the expedition's one remaining tent. The situation was dire, to say the least.

Eventually, Kermit devised a way to lower the party's boats over some waterfalls and saved the surviving members of the expedition. As a result, they succeeded finally in mapping a previously uncharted river, which the Brazilian government renamed after TR. He and his colleagues had paid a heavy price for the honor.

Even though TR did not pay for the trip with his life immediately, the illnesses and injuries he incurred certainly played a role in his deteriorating health over the next few years. That was not a concern for him in early 1914, when it came time for him to return home. He had another task: stopping President Woodrow Wilson from leading the United States into danger.

Anti-Wilson

After TR returned from South America, he began filling pages of various publications with articles and editorials on a wide range of topics. Initially, they were narratives of his expedition, some of which he had been writing while traveling. As 1914 wore on, his focus changed to politics, particularly criticizing the president and his policies.

ESSENTIAL

Among the articles TR published in late 1914 were "Women and the New York Constitutional Convention" (*Outlook*, August 8), "The Right of the People to Review Judge-Made Law" (*Outlook*, August 8), "The Danger of Making Unwise Peace Treaties" (*New York Times*, October 10), and "The Navy as a Peacemaker" (*New York Times*, November 11). He was making his views of Wilson's policies public.

TR was not attacking President Wilson personally, even though he disagreed with him on almost everything. Personal attacks would come later, especially in the presidential election campaign of 1916. In true political fashion, he disguised his messages nicely as he presented opposing views.

In one article, published in the August 8, 1914, issue of *Outlook*, he wrote:

However great our regret that we have not as a nation during the last few years adhered as effectively as we ought to have adhered to the policies which alone can make the United States a real and efficient factor for the peace of righteousness throughout the world . . .

Then, he wrote, "As regards any actions affecting only our immediate interests in this crisis, I shall, wherever possible, simply support the position the Administration takes." That was the politically experienced TR talking: take a slap at the president's policies, but swear to uphold them.

TR was especially critical of what he considered Wilson's timid response to American involvement in World War I, which began in the summer of 1914. At first, the president encouraged Americans to stay out of it, even in the face of attacks on American ships and citizens, such as the sinking of the *Lusitania*.

FACT

The German submarine U-20 torpedoed the *Lusitania* on May 7, 1915, 11.5 miles off the coast of Kinsale, Ireland. The ship sank in eighteen minutes; 1,198 passengers, including 128 U.S. civilians, died in the sinking. Although the event was not the direct cause for the United States' entry into the war, it did play a role.

The United States' role in the war played into the presidential campaign of 1916.

The Presidential Campaign of 1916

The Bull Moose Party encouraged TR to head its ticket in the 1916 presidential election. But he declined. He had learned a lesson from his third-party experience in 1912 and recognized that his chances of winning under the Bull Moose banner were small. He wanted the Republican Party nomination.

The Republicans avoided a fight over nominating TR. There were seventeen names in play at the convention in Chicago, including TR's 1912 rival Robert LaFollette. The party shunted the progressives aside and selected a compromise candidate, Supreme Court Justice Charles Evans Hughes. The vice-presidential nominee was Charles Fairbanks, who had served in that position with TR during his 1904–1908 term.

The Progressive and Republican parties held separate conventions in Chicago in 1916. TR attended the Progressive meeting. Representatives from both factions tried to arrange a joint meeting to nominate TR, but the Republicans declined and nominated Hughes on the third ballot. TR met with Hughes after his nomination, then withdrew from the race.

TR threw his support to Hughes and campaigned actively on his behalf. His speeches tended to be bombastic and pro-war. Whether that helped Hughes is a matter of speculation. TR did launch direct criticisms against President Wilson, which did not help Hughes's candidacy in some quarters.

In one campaign speech on Hughes's behalf in Chicago on October 26, 1916, titled "True Americanism and National Defense," TR said, "Before entering into power Mr. Wilson announced that he was going to insist on 'pitiless publicity,' but as a matter of fact we have never had an Administration where there has been so much furtive and underhand work." He also attacked the president's handling of the navy.

Unprepared for War

TR suggested that the Wilson administration had neglected the navy to the point that it had affected "the efficiency of the fleet and the enthusiasm of its officers and men." Two days earlier, in Denver, in his oration, "Preparedness: Military, Industrial and Spiritual," he attributed the country's lack of preparation for war to "evil leadership given our people in high places." He opined that "Mr. Wilson has not only been too proud to fight, but has also been too proud to prepare."

TR's charges were not always accepted unilaterally. People did challenge him on occasion.

In one of his last campaign speeches, on November 4, in Bridgeport, Connecticut, he went all out. He criticized Wilson's foreign policy, rallied for United States intervention in Mexico's internal political upheavals, and attacked hyphenated citizenship such as Irish-American, Italian-American, etc. TR said there was "no room in this country for those whose loyalty was 'fifty-fifty.'"

In his October 26, 1916, speech in Chicago, TR included an oft-stated opinion regarding what constitutes an American: "To divide our citizens along politico-racial lines is to be guilty of moral treason to the Republic." Words like that incurred allegations of racism and anti-ethnic feelings against TR, which are still leveled against him today.

He even took a swipe at Secretary of War Newton D. Baker, who he labeled "a noble gentleman who, I understand, knits well." That was an apparent slap at Wilson's reluctance to enter the war. The Bridgeport audience did not take too kindly to TR's comments. There was some heckling, but it was not the first time political opponents had chided TR.

Possibly, Hughes lost the presidential race because he allegedly snubbed TR's 1912 running mate, Hiram Johnson. While Hughes was campaigning in Long Beach, California, he and Johnson stayed in the same hotel. Hughes ignored Johnson, though. That may have cost him enough votes to lose California, its thirteen Electoral College votes—and the election. (Wilson carried the Electoral College vote, 277–254.)

If nothing else, his fiery speeches were attracting attention. But, they may not have been conducive to winning support for Hughes. President Wilson won the election, TR and Hughes went back to their private lives, the United States entered the war—and TR had the audacity to petition the president to rejoin the army.

Trying to Return to War

Finally, President Wilson found that he had no choice but to involve the United States in World War I. German submarines were sinking American merchant ships at an alarming rate, and Germany had invited Mexico to join it in the war against the United States.

ESSENTIAL

German Foreign Minister Zimmermann sent the German minister in Mexico an enciphered message on January 16, 1917, that proposed a German-Mexican alliance. Germany offered to Mexico the return of the territory it lost in the Mexican-American War. However, British intelligence intercepted, deciphered, and forwarded the message to American authorities on February 24. Its contents raised some eyebrows in the United States.

Finally, Congress declared war on Germany, only a month after the president—who ran on the slogan that he kept the country out of it—began his second term. Two months earlier TR had requested permission from the president to raise, equip, and lead a division of volunteers for service in France.

TR fully expected that he would become involved in World War I. In a May 18, 1917, letter to President Wilson, he wrote:

I respectfully ask permission immediately to raise two divisions for immediate service at the front under the bill which has just become law, and hold myself ready to raise four divisions, if you so direct. I respectfully refer for details to my last letters to the Secretary of War [Newton D. Baker].

With his usual optimism, TR believed his request would be granted. He already had his officers picked out. He wrote to President Wilson:

If granted permission, I earnestly ask that Captain Frank McCoy be directed to report to me at once. Minister Fletcher has written me that he is willing. Also if permission to raise the divisions is granted, I would like to come to Washington as soon as the War Department is willing, so that I may find what supplies are available, and at once direct the regular officers who are chosen for brigade and regimental commands how and where to get to work.

The secretary of war to whom he referred was the same man who he suggested "knit well" in 1916. TR corresponded with Baker by letter as he tried to drum up interest in his military leadership. However, there were too many factors working against him to get Baker and Wilson to go along with his request.

TR was fifty-nine years old, a bit old for military duty. He was in poor health, and he already had one bullet in him. TR had insulted both Baker and President Wilson during the 1916 presidential campaign—and before it. The odds were that his request would be denied. It was.

Permission Denied

President Wilson did not waste any time making a decision. He sent TR a terse note two days later, stating:

I very much regret that I cannot comply with the request in your telegram of yesterday. The reasons I have stated in a public statement made this morning, and I need not assure you that my conclusions were based entirely upon imperative considerations of public policy and not upon personal or private choice.

It had been a gallant, heroic, and perhaps quixotic effort on TR's part, but he would have to fight the war vicariously through his sons, all of whom volunteered for military service.

TR recounted his efforts to raise and lead volunteers in his feisty book, *The Foes of Our Own Household*, published in 1917. In that book, he explained precisely why the United States should be involved in the war and why Germany needed to be punished. He laid out concise plans for individual and collective participation—including his own.

There was nothing else for TR to do. He notified his supporters that they would not be going to war. He told them:

It was decided unanimously that in view of the decision of the President the only course open to us is forthwith to disband and to abandon all further effort in connection with the divisions, thereby leaving each man free to get into the military service in some other way, if that is possible, and, if not, then to serve his country in civil life as he best can.

Ever the good soldier, he concluded, "As good American citizens we loyally obey the decision of the Commander-in-Chief of the American Army and Navy." He returned to heckling the president and planning a possible presidential run in 1920. TR would not live long enough to carry out his plan.

Running Again

In a way, President Wilson might have been better off accepting TR's offer to go to France. There, TR would have been out of the president's hair for a while. Instead, TR contented himself with attacking the president's policies and setting himself up for a possible presidential run in 1920.

TR became more outspoken against Wilson's policies as the war dragged on. He used his continuing personal popularity to promote the united Republican Party principles in an effort to sway the congressional elections of 1918 back into the party's power. (The Progressive Party had all but disappeared by 1918.) He succeeded.

FACT

The Republicans gained twenty-five seats in the 1918 House of Representatives election. The Democrats lost twenty-two. That gave the Republicans a 240–192 majority in the House. (There were also one Prohibition Party member, one Farmer-Labor Party member, and one Socialist, who the House refused to seat.) The Republican majority put added pressure on President Wilson as he sought a suitable peace treaty.

The outcome of the election not only gave the Republicans more leverage in domestic and foreign policies, but it re-established TR as a viable presidential candidate in the upcoming 1920 election.

TR Lays Out His Platform

TR was sounding like a candidate in 1918. An article in the October issue of *Metropolitan* magazine, "The Men Who Pay with Their Bodies for Their Souls' Desire," resembled a campaign platform. Although it sounded like a paean to the troops returning from the war, it laid out a plan for everything from education to unemployment insurance.

In the article, TR called for the implementation of many ideas he had been proposing for years. "The teaching in the schools should be only in English; in this country there is room for but one flag and but for one language," he averred. He suggested that there should be universal military service and "training and service in the duties of peace"—for men and women.

Other recommendations included preparing shipping for times of peace, dealing on a national scale with factory and industrial conditions, and providing old age, health, and unemployment insurance for workers. He was outlining a wide political agenda.

Criticism Continues

At all times TR was particularly critical of President Wilson's proposal for a League of Nations, which he had offered after the war ended. He wrote in a January 1919 *Metropolitan* magazine article, "If the League of Nations is built on a document as high-sounding and as meaningless as a speech in which Mr. Wilson laid down his fourteen points, it will simply add one more scrap to the diplomatic waste paper basket."

The speech to which TR referred was delivered by President Wilson to Congress in January 1918. In it, he outlined the fourteen points that formed the basis for a peace program and the November 1918 armistice between Germany and the allied countries. Point fourteen read, "A League of Nations should be set up to guarantee the political and territorial independence of all states."

The armistice might have served as an issue of contention for TR in the 1920 presidential election. Sadly, he did not get to use it.

The Final Editorial

The March 19, 1919, issue of *Metropolitan* magazine carried an article by TR, titled "Bring the Fighting Men Home." The editor added a note to it:

> *On Thursday, January 2nd, Colonel Roosevelt dictated the article to his secretary Miss Stricker who took it to him on Saturday, January 4th. One of the last things he did on the Sunday before his death was to correct the typewritten copy.*

There was one final irony in TR's death. His last editorial reflected the deeply religious old political and military warrior's final act. The God he so deeply respected did indeed bring the fighting man home.

Theodore Roosevelt died at his home in Sagamore Hill, New York, on January 6, 1919, of a pulmonary embolism. The world had lost a great leader—but it retained fond memories of a lasting legacy.

16-1 TR and his party planned to travel how many miles on their South American river expedition, not including the voyages there and back?

A. 875
B. 60,000
C. 38,000
D. 109,000

16-2 How many miles did the party actually travel, not including the voyages there and back?

A. 875
B. 109,000
C. 15,000
D. 60,000

16-3 On one occasion during the River of Doubt expedition a snake almost killed TR.

A. True
B. False

16-4 Sir Edward Grey was:

A. the inventor of Earl Grey tea.
B. the brother of American author Zane Grey.

C. the Socialist Party candidate in the 1912 election.
D. an eighteenth- and nineteenth-century British politician and statesman.

16-5 Even though Germany did not play a role in the 1845–1846 Mexican-American War, it offered to return land to the Mexicans in exchange for their help in WWI.

A. True
B. False

16-6 Woodrow Wilson was the president of what university before becoming president of the United States?

A. Yale
B. Dakota Wesleyan
C. Princeton
D. Cambridge

ANSWERS

16-1. B

16-2. C

16-3. True: A coral snake sank its fangs into TR's boot one night. But it could not penetrate its thick leather, so TR lived to explore some more. So did his boot.

16-4. D

16-5. False: Germany offered the land if Mexico would join it in the war against the United States. Germany did not actually have any Mexican land to offer.

16-6. C: He served from 1902-1910 as the university's thirteenth president.

CHAPTER 17

Theodore Roosevelt's Literary Bent

"Far and away the best prize that life has to offer is the chance to work hard at work worth doing."

TR was one of the most well-rounded people of his era. He developed interests in a variety of disciplines as a youth and expanded his areas of academic and practical expertise as he grew older and more experienced through memberships in elite organizations such as the American Academy of Arts and Letters and the American Historical Association and the friendships he cultivated. His memberships in prestigious organizations and his access to people through his books, articles, and literary positions gave him more opportunity to influence events. He used them shrewdly.

Eclecticism

Few people in TR's circle of associates were as well-versed as he was across the spectrum of academic and literary pursuits. Nevertheless, the people with whom he associated helped him develop his knowledge and skill sets even more.

More importantly, TR and his associates used their knowledge to help educate people at all levels of society. Sometimes their efforts went unrecognized. At other times, they led to controversy. In many cases, they were long-lasting. In fact, some of TR's initiatives and innovations are still affecting society today.

"Nature Fakers"

A controversy arose in the United States in the early 1900s over whether animals were governed by instinct, instruction, or intuition and how they should be presented in literature. Most people really did not care.

Readers enjoyed stories like Anna Sewell's *Black Beauty*, published in 1890; Jack London's *White Fang* (a sequel to his 1903 best seller, *The Call of the Wild*, which appeared in serial form in *Outing* magazine prior to its publication in book form in 1906); and William Long's *Brier-Patch Philosophy* (appearing in *Harper's Monthly* starting in early 1905 under the pseudonym Peter Rabbit). As innocuous as such stories were, they generated significant literary controversy.

Writers Versus Naturalists

Stories of the generic genre irritated true naturalists such as John Burroughs and William Morton Wheeler, who abhorred the fact that writers untrained in animal science were leading people to believe erroneously that some critters had human tendencies. Worse, as Burroughs and his supporters suggested, these pseudo-naturalists were writing more to earn money than to educate readers about what really drove animals to do what they did, namely instinct.

TR read most of the articles and stories, but he stayed out of the debate for the first three years it raged. He was too busy settling matters between Russia and Japan, preparing the "Great White Fleet" for its trip around the world, overseeing the construction of the Panama Canal, and carrying out his other presidential duties to get involved in discussions about instinct versus intellect as they applied to animals.

FACT

The press was only too happy to keep the argument going. Noted publications of the time such as *Harper's Monthly*, *Science*, and the *New York Times* ran articles and essays in which supporters of both viewpoints exchanged insults, charges of carelessness in documenting their facts, and challenges to provide scientific evidence of their observations.

He believed that animals existed solely to satisfy human needs, especially in the name of progress, so it didn't matter what prompted them to act. Eventually, he had enough of the debate and jumped into it, ostensibly to protect his friend John Burroughs.

TR Joins the Fray

TR had never been shy about engaging in a healthy debate, especially when it involved a topic of which he knew a thing or two. Natural history was one of them.

Ever since TR had acquired the seal's skull and shot his first buffalo, he had retained his fascination with natural history. In fact—and identifying facts as opposed to fiction was the gist of the "Nature Fakers" controversy— it was their mutual interest in natural history that began TR's friendship with Burroughs, which started when they explored Yellowstone Park together in 1903. It was only natural that Roosevelt would try to defend him.

The catalyst that finally drew TR into the debate was a book by writer, naturalist, and Congregational minister William Joseph Long, titled *Northern Trails*. In it, Long described how one of his subjects, a wolf named Wayeeses, killed a caribou by impaling its heart with his teeth.

As a hunter, TR knew that it was a physical impossibility for a wolf to do that. So even though he was a religious man and the author was a minister, TR took a stance. He never let religion stand in the way of a good argument, so the president wrote a letter to the publisher with a copy to Burroughs in which he pointed out that Long's description was inane. TR's personal involvement in the "Nature Fakers" controversy had begun.

QUOTE

Even a wolf can't do the impossible. William Joseph Long described in *Northern Trails* how a wolf killed a caribou. "A terrific rush, a quick snap under the stag's chest just behind the fore legs, where the heart lay; then the big wolf leaped aside and sat down quietly again to watch." An exciting account—but an implausible feat according to TR.

In an October 3, 1905, letter to Burroughs, which also appeared as a dedication in his book published that same year, *Outdoor Pastimes of an American Hunter*, TR made plain his feelings about writers like Long:

From the days of Aesop . . . to the present time, there has been a distinct and attractive place in literature for those who write avowed fiction in which the heroes are animals with human or semi-human attributes. This fiction serves a useful purpose in many ways, even in the way of encouraging people to take the right view of outdoor life and outdoor creatures; but it is unpardonable for any observer of nature to write fiction and then publish it as truth, and he who exposes and wars against such action is entitled to respect and support.

The book opened the floodgates. TR became a crusader against nature fiction writers such as Long, Jack London, the Canadian poet Charles G. D. Roberts, and Ernest Thompson Seton. He charged them with writing "unnatural history."

The Writers Fight Back

In an effort to tone down the debate, or at least his part of it, TR changed direction. He said that perhaps the nature writers were not to blame for what they wrote. Instead, it was the publishers who provided them space and the school boards that used the stories who were at fault.

London labeled TR in a *Collier's* magazine article as "homocentric" and "amateur." Long suggested that the president had no room to talk when it came to understanding nature. He wrote, "I find after carefully reading two of his big books that every time he gets near the heart of a wild thing he invariably puts a bullet through it."

Eventually, TR stopped blaming anybody for anything they wrote about nature and withdrew from the debate. Once he did that, some of the other people involved lost interest as well. TR returned to his presidential duties.

About the only significant outcome of the debate was TR's contribution to the lexicon of the day; he coined the term "nature fakers." He took the name from an article in the June 1907 issue of *Everybody's Magazine* by journalist Edward B. Clark, which was based on his interview with the president.

Clark entitled the article "Roosevelt on the Nature Fakirs." TR changed the spelling of fakirs in an essay he wrote, in which he charged that "nature fakers" completely "deceive many good people who are wholly ignorant of wild life." The term caught on, and TR got the credit for it.

American Historical Association

TR was not only a student of history, but a practicing historian as well. While he was president of the United States, he pushed for the preservation of historical records, which made him an ideal candidate for the leadership of the AHA. He became the association's twenty-seventh president in 1912. One of his primary duties as president was the same as that of his predecessors and successors: give an address at the annual meeting.

FACT

The AHA, founded in 1884, is composed of U.S. historians and professors of history. It exists to promote historical studies, the teaching of history, and the preservation of and access to historical materials. AHA publishes *The American Historical Review* five times a year, presenting scholarly articles and book reviews. Congress granted AHA a charter in 1889. TR was not always happy with the organization—or the way history was presented. He believed that historians in the late nineteenth and early twentieth century were too scientific in presenting their topics. But his membership did provide him with the "bully pulpit" to espouse his views on the importance of history and its role in the education process.

The Importance of Imagination

TR told members in a December 27, 1912, "State of the Union" address in Boston that historians had to have imagination if they were going to be storytellers and entice the general public into developing an interest in what created their world. He declared, "The imaginative power demanded for a great historian is different from that demanded for a great poet; but it is no less marked. Such imaginative power is in no sense incompatible with minute accuracy."

As he explained, "On the contrary, very accurate, very real and vivid, presentation of the past can come only from one in whom the imaginative gift is strong."

QUESTION

Should history be considered literature or a science?
TR addressed that question in his December 27, 1912, speech in Boston: "There has been much discussion as to whether history should . . . be treated as a branch of science rather than of literature . . . There is, however, a real basis for conflict in so far as science claims exclusive possession of the field." TR was clearly on the side of history as literature.

He urged professors and historians to lighten up and become a bit more romantic in order to foster a love of history among nonprofessionals, rather than analyzing it scientifically in esoteric journals such as *The American Historical Review*, which few people other than themselves read or understood. There was a certain irony in his suggestion. TR was less than enthralled with the "nature fakers" who used that romantic approach in their natural history storytelling. Nevertheless, he averred that historians apply a bit of it in their writing.

In TR's opinion, historians' purposes were to be great moralists and to "thrill the souls of men with stories of strength and craft and daring." He said that he hoped when the history of his era was written, "It will show the forces working for good in our national life outweigh [those] working for evil." That summed up his personal philosophy about government and history. TR worked for good throughout his lifetime, in every capacity in which he served.

The National Institute of Arts and Letters

TR was a great "joiner." If there was a prestigious club he could join, he would. If such a club invited him, e.g., the British Royal Society, all the better. His eclecticism qualified him for a variety of associations. Among them were The National Institute of Arts and Letters and the American Academy of Arts and Letters

The American Academy of Arts and Letters, created in 1898, was called the National Institute of Arts, Science and Letters. By 1900, the "Science" part was dropped, and eventually the organization morphed into the American Academy of Arts and Letters. Name changes notwithstanding, TR was one of the first fifteen members.

The NIAL held its first meeting in February 1899 in New York City. It had a maximum membership of 150. The primary qualification for membership was the completion of notable achievements in art, music, or literature. TR qualified through his accomplishments in literature. Thus, he became an original member. In 1904, he was among the first fifteen NIAL members elected to the organization's AAAL offshoot.

According to the original organizational structure, the first 150 members of the institute were to elect thirty of their group to the academy, an elite subset. The numbers were increased in 1904 to 200 regular and fifty elite members. As the numbers grew, so did the organization's prestige. By 1907, the numbers had risen to 250 regular and fifty elite members (where they remain today).

Eventually, TR used some of his influence to try to get the group a federal charter. That created a bit of controversy. He relished the chance to get the institute and the academy more recognition. It was a bit of a surprise that his last controversy as president would arise from such an innocuous attempt to gain recognition for a literary organization.

The "Immortals"

In January 1909, as TR was leaving office, his friend, Senator Henry Cabot Lodge of Massachusetts, an historian in his own right, introduced a bill to incorporate the National Academy of Arts and Letters and the National Institute of Arts and Letters. The list of incorporators included Lodge, TR, and what the *New York Times* called in a January 18, 1909, article, "A Slur on the Immortals," "a galaxy of leading writers, scientists, sculptors and artists." The newspaper did not take the organizations as seriously as they took themselves.

The members of the Institute of Arts and Letters objected to being called "Immortals," because it made them sound like elite French academicians. They considered themselves to be nothing more than a group of artists pursuing practical policies for their mutual benefit as part of an official organization—preferably one with a federal charter.

According to Lodge, TR, et al., the incorporation would benefit the country. They included in their bill a provision that the government might call on members of either organization to get advice on literary matters when needed. A Judiciary Committee deleted the provision. Worse, it denied the "immortals" a charter, offering to incorporate the groups in Washington, D.C., to deprive them of national recognition. The slap in the face did not deter TR or Lodge.

Within a few days of the Judiciary Committee's ruling, TR issued an executive order to form a National Fine Arts Council and appoint an Advisory Arts Committee to the Government, which individuals involved claimed was independent of the attempts to incorporate the institute and the academy.

According to a spokesperson for the Executive Committee of the Academy of Arts, it was sheer coincidence that "all the painters and sculptors of the President's National Fine arts Committee, and eight of the twenty-one are architects, are members of the National Institute of the Arts, but the movements are entirely independent and without the slightest combination."

Receiving the Charter

Coincidence or not, the organizations did not get their charters before TR left office. The National Institute of Arts and Letters was incorporated by Congress in 1913, one of the last papers signed by outgoing President William H. Taft, TR's successor. The American Academy of Arts and Letters was incorporated in New York state in 1914 and received its federal charter in 1916.

In any case, TR was not affected. He had earned his way into both organizations, did what he could to help them while he was in office, and remained a member in good standing, since acceptance carried with it a lifetime membership.

Author

TR wrote more books and magazine articles in his sixty years than some people can read in a longer lifetime. His first published article, "Fall Meeting of the Athletic Association," appeared in the October 1879 issue of the *Harvard Advocate*. It was five years before his next piece, a letter to the editor about Chimney Butte Ranch, showed up in print in *Forest and Stream* (December 1884).

Only five months later, *Century* magazine printed TR's first "real" article, "Phases of State Legislation." After that, there was no stopping him. Seemingly, the only times he stopped producing articles for magazines were when he was writing books.

QUOTE

Social reformer Jacob Riis elegantly summed up TR's writing style. He wrote, "Critics sometimes say that his books are not 'literature,' by which they apparently mean words strung together to sound well. They are not. But what he writes no one can misunderstand, and the style seems to the reader unimportant, though it is notably direct, terse and vigorous."

Critiques

Certainly, when TR was writing *The Naval War of 1812*, he had no way of knowing that he would someday become assistant secretary of the navy and open himself up to some of the same criticisms he heaped on American commanders and political leaders during the war. In Chapter VIII of *The Naval War of 1812*, he discussed their extreme caution, sometimes "verging on timidity." And, he claimed that the land segment of the war was not worth studying.

In *The Naval War of 1812*, TR wrote:

But a short examination showed that these operations were hardly worth serious study. They teach nothing new; it is the old, old lesson, that a miserly economy in preparation may in the end involve a lavish outlay of men and money, which, after all, comes too late to more than partially offset the evils produced by the original short-sighted parsimony.

TR also observed, "At present people are beginning to realize that it is folly for the great English-speaking Republic to rely for defence [sic] upon a navy composed partly of antiquated hulks, and partly of new vessels rather more worthless than the old." Those words would help him later on in life when building a strong navy became his responsibility.

Perhaps it was the arrogance of his youth and inexperience in political and military matters at the time that encouraged him to include these observations, but he stored the lessons he learned and applied them in later years. That was one of his strong points: He learned from everything he did and used his knowledge for positive purposes later. And, more often than not, what he learned became the subject of subsequent books and articles.

TR Takes TJ to Task

In his preface to the third edition of *The Naval War of 1812*, TR chastised presidents Thomas Jefferson and his successor James Madison for their lack of preparation for war. (The fact that the book was printed in a third edition lent credence to the historical value of his work to readers.)

He stated, "It was criminal folly for Jefferson, and his follower Madison, to neglect to give us a force either of regulars or of well trained volunteers during the twelve years they had in which to prepare for the struggle that any one might see was inevitable."

Again, he could not see into the future, but he faced some of the same monetary restraints as Jefferson and Madison did almost 100 years prior to his presidency.

All in all, TR's first book was a success. It did not make him rich, but it helped him build a reputation as a scholar and military tactician, two talents he developed more fully as he took on more and more responsibility in his many political positions. It certainly encouraged him to accelerate his writing career, especially in the publication of books.

FACT

There was a three-year gap between the publication of *The Naval War of 1812* and his next book, *Hunting Trips of a Ranchman, Parts 1 and 2*. After that, he produced books almost every year, regardless of what his job happened to be at the time.

Topics ranged from biography (*Thomas Hart Benton*) to history (*Hero Tales from American History*), which he co-authored with Henry Cabot Lodge, his future conspirator in the charter fiasco; nature (*The Deer Family*, with T. S. Van Dyke, D. G. Elliot, and A. J. Stone); and politics (*American Problems* and *The New Nationalism*). The latter two appeared in 1910, along with his *Presidential Addresses and State Papers, 8 Volumes* shortly after he left the presidency. If nothing else, readers had a clear history of TR's years as U.S. president and a keen insight into what was wrong with America.

Post-Presidency Writings

TR's post-presidency writings for the most part veered away from political topics and homed in on "self-help" topics. He had packed a lot into his first half century on earth, and he wanted to share what he had learned with others.

One passage from his 1912 book, *Realizable Goals*, which was a collection of talks he delivered as part of the Earl Lectures of Pacific Theological Seminary at Berkeley, California, in 1911, provided a look at the one tenet that ruled his life:

> *What is necessary is to tell [young people] that their first duty is to earn their own livelihood, to support themselves and those dependent upon them; but that when that first duty has been performed there yet remains a very large additional duty, in the way of service to their neighbor, of service to the rest of mankind.*

Those words epitomized Theodore Roosevelt's personal philosophy, which he was never loath to reveal in his writings. In retrospect, his books were just one more block in his "bully pulpit's" foundation—and a valuable part of his considerable legacy. But his writing went far beyond just books.

FACT

During his lifetime, TR produced an estimated 2,000 articles about history, politics, travel, and nature for magazines such as *The Century, Scribner's, Metropolitan, McClure's, Atlantic Monthly,* as well as numerous newspapers. He also penned more than 150,000 personal letters, many of which were included in the book *Theodore Roosevelt's Letters to His Children*, edited by Joseph Bucklin Bishop and published in 1919, the year of TR's death.

One article in particular proved how truly eclectic TR was: "Some Recent Criticism of America" appeared in the eponymously named *Eclectic Magazine* in November 1888.

New "Outlook"

As his presidency ended, TR cast about for new opportunities. He settled immediately on one that gave him a chance to remain in the public's eye and continue to espouse his views on matters he deemed important. TR accepted a position as contributing editor of *Outlook*, a leading journal of the time, with which he had a longstanding relationship.

FACT

TR's first article for *Outlook*, "The Higher Life of American Cities," was included in the December 1895 issue. His choice to work with *Outlook* was so important that the *New York Times* trumpeted it in a March 5, 1910 article, "Roosevelt Begins Work As An Editor."

TR stated plainly in his first editorial that the magazine would be his vehicle to support people who believed in "a wise individualism" because the magazine owners "preach the things that are most necessary to the salvation of this people." Those ideas were not necessarily a new outlook for TR, who had been espousing them for most of his life. He was off on a new adventure.

Additional Success

TR's first eleven pieces as contributing editor for *Outlook*, which were published quickly in book form, demonstrated his eclecticism at its finest. Topics ranged from "A Scientific Expedition" to "Where We Cannot Work With Socialists," "Where We Can Work With Socialists," "The Japanese Question," and "The Thraldom of Names," a warning to readers not to fall for labels. They were the first of many.

Roosevelt enjoyed a long relationship with the *Outlook*. His final article, "The Wild Animals of North America," appeared in the November 1918 issue. Between 1895 and 1918, TR wrote almost 200 articles for that one magazine. His experience there provided him—and America—with a new outlook on a wide range of topics, some of which have remained relevant long past TR's heyday.

17-1 American novelist Jack London was:

A. a pioneer in the increasingly popular field of commercial magazine fiction at the turn of the twentieth century.

B. one of the first fiction writers to gain an international celebrity status.

C. among the first writers to earn a large fortune from his fiction.

D. on the opposite side of the fence from Theodore Roosevelt in the "Nature Faker" argument.

17-2 The American Historical Association grants an award occasionally to honor a public official or other civil servant who has made extraordinary contributions to the study, teaching, and public understanding of history. The award is named in honor of two former U.S. presidents. Ironically, TR shares the name with another president with whom he did not have the most cordial relationship. Who is it?

A. William Howard Taft

B. William McKinley

C. Woodrow Wilson

D. Franklin Delano Roosevelt

17-3 How many books did TR write in his lifetime?

A. 28

B. 10

C. It depends on who is counting

D. 51

17-4 TR wrote all the letters included in the 1919 book, *Theodore Roosevelt's Letters to his Children*, to his children.

A. True

B. False

17-5 "Yellow Journalism" is:

A. writing about health-related topics.

B. a style that exploits, distorts, or exaggerates the news to create sensations and attract readers.

C. a journalistic approach that concentrates on one color in the rainbow.

D. news reporting that focuses on facts.

ANSWERS

17-5. B. The term became popular around 1900 to describe some major New York City newspapers competing for circulation. It is applied today to describe negatively any journalism that presents news unprofessionally or unethically.

17-4. False: As editor Joseph Bucklin Bishop explained, he wrote most of them to the children as "messages of constant thought and love, for they were never for a moment out of his mind and heart." But he wrote a few others to friends or relatives to brag about the children, of whom he was extremely proud.

17-3. C. Some people list different volumes under one title as all as one individual book. Others list them all as individual books. At least two of the books attributed to him may have been written or edited by someone else. In any event, he wrote somewhere between 40–50 books.

17-2. C

17-1. All of the above

CHAPTER 18

The People Who Helped Shape Theodore Roosevelt

"It is not the critic who counts; not the man who points out how the strong man stumbles, or where the doer of deeds could have done them better. The credit belongs to the man who is actually in the arena, whose face is marred by dust and sweat and blood . . . " From Theodore Roosevelt's speech "Citizenship in a Republic"

TR was not a completely self-made man. He epitomized the ideal that no individual can be successful without the help of the right friends and champions. Throughout his life he had a knack for befriending and working with the people who could best guide him through specific situations. The process began with his father and siblings and continued throughout his lifetime. It was not always the same people at his side when he needed them. The cast may have changed at times, but their allegiance to one another did not.

Forming Friendships

TR was always candid about his relationships with other people. He stated that his father was the greatest man he ever knew, and he spoke of his warm relationships with his brothers, sisters, and children. His long-lasting relationships with his family extended well beyond their inner circle—and not only with people who were alive.

TR had a penchant for "taking advice" from characters from literature and history. He was an avid reader who learned a great deal about life from historical figures. His letters and books are replete with references to kings, presidents, and other significant personages in history, many of whom in one way or another helped him solve problems or create solutions.

QUOTE

Abraham Lincoln was one of TR's favorite mentors. He told his son Kermit in an October 2, 1903, letter: "It is a great comfort to me to read the life and letters of Abraham Lincoln. I am more and more impressed every day, not only with the man's wonderful power and sagacity, but with his literally endless patience, and at the same time his unflinching resolution."

TR's friends fell into two categories: professional and social. He maintained some relationships on a professional or advisory basis only, such as those with politicians, artists, and naturalists. Others, like those with Seth Bullock, Henry Cabot Lodge, and Leonard Wood, were business-like when necessary, but social as well.

Some of his friendships and relationships lasted for decades. One in particular dated back to his early childhood, led to his second marriage, and changed his life forever. That was his marriage to and friendship with Edith Carow.

Overall, the list of people who he numbered among his closest friends and champions is long. There were several people among them who bear special mention because of their ability to help shape his thinking and make decisions on a variety of issues. They were his sounding boards, whose advice he sought and valued.

Benefits of Listening

There is little doubt that the people with whom TR associated had a significant impact on his philosophies of life and their application to make sure things got done. Not only did he listen to his friends, but he integrated their advice into his endeavors. That is evidenced by the constant appearance of certain people's names throughout TR's political and private lives.

Names like Seth Bullock, Gifford Pinchot, and Henry Cabot Lodge appear frequently in accounts of TR's life. They entered his life at different periods; many remained friends until they or TR died. Others moved in and out at crucial periods in his life.

Regardless of when they entered and exited TR's life, numerous people helped shape his careers in the many fields he worked—and as a human being. That was because TR learned early a salient lesson about life: listen to what other people have to say, apply that which is practical, and pay them back in kind.

FACT

The book *Theodore Roosevelt's Letters to His Children* is a prime example of TR's penchant for sharing experiences and providing advice to his children. It also demonstrates his lifelong practice of seeking guidance from other sources as a way to steer his own destiny.

In retrospect, TR's greatest accomplishments would not have been possible without the advice of his close friends and associates. Or they would have been diminished significantly. That is true of every phase of his life.

Seth Bullock

TR and Seth Bullock worked together on conservation and military projects for about thirty years. They met in the Badlands during TR's ranching phase. Even though Bullock was about eleven years older than TR, they had one significant common bond: they were both lawmen. Their friendship lasted throughout their lifetimes. (Both men died in 1919.)

Bullock was an effective and feared lawman. He was named the sheriff of the newly organized Lawrence County in March 1877. Bullock did not brook any nonsense from local "bad guys." He cleaned up the county, for which he earned TR's—and practically everyone else's—respect.

FACT

Bullock and TR met in 1884. TR had nabbed a horse thief whom Bullock wanted. Later, on a business trip to Deadwood, South Dakota, TR and two friends met Bullock. The trio had been on the trail for two weeks. Bullock thought they were gamblers and stopped them for questioning. They shared some stories about the thief's capture. Their meeting was the beginning of a long friendship.

The pair crossed paths often during their later years. They traveled together through national parks, served in the Spanish-American War—although not together—and honored one another's achievements. Captain Bullock enlisted as a member of the Rough Riders, but he remained at a training camp in Louisiana with "Grigsby's Cowboys."

After the war, when TR was president, he appointed Bullock as U.S. marshal for South Dakota. Bullock retained the position for nine years.

They shared the same political philosophy as well. Bullock served as a member of the Montana Territorial Legislature between 1871 and 1873 and later on with the Republic Central Committee in South Dakota in 1888. One of their closest ties was a mutual appreciation for conservation. Bullock played a significant role in creating Yellowstone National Park—the first such park in the United States.

Bullock and the Family

Bullock was drawn into the Roosevelt family circle as their friendship developed. TR sent his children to Bullock's ranch in South Dakota on occasion to give them a taste of Western life, and the two men socialized along with their wives. TR considered Bullock one of his most valued friends—and vice versa.

Bullock was devastated when TR died in 1919. As a true measure of the friendship, Bullock worked with the Society of Black Hills Pioneers to erect a monument to his deceased friend. The monument, located a few miles outside Deadwood, was dedicated on July 4, 1919. It was the first memorial erected in TR's honor in the United States.

QUOTE

TR yearned for Bullock's company at times. He wrote, "When, after the close of my term, I went to Africa, on getting back to Europe I cabled Seth Bullock to bring over Mrs. Bullock and meet me in London, which he did; by that time I felt that I just had to meet my own people, who spoke my neighborhood dialect."

A few months after the monument was dedicated, Bullock joined his friend in death. Their relationship was a true definition of a symbiotic and long-lasting friendship, the type TR shared with a few other people in his lifetime.

Gifford Pinchot

Gifford Pinchot and conservation are synonymous in American history. He introduced a scientific method to forestry management that revolutionized the practice and intrigued TR.

FACT

Gifford Pinchot graduated from Yale University in 1889, after which he studied at the French National Forestry School for one year. He returned to the United States and began what he called "the art of producing from the forest whatever it can yield for the service of man." He used his self-coined term the "conservation ethic" to carry out his work.

The avid conservationists started working together when TR was governor of New York state. Based on Pinchot's growing reputation as a conservationist, TR sought his advice on conserving forests. He acknowledged that Pinchot's suggestions shaped his recommendations about forestry.

Theodore Roosevelt with Chief Forester Gifford Pinchot on river steamer *Mississippi*, 1907

The two men continued their working relationship after TR became president. Pinchot was in charge of the Forestry Bureau at the time. President Roosevelt reorganized the service and renamed it the U.S. Forest Service.

During his first term in office, Pinchot became TR's "moving and directing spirit in most of the conservation work, and as counsellor and assistant on most of the other work connected with the internal affairs of the country." TR considered him the most invaluable member of his staff.

Much to his chagrin, TR's successor, President William Howard Taft, dispensed with Pinchot's services in January 1910 because Pinchot spoke out frequently against the president's policies.

Pinchot and TR also got involved in a 1907 controversy. Congress felt that the two were conserving too much Western forestland. It passed a bill to stop the creation of any more forest reserves in the region. Minutes before the ban took effect, TR designated 16 million acres of new national forests, which became known as the "Midnight Forests."

Pinchot and TR partnered for years in saving resources for the nation. Their professional relationship evolved into a friendship that endured—and paid significant benefits for conservationists across the globe. They frequently walked together, played tennis, and had dinner at the White House. It is safe to say that the two men had profound effects on one another in their social and professional relationships—and on the country in general.

Henry Cabot Lodge

Perhaps no one person other than Thee had a bigger influence on TR's career than Henry Cabot Lodge. Even though Lodge was eight years older, he exercised a profound impact on TR's career.

Both Lodge and TR were Harvard graduates. That was a significant bond, as far as TR was concerned. But Lodge was more interested in TR's potential—which he fostered as much as possible—than where he had graduated from.

The two men formed a bond in Washington when TR served as Civil Service commissioner. TR described Lodge as one of his "especial cronies." Like TR, Lodge, then a member of the House of Representatives, abhorred the spoils system. (Lodge was elected to the U.S. Senate in 1893 and served there until 1924.) When TR began to crack down on it, Lodge was one of his most ardent supporters.

They also supported one another in the days leading up to the Spanish-American War, when TR consulted the senator frequently on matters pertaining to naval preparations. Lodge was one of the few proponents of the war in the U.S. Senate. Their cooperation was mutually beneficial.

FACT

On February 25, 1898, when TR was preparing his telegram to Admiral Dewey to order the Asiatic fleet to Manila, Senator Lodge happened to be in his office. As TR noted, "Lodge called on me just as I was preparing the order." Dewey said that the telegram was the first step regarding naval war preparations—and Lodge and TR were the first two to know about it.

Their close relationship continued while TR was president. He confided in Lodge on almost every domestic and foreign issue. They did not disagree often, so TR felt very comfortable with Lodge's advice and guidance. There were times when it was almost TR and Lodge against the world.

Lodge on TR's side

When TR was trying to create a treaty with Santo Domingo to get the Panama Canal built, the opposition to it was extreme from all sides. Democrats, the press, businesspeople, and even members of TR's own party rebelled against his efforts, allegedly on constitutional grounds. Lodge was among the few people who stood beside the president. His support epitomized the allegiance Lodge had to TR and explains why they got along so well for so long.

As was the case with so many of his advisors and champions, Lodge was also a social companion. It was not unusual for the Roosevelts and the Lodges to get together for meals and amusement, especially on holidays.

They spent Christmas together in 1902, ending the day with dinner at the White House and dancing later in the East Room, "closing up with the Virginia Reel." Six years later, on Thanksgiving Day in 1908, the Lodges and Roosevelts went on a three-hour horse ride and ate dinner in the new State Dining Room.

The highlight of the day for TR was dancing the waltz with Mrs. Lodge and his all-time favorite friend and mentor, Edith, who, he told Kermit, "looked just as pretty as a picture."

TR enjoyed his friendships and working relationships with the Lodges and his other longtime companions. He prized loyalty, a trait that he and Henry Cabot Lodge shared. So did TR and Leonard Wood, who was apt to be nearby whenever the Lodges and Roosevelts socialized.

Leonard Wood

Like many of TR's closest friends, Leonard Wood was a graduate of Harvard. That was not the most important criterion TR considered when selecting his friends; it often happened to be coincidental. Other factors included age, political philosophy, and physical prowess—especially the latter.

People had to be able to keep up with TR while riding horses, taking strenuous walks, playing tennis, or whatever physical activity he fancied at any given moment. The "strenuous life" continued to play an important role in his regimen, practically until the day he died.

FACT

Leonard Wood, who attended Harvard Medical School, received his medical degree from Boston City Hospital in 1884, where he interned. As an army doctor, he was the personal physician to presidents Grover Cleveland and William McKinley through 1898. Wood was not TR's White House physician: that was Rear Admiral Presley M. Rixey. (Andrew Lambert was TR's personal physician in New York.)

Wood was born roughly two years after TR. They did not meet until TR went to Washington, D.C., to serve as secretary of the navy. Their blooming friendship set the stage for TR's army career and subsequent heroics in Cuba.

Theodore Roosevelt with General Leonard Wood

TR relied heavily on Wood's military background and organizational skills to form the Rough Riders and prepare them for the Spanish-American War. He said about Wood, "He had every physical, moral, and mental quality which fitted him for a soldier's life and for the exercise of command." TR felt that he could learn something from his friend, while doing his share of the work.

Mutual respect between the two grew as the regiment's evolution progressed from raw recruits to efficient fighting machines and seasoned veterans, all in the space of a few months. Wood demonstrated his respect for TR's courage and military leadership by supporting the recommendation for his Medal of Honor.

A Temporary Separation

After the fighting in Cuba ended, the two men parted ways for a while. Wood stayed in Cuba to serve as its military governor. He did not return to the United States until 1902, as a brigadier general.

QUOTE

Wood and Roosevelt were two of a kind, according to their commanding officer in Cuba. He wrote: "The conduct of Lieutenant-Colonel Roosevelt . . . deserves my highest commendation. Both Colonel Wood and Lieutenant-Colonel Roosevelt disdained to take advantage of shelter or cover from the enemy's fire while any of their men remained exposed to it—an error of judgement but happily on the heroic side."

Wood earned even more respect from TR for his administration of the island. According to TR:

"Leonard Wood was left in as Governor for two or three years, and evolved order out of chaos, raising the administration of the island to a level, moral and material, which it had never before achieved." That was what he was trying to do in his various government roles.

The Philippines Fiasco

Things did not always go smoothly with TR and Wood. As with any of his relationships, there were peaks and valleys. An incident in the Philippines in 1906 placed the pair in a corner, although the problem lay more with TR's opponents than with them.

In 1906, Wood's troops killed approximately 600 Moros, including men, women, and children, hiding inside a crater. TR praised Wood for his brilliant leadership. He sent the general a telegram on March 10, 1906, that said, "I congratulate you and the officers and men of your command upon the brilliant feat of arms wherein you and they so well upheld the honor of the American flag."

FACT

The United States annexed the Philippines after the Spanish-American War, which was unpopular with many vocal Americans, e.g., Mark Twain and William Jennings Bryan. Filipino forces fought U.S. troops in battles for their independence throughout TR's administration. Wood led a violent American campaign against one tribe in particular, the Moros, which incurred the wrath of TR's opponents.

The press in the United States and his political opponents excoriated both men. Many of them stressed that Wood should not be leading troops since he had a medical background. Moreover, they said, TR appointed Wood to his position as commander in the Philippines out of friendship, not because the general had any military acumen.

TR, who stood by his friends in most cases, wisely let the matter die. The case was a prime example of how much TR valued friendships and why they lasted so long.

Wood and TR survived the incident and the resulting bad press. Wood stayed in the army until 1921, retiring as a major general. He and TR remained four-star friends until Roosevelt died. Wood was among the mourners at TR's funeral, along with Henry Cabot Lodge. That was a testament not only to TR, but to friendship.

Jacob Riis

TR began a long friendship with Riis when he was a young man, but it evolved to a higher level when he started his police commissioner stint in New York City. The two men conducted night police patrols of the city together.

Riis enjoyed their time together immensely. "For two years we were to be together all the day, and quite often most of the night, in the environment in which I had spent twenty years of my life," he wrote. "And these two were the happiest by far of them all."

Riis provided an invaluable service for TR. He had grown up in the slums of New York City, where he had lived in boardinghouses run by the police department for poor people, which TR closed during his regime as commissioner.

Riis knew the slums of the city backward and forward and took TR to places he might never have found on his own. The visits gave TR fresh insights into the depressed conditions in which some New York City residents lived and prompted him to make some major changes to improve their lives.

"The midnight trips that Riis and I took . . . gave me personal insight into some of the problems of city life," TR acknowledged. "It is one thing to listen in perfunctory fashion to tales of overcrowded tenements, and it is quite another actually to see what that overcrowding means, some hot summer night, by even a single inspection during the hours of darkness."

Jacob Riis revealed in his biography of TR that New York City Police Chief Byrnes warned the new commissioner that police work would break him. "You will yield. You are but human," Byrnes said. Riis reported that it did no such thing. TR's answer "was to close the gate of the politicians to police patronage," which was his plan all along.

The First Patrol

The first time TR and Riis went on patrol together, they discovered that 90 percent of the patrolmen assigned to duty were nowhere to be found. Riis commented on that in the newspaper the next day. His story had the desired effect.

Starting the next day, and throughout TR's term as police commissioner, more cops started taking their jobs seriously—and patrolling their beats lest he should find them missing.

As a result of their working arrangement, Riis and TR formed a mutual admiration society. Riis, in summing up TR's work as police commissioner, wrote, "We rarely realize, in these latter days, how much of our ability to fight for good government, and our hope of winning the fight, is due to the campaign of honesty waged by Theodore Roosevelt in Mulberry Street [the Police Department's headquarters]."

A Tribute to Riis

Riis rated high among TR's friends and influences. TR credited Riis with opening his eyes wider to the problems of tenement living and the need to resolve them.

Jacob Riis died on May 26, 1914. Immediately, TR petitioned to change the name of Telawana Park in New York to Jacob A. Riis Park. By July 1914, the change was completed. TR made possible a memorial to his friend and to one of the United States' most prominent social reformers. The park is now part of the Gateway National Recreation Area in New York.

Years after TR left the White House, he said that his "whole life was influenced by my long association with Jacob Riis, whom I am tempted to call the best American I ever knew." That was the level of esteem TR held for Riis the reformer—and for Riis the friend.

Muir and More Friends

Just as TR formed a series of friendships throughout his life that were durable and mutually rewarding, he also participated in some that were temporary and expedient. The latter category was important to him because of what he learned from each friend and how the knowledge shaped his life, regardless of how long the friendships lasted.

Among the people who entered his circle of friendship at critical times in his life and faded away as time went by and circumstances changed were people like John Muir; members of the Rough Riders, whose reunions he attended on occasion; and William Howard Taft, who was a surprise attendee at TR's funeral.

The people TR called friends throughout his lifetime were a diverse group. They ranged from former presidents to the cowboys he fought with in Cuba. Regardless of who they were, they all shared a common bond: they helped shape TR's life—and vice versa.

QUIZ

18-1 John Owens of Newcastle, Wyoming, is a side note in the Theodore Roosevelt saga. He was:

A. the first outlaw TR arrested in the Badlands.
B. a medal winner in the 1936 Olympics in Berlin, Germany.
C. the governor of Wyoming during the Spanish-American War.
D. a cowboy in Seth Bullock's "posse" who missed TR's 1905 inaugural parade.

18-2 Until 1900, the New York State College of Forestry at Cornell and the Biltmore Forest School in Asheville, North Carolina, were the only two schools of forestry in the United States:

A. available for forestry students.
B. that contained the letter "e" in their names at least three times.
C. that received endowments from Gifford Pinchot's father, James.
D. that granted TR honorary degrees.

18-3 Who was the first person to earn a PhD in political science from Harvard?

A. Theodore Roosevelt
B. Henry Cabot Lodge
C. Gifford Pinchot
D. Seth Bullock

18-4 Which one of TR's closest friends was Georgia Tech's football team captain, second football coach, and the star of its first football victory, a win over the University of Georgia?

A. John Muir
B. "Ramblin" Wreck
C. Leonard Wood
D. "Buffalo Bill" Cody

18-5 Jacob Riis was:

A. the inventor of a peanut butter-based candy bar.
B. a shortstop for the Brooklyn Dodgers.
C. a famous nineteenth-century social reformer in New York City.
D. the premier of Denmark in 1898.

ANSWERS

18-5. C

18-4. C: On November 4, 1893, in the first football game between the schools, Georgia Tech beat the University of Georgia, 28-6, in Athens, Georgia. Leonard Wood, then stationed at nearby Fort McPherson, enrolled at Tech just in time to play in the game. He scored the school's first touchdown in history during that game—and left the school a few weeks later.

18-3. B

18-2. A

18-1. D: Sheriff John Owens left the "Cowboy Brigade" in Broken Bow, Nebraska, due to illness. The Newcastle News-Journal on March 3, 1905, reported that he "cried when he had to give up and leave his associates." The account highlights the affection the cowboys felt for one another—and for TR.

248

CHAPTER 19

Theodore the Family Man

"... compared to this home life everything else was of very small
importance from the standpoint of happiness."
(Theodore Roosevelt to his son Kermit)

TR recognized that families were important. He made sure
that his own children received every opportunity to succeed in life. All of them did, although none were ever as
famous as their father. His sons Theodore Jr., Quentin, and
Archie became military heroes. Theodore Jr., like his father,
earned the Medal of Honor. Quentin, an aviator, was shot
down by German fighter pilots in WWI. The Germans gave
him a burial with full battlefield honors despite his enemy
status. That epitomized the respect people throughout the
world had for TR.

The Roosevelt Family Heritage

The Roosevelt family arrived in America from the Netherlands around 1660, under the name van Rosenvelt. The name was changed to Roosevelt by a second-generation family member, Nicholas Roosevelt, in the late 1600s. Nicholas also established a family tradition when he became an alderman.

FACT

The list of families to which the Roosevelts are connected is like a "Blue Blood Hall of Fame" roster. It includes the Delanos, DuPonts, Astors, Alsops, Arnolds, and Longworths. The Roosevelts who did not marry into those families often chose members of other noted clans, i.e., TR and Edith Carow, and Quentin and Flora Whitney, who never reached the altar because of Quentin's untimely death.

Two of Nicholas's children and their families split into two branches, one based at Oyster Bay, Long Island, the other at Hyde Park, New York. The Oyster Bay clan became Republicans; their cousins in Hyde Park gravitated toward the Democrat Party. Both factions grew prosperous and became serious about their duties and obligations to society. The die was cast for TR. He could not escape his fate as a "do-gooder."

From almost the moment the first Roosevelts stepped off the boat in America, they became involved in business as merchants and planters and in politics. Some of them served in the military during the American Revolutionary War—"without distinction," as TR noted. Others were members of the Continental Congress or other legislative bodies. TR was destined to continue the family's activities in politics.

Passing on Family Values

Both of TR's parents came from aristocratic families. His mother's family was included on the list of wealthy, elite Georgia planters. They established a pattern for their children, which included formal and informal schooling and field training. Thee set the pattern for TR and his siblings.

TR downplayed the influence his mother played in his life. He said that she was a "sweet, gracious, beautiful Southern woman, a delightful companion and beloved by everybody." She was a most devoted mother with a great sense of humor, he recalled, but for the most part it was his father from whom he learned the most in life.

FACT

One memory TR had about his mother's sense of humor revolved around her Civil War Southern loyalty. She disciplined him one day, unjustly in his opinion. As retribution, he prayed loudly that night in her presence for the Union's success in the war. She laughed and warned him not to do that again, lest she tell his father. He heeded her advice, and Thee did not learn about the incident.

TR overlooked the role she played in his life as he grew older, especially when he went to college. She did not want TR living on campus with the other students, which created some uncomfortable moments for him. Many of his classmates found it a bit odd that one of their peers was so pampered and antisocial.

There was a fine line between protection and overprotection in their view. His mother crossed that line. It was just one more obstacle that TR had to overcome in his struggle to become independent and accepted. That helps explain why he gave more credit to his father than his mother for molding him into a productive member of society who could stand on his own two feet.

Like Father, Like Son

TR always recalled fondly the lessons he inculcated from his father. Thee taught him and his siblings about their duties to society. His father was religious, brave, gentle, tender, unselfish, and, most of all, loving. He instilled those same virtues in his children.

And Thee made it clear there were certain things he would not tolerate in them. Selfishness, cruelty, idleness, cowardice, and lack of truthfulness topped the list. Thee relied on discipline and love to drive those virtues and vices into his children's minds.

Above all, Thee made his children feel protected. TR always felt safe with Thee, but he knew that the protection only went so far. Thee expected the children to fight their own battles when necessary. He knew he would not be around forever to help them. Self-dependence was one of the biggest gifts he gave his children. It was one that TR learned well.

Thee was not averse to giving his children little gifts every now and then. That practice reinforced the notion of giving, even if the little things he gave had no extrinsic value but served merely as reminders of a father's love for his children. TR passed the same types of gifts to his children later on.

TR invented his own reward system with his children. He remembered one in particular. Whichever child brought him his bootjack, a small tool that helped people pull their boots off, after he returned from a horse ride got to walk around the room in TR's boots. That was a significant reward; it took someone special to fill his shoes.

In addition to passing down his own values to his children, Thee applied them outside the home. He worked hard at his business during the day and redirected his industriousness to social reform and charity works at night and on the weekends. He did not just give money to people or underwrite buildings. He visited the poor and downtrodden and took the children with him.

TR Tags Along

When Thee visited the hospitals, homes for orphans, the YMCA, and other places in which he had an interest, the kids went along. Often, when he taught a Bible class at Madison Square Presbyterian Church, as he did many Sunday nights, TR was there. Later, when TR was at Harvard, he taught Sunday school classes.

TR emulated his father in many ways later in life. He may have done so in word only during his formative years by paying lip service to fighting graft and corruption and protecting the weaker elements of society. Later, he became more serious about helping those who needed help.

The ideas he formed about seeking social justice came largely from his father. He simply carried them out on a much larger stage when the opportunity arose.

ESSENTIAL

Nathan Miller described TR's father in his book, *Theodore Roosevelt, A Life*, as "either founder or early supporter of almost every humanitarian endeavor in [New York] city." He added, "In extending a hand to those less fortunate than himself, he acted from a disciplined sense of obligation as a Christian and a gentleman. Good fortune, he believed, must be balanced with productive work and service."

Carrying the Torch

TR's letters to his children are filled with pieces of advice regarding success, how to achieve it, and what he expected of them. He was accomplishing two purposes through the letters: expanding on the advice handed down to him and integrating it with his own experiences.

President Theodore Roosevelt with his boys, 1904

In one letter to Theodore Jr., TR sums up his attitude about life in general and what he hoped his children would do: "I always believe in going hard at everything, whether it is Latin or mathematics, boxing or football, but at the same time I want to keep the sense of proportion. It is never worthwhile to absolutely exhaust one's self or to take big chances unless for an adequate object."

There was a lot of TR and his father in those letters. He discussed every conceivable subject in them, but the underlying theme in almost every one was to "do your best" and "you and the world will be better for it."

He mentioned Edith often, but as a sort of postscript. "Mother has gone off for nine days . . ." "Mother and I have just come home from a lovely trip to Pine Knot . . ." "Mother was away [so] I made a point of seeing the children each evening for three-quarters of an hour or so . . ." It was a throwback to his own upbringing: "Mother" was in the background, while "Father" dispensed the advice to the children.

But, that was TR: always in charge—except when Edith took a page out of his book and made decisions such as buying Pine Knot, introducing innovations in the White House, and deciding when he needed a vacation.

FACT

TR may have been deluding himself at times about who was in charge. In an April 30, 1906, letter to Kermit, he wrote: "On Saturday afternoon Mother and I started off . . . Mother having made up her mind I needed thirty-six hours' rest, and we had a delightful time together, and she was just as cunning as she could be." Edith suggested; TR obeyed.

Regardless of whom he was writing to, and what the subject was, one thing shone through: TR was a proud father overseeing a mostly happy family.

TR, Edith, and Family Life

His children were the focal point of TR's life. Whether they were at Oyster Bay or in the White House, he made time for them. When he was away, he missed Edith and the children.

Fortunately for TR, he served as president at a time when the position did not require extensive travel, especially outside the country. So he could do a lot of his work at Oyster Bay or in Washington, D.C., and live and play with Edith and the children when they were growing up. Much of that "work" involved corresponding with his family.

A May 10, 1903, letter TR wrote from California to Quentin demonstrated how homesick he could get when he was traveling: "I am very homesick for mother and for you children; Whenever I see a little boy being brought up by his father or mother to look at the procession as we pass by, I think of you and Archie and feel very homesick." Homesickness and "presidenting" went hand in hand.

President Theodore Roosevelt and Family, 1903

Strangely enough, TR had nicknames for his children that he might not have tolerated when he was a child. At one time or another he called Quentin "Quenty-Quee," Theodore "Ted," Archibald "Archiekins," and Ethel "Etheley-Bye."

He did not use a pet name for Alice, to whom he seldom wrote. That may have been because she was practically a grown woman by the time TR became president. In fact, he did not write to the girls in general as often as he did to his sons.

Living in a Zoo

TR and his family did not live far from the National Zoo in Washington, D.C. They did not have to go there often. The White House was a miniature zoo of sorts, which was one of the factors that created camaraderie among the family members.

There was a parade of dogs, rabbits, owls, eagles, guinea pigs . . . the list went on. Some of them were children's pets. Others, such as the eagle and the owl, were gifts to TR, which he donated to the real zoo.

FACT

When a pet died at the TR White House, it got a proper burial. On May 27, 1904, "poor Peter Rabbit died and his funeral was held with proper state. Archie, in his overalls, dragged the wagon with the little black coffin. Mother walked behind as chief mourner, she and Archie solemnly exchanging tributes to the worth and good qualities of the departed. Then he was buried, with a fuchsia over the little grave." The family never got the chance to do the same for Quentin.

The entire family rallied around the menagerie that populated the White House and the family home at Sagamore Hill. They were just as fond of reading about animals as they were playing with them.

Books, Books, and More Books

TR had been brought up with books as constant companions. He made sure the tradition continued with his children. They read and discussed books constantly, ranging from classics to children's stories. TR knew some of the authors and made sure that they met his children.

Alice and Kermit in particular were great fans of Joel Chandler Harris, who was known for his "Uncle Remus" stories, which delighted them. He recorded many stories from the African-American oral tradition. By doing so, Harris revolutionized children's literature. TR and Edith read his stories to their children, most of them repeatedly.

There were regular book review sessions among them. TR never passed up an opportunity to express his opinions on Charles Dickens, William Makepeace Thackeray, and other authors. He entered discussions on the merits of the authors and their characters, the plots, and other aspects of literature.

A lot had changed since his days in the Badlands, when he professed his lukewarm interest in novels. The opportunity to discuss them with his children changed his mind about a lot of things in life.

Physical Activity

TR was proud of his children's physical prowess, especially the boys' participation in organized sports. He sent them off to Harvard with his blessings and praised them for their athletic endeavors. But he was not going to let them pursue the "strenuous life" without engaging in physical activity himself.

FACT

In 1904 TR took up Japanese wrestling. He worked out with two Japanese wrestlers three times a week to stay in shape. He admitted that he was not built well enough or at an age where he could keep up with them for long, but he had still not lost his desire to work on his physical well-being. The experiment lasted about one month.

He may have been the president of the United States, but he was not going to restrict himself to wrestling with problems. He took up wrestling—literally.

Even though the Roosevelt family life seemed "Edenesque" at times, there were a few of the proverbial skeletons in the closet endemic to most families.

A Problem or Two

Alice did not always fit well into the family structure. There had been friction between TR and Alice ever since she was a child. Bamie had done a great job raising her while TR was in the Badlands trying to forget Alice Hathaway Lee Roosevelt. Even though Edith had gladly consented to raise Alice as her own, there was always a wall between them.

After Alice got married at the White House on February 17, 1906, Edith sent her off with some less than friendly words. According to Stacy A. Cordery, author of a biography of Alice Roosevelt Longworth, Edith said, "I want you to know I am glad to see you leave. You have never been anything but trouble."

TR did not live to see the type of life Alice led after she left the White House. He did hear, however, one of her quips about a major episode in his life. She and her husband, Ohio representative Nicholas Longworth, went to Cuba for their honeymoon. They visited Kettle Hill, where TR had led his charge in 1898. She said she found the hill "mildly sloping."

Alice may have been a disappointment at times to TR. So was—or would have been—Kermit, who committed suicide on June 4, 1943, after struggling with alcoholism and depression. That, too, occurred after TR's death. Only one of his children, Quentin, died before he did. He died a hero's death. Quentin was just one hero among many in the Roosevelt family.

A Family of Heroes

TR and Edith raised their children to be patriotic and philanthropic. They had a duty to make the world a better place for everyone, at least to the extent of their abilities. That lesson never shone through more than when World War I began. Supporting the effort was a family affair. The immediate family did its part during the war—and paid a huge price.

All four of TR's sons fought in Europe. Archie, an army infantry officer, was wounded in March 1918. Kermit served with the British Expeditionary Force. Theodore Jr., also an army infantry officer, was gassed once and wounded on July 18, 1918. All three also served in World War II. Quentin was killed in action on July 14, 1918.

Almost everyone pitched in. Ethel, who was married to Dr. Richard Derby, served overseas as a Red Cross nurse at the American Ambulance Hospital in Paris, where her husband was a surgeon. Later, he served with the U.S. Army Medical Corps. He caught pneumonia in 1918 while in the army.

Theodore Jr.'s wife, Eleanor Alexander Roosevelt, volunteered with the YMCA and worked in Paris. TR had a lot to be proud of, even if he could not serve on the front lines himself. But Quentin's death meant heartbreak for Edith and TR.

The American Ambulance Field Service was made up of a small group of noncombatant ambulance drivers and medical specialists who volunteered for duty in France in WWI. Inspector General of the Field Service A. Piatt Andrew said of them, they "can best be thought of as only a symbol of millions of other Americans, men and women, who would gladly have welcomed an opportunity to do what these men have done—or more."

There was no doubt that the Roosevelts would do their part. Shortly after a German U-boat sank the *Lusitania*, Theodore Jr. wrote to his brother Kermit, "I believe war is thoroughly possible . . . Should war be declared of course we all will go." Their part in the war was preordained.

Worldwide Respect for TR

There was no doubt that TR had earned the world's respect by the time World War I started. It was a war he believed had to be fought, and he made no secret of that. He had encouraged President Wilson to get the country involved and had even offered to raise a regiment and lead it into battle. Wilson declined, and TR had to participate vicariously through his sons' military exploits.

Quentin was at Harvard when WWI began. He dropped out to join the army and train as a pilot. Two German aviators shot him down behind their lines in France on July 14, 1918—Bastille Day.

At first, the Germans did not know who he was. As far as they knew, he was just another American pilot who had died fighting for freedom. They learned quickly that was not the case.

Thirteen years before Quentin died in WWI, TR wrote a letter to Kermit regarding the reading of novels. One passage was a precursor of Quentin's death: "I quite agree with you that if the hero has to die he ought to die worthily and nobly, so that our sorrow at the tragedy shall be tempered with the joy and pride one always feels when a man does his duty well and bravely."

Once the Germans discovered that the deceased pilot was TR's son, they buried him with honors where he had fallen. Approximately 1,000 Germans formed an honor guard near the crash site. They marked his grave with a wooden cross and the wheels and propellers from his plane.

The cross carried these simple words: "Lieutenant Roosevelt, buried by the Germans."

Allegedly, Germans found a letter on Quentin's body from his fiancée, Flora Payne Whitney. That is how they identified him. She had wanted to travel to Europe to marry Quentin while he was stationed there. Permission was denied. Married or not, she had a hand in identifying her sweetheart's body and ensuring that he was buried with dignity and respect.

Inwardly, TR and Edith accepted Quentin's death with a great deal of sadness. Outwardly, they put on a brave front for the world. He issued a simple statement saying, "Quentin's mother and I are very glad that he got to the front and had a chance to render some service to his country and show the stuff that was in him before his fate befell him." He had done the same himself twenty years earlier.

Letters

Ten days after Quentin died, TR wrote two letters, one to French statesman and scholar Gabriel Hanatoux, the other to his son Archie. He said essentially the same thing to both men. To Hanatoux he wrote, "It is very hard for the old to stay . . . whereas the young die in their glorious golden morning. It is bitter for me to sit at home in ease and comfort and have my four sons and my son-in-law and all the young kinsmen I have at the front facing death and enduring hardship."

He said to Archie, "It is very dreadful; it is the old who ought to die, and not fine and gallant youth with the golden morning of life still ahead; but after all he died as the heroes of old died." But, he concluded with the same convictions he had about the family's participation in World War I, "If our country did not contain such men it would not be our country."

The fact that the Germans, although they were fighting the Americans at the time, buried Quentin with honors was a grand measure of respect for TR. He did not have long to appreciate it. TR died six months later, leaving behind a legacy filled with respect.

QUIZ

19-1   The French celebrate Bastille Day every July 14th. Why is the day so significant in French history?

A. It was the day King Louis XVII was born.
B. It is the anniversary of the storming of the Bastille on July 14, 1789, which marked the birth of the modern French nation.
C. It was the day Marie Antoinette opened the Bastille on July 14, 1858.
D. July 14 is the day the French bottle the year's crop of champagne.

19-2   When TR was at Harvard he lived in the dormitories with other students.

A. True
B. False

19-3   The National Zoo was established in what year?

A. 1776
B. 1861
C. 1889
D. 1919

19-4   TR's daughter Alice married U.S. Congressman Nicholas Longworth in 1907. The father of her first child was:

A. Nicholas Longworth
B. Hiram Johnson
C. William Borah
D. Uncle Remus

CHAPTER 20

TR's Legacy

"I have never in my life envied a human being who led an easy life; I have envied a great many people who led difficult lives and led them well."

Theodore Roosevelt created a legacy that is manifested in a variety of ways for a range of accomplishments. He is noted for his deeds as a politician, natural history expert, writer, father, and family man. Contemporary people who know him only by reputation continue to honor his memory by naming parks, ships, and assorted memorials after him. TR may be dead, but reminders of his accomplishments are not. He left a large footprint on the earth in his sixty years of life—and mighty big shoes to fill.

Face on a Mountain

As long as Mount Rushmore and old movies exist, so will the memories of Theodore Roosevelt. Memories, in the form of a legacy, are the true gauge of how significant an impact a person has had on the world he has left behind. Few people in history have left as large a footprint as did Theodore Roosevelt.

FACT

Sculptor Gutzon Borglum advocated for TR's inclusion on Mount Rushmore when he got involved in the project to carve the profiles of four former U.S. presidents on the mountainside. Borglum had campaigned for TR and exhibited a statue of Abraham Lincoln in the White House after he was elected. The publicity and his acquaintance with TR served as his entry into the Mount Rushmore project. Consequently, TR was perpetuated in stone.

One of the most recognizable reminders of TR is his profile carved on Mount Rushmore, in Keystone, South Dakota. His face is there alongside Thomas Jefferson's, George Washington's, and Abraham Lincoln's. Every time Mount Rushmore appears in a television ad or his image or persona is featured in movies, such as the *Night at the Museum* films, people are reminded of TR.

But sculptures on mountainsides and portrayals in movies do not tell the real story of historical figures. That is true where the legacy of Theodore Roosevelt is concerned.

An Unparalleled Legacy

One movie that prominently featured Mount Rushmore was *North by Northwest*, starring Cary Grant as Roger Thornhill. During a chase around the profiles, Thornhill said, "I don't like the way Teddy Roosevelt is looking at me." That may have been a throwaway line in a movie, but it explains in part why TR is so well-remembered. He made a lot of people uncomfortable over his lifetime as he built his legacy—but many more pleased.

TR is remembered for his determined campaigns to eliminate greed and corruption in his political positions such as New York state assemblyman, New York state governor, New York City police commissioner, and president of the United States. He fought for social justice and righteousness incessantly, in and out of office—and he did it all from a standpoint of character and righteousness.

"Character" and "righteousness" epitomize TR's life; they steered every action he undertook. Those traits may not have seemed evident to everybody with whom he was involved, but they were the basis of his personal ethos.

Character Counts

One of TR's most significant legacies was the impact he had on the office of U.S. president. He altered the U.S. political system by drawing attention to the role of the president in the government structure and making character as important as the issues. That was due in part to his personality—and changing technology.

TR recognized that the "bully pulpit" he had inherited as the result of President McKinley's assassination provided him with an opportunity to influence the people of the United States and the role the country played in the world. He applied his "big stick" philosophy across the globe and let the world know the United States was going to flex its muscles whenever it was required to do so.

QUOTE

TR wrote to John Hay in 1897, "Is America a weakling, to shrink from the work of the great world powers? No! The young giant of the West stands on a continent and clasps the crest of an ocean in either hand. Our nation, glorious in youth and strength, looks into the future with eager eyes and rejoices as a strong man to run a race."

Modern technology, as it was evolving in the early 1900s, helped him in the process. His work to get the Panama Canal completed facilitated the deployment of military troops and equipment to "hot spots" around the world. Improved communication devices made it easier for commanders and politicians to make decisions faster. TR was acute enough to recognize the value of communications and "big sticks."

Using Technology

TR applied the benefits of modern technology to facilitate his communications with Americans. He recognized the value of mass media before most politicians did and used it to his advantage. Film and recording devices made it possible for him to reach wider audiences wherever he went. Voters and constituents got to see and hear TR more often and gauge his character for themselves. That helped him immensely as he built a legacy based on deeds and character.

QUOTE

TR wrote in his autobiography, "No man can lead a public career really worth leading, no man can act with rugged independence in serious crises, nor strike at great abuses, nor afford to make powerful and unscrupulous foes, if he is himself vulnerable in his private character."

In the long run, the label "First Modern President" applies to TR. That would be just one more "first" he accomplished in his lifetime.

Pushing Reform

TR and reform were synonymous. He instituted reform in whatever political or appointed office he assumed, starting with his three terms as New York state assemblyman.

Readers of his autobiography will notice that the word "reform" appears in ten of the fifteen chapters. That fact highlights the importance TR placed in reform in every chapter of his life—and of the need for change in every aspect of American society.

The reforms TR started in New York state and across the country are still in place today. He was among the first politicians in the nation's history to see the connections among efficiency, individual character, merit, and corruption. His goal was simple: separate politics and corruption from individuals' opportunities to acquire government jobs based on merit, rather than political party affiliation.

Significantly, TR did not see reform as a one-party issue. He worked with Democrats and Republicans alike to implement reforms in every aspect of life for the benefit of society. His ability to work across party lines when it was expedient was one of his many talents and caused people to wonder at times whether he was truly a Republican or a Democrat.

In one case, TR worked closely in the New York State Assembly with a Democrat named Pete Kelly. He explained how that benefited both men: "We began to vote together and act together, and by the end of the session found that in all practical matters that were up for action we thought together. Indeed, each of us was beginning to change his theories, so that even in theory we were coming closer together."

TR carried his willingness to work with people of all political "isms" into every campaign and position. The fact that he formed his own political party in 1912 was evidence that he did not always agree with the Republicans with whom he was affiliated. And, he learned from Democrats as well as Republicans.

Working Across Party Lines

His ability to work across party lines manifested his willingness to learn and apply the lessons to the betterment of society—all society. His zeal for reform was an offshoot of his bipartisan nature. He worked well with people of different political beliefs whenever he found it necessary to do so. The civil reforms he enacted were—and still are—proof of that.

The civil reform changes TR initiated in New York state in the 1880s and continued in his tenure in Washington, D.C., set the tone for government merit programs across the country. They are still in place. That is one more tribute to his forward-thinking ways.

Conservation

Visitors to national parks get a firsthand glimpse of TR's legacy. He accelerated the conservation movement in the United States, which led to the formation of national game preserves, bird reservations, and national forests. He would have done more if Congress had not stopped him.

FACT

> When TR took office, several natural resources problems required resolution: approximately 80 percent of America's forests were depleted; a large portion of the country's farmland was unproductive due to overuse; mining companies were extracting too much oil, gas, and minerals from the ground; and private enterprises controlled water rights. TR had to resolve these problems if the nation was to have a future.

TR became an activist to ensure the preservation of natural resources. He had seen firsthand in his days as a "cowboy" and a legislator the damage nature could suffer if humans were left to devastate it without a system of checks and balances. He implemented those checks and balances.

As president, TR and his associates preserved 170 million acres of land for public use. He concentrated on Western lands. Year after year, he designated large areas as national landmarks, sometimes after protracted battles.

The first national park TR created was Crater Lake in Oregon. Environmental activist William G. Steel lobbied unsuccessfully for seventeen years to get Crater Lake designated as a national park. He and fellow activist John B. Waldo persuaded President McKinley to declare it a part of a federal forest preserve. It took TR to designate it as a national park.

TR's ability to look into the future while others were mired in the past was his forte in pushing for conservation. Some congressmen could not see the need for national parks because they were costly to a government that had a limited income, inaccessible to a large portion of the population, and difficult to maintain. TR saw beyond those arguments.

Looking Ahead

TR forecast correctly that automobiles would change the face of the country's future. He predicted that they would become more widely available to Americans, which would open access to the parks. He was right.

FACT

One U.S. congressman in particular, Speaker of the House David Henderson (R-Iowa), held up attempts to create national parks by not allowing floor votes. TR used his considerable powers of persuasion to get Henderson to change his mind. Henderson relented and allowed a vote. On May 22, 1902, TR signed a law creating Crater Lake National Park.

From that point on, the number of national lands set aside for future use rose steadily. TR solidified his reputation as a conservationist as a result. His reputation in that regard endures—and will continue to do so as long as the land stays preserved.

Creating a World Power

The government and people of the United States spent their first 125 years trying to define their role in the world. For the most part they stayed out of international politics, with occasional forays into wars with the Barbary Pirates between 1801 and 1815, Mexico in 1846–1848, and Spain in 1898. It was not until TR became president that the United States began its ascendancy as a world power.

Years after TR left the White House, President Wilson was still talking about the navy in terms of defense. In his annual message to Congress on December 8, 1914, he said:

A powerful Navy we have always regarded as our proper and natural means of defense; and it has always been of defense that we have thought, never of aggression or of conquest. But who shall tell us now what sort of Navy to build? We shall take leave to be strong upon the seas, in the future as in the past; and there will be no thought of offense or provocation in that. Our ships are our natural bulwarks.

Since TR's first day on the job as assistant secretary of the navy, he had pushed for a strong offensive navy. Historically, the U.S. Navy had been a defensive force. TR made it clear to anyone who would listen—and to some who would not—that the way to earn respect from other nations with strong armed forces was to create a powerful navy. And, he stressed, there should be shortcuts such as a canal between major oceans to make travel across the globe easier.

TR had an ulterior motive in building a strong navy and a canal. He wanted to export American ideals and values around the globe, which could not be done on ships. It could, however, be done through diplomacy and shows of force, such as the deployment of the "Great White Fleet." TR's use of both was one area in which his "big stick" strategy played a role.

ESSENTIAL

Until the aftermath of the Spanish-American War, the United States had never had any territory outside North America to administer. Once the federal government took responsibility for the Philippines, Guam, Puerto Rico, Cuba, and Hawaii after 1898, it had to play a bigger role in international politics to protect American interests in those jurisdictions. That was a major reason TR increased U.S. involvement in global affairs.

President McKinley had started the job of expanding the United States' international presence. TR took it a step further. He did not restrict his efforts to export American ideas and values to his years in the White House. TR continued to push for U.S. involvement in world affairs when it became evident to him that World War I would become a reality.

TR's insistence on letting the world know that the United States was willing to use diplomacy when necessary to keep peace among nations or military power to protect its interests led to a new role for the country. He was the first United States president to establish the country as a world power, and his persistence and statesmanship set a precedent that every one of his successors has followed, albeit reluctantly at times.

Science and Natural History

Few American presidents prior to 1901 gave much thought to the role of nature in politics. TR was an exception. He heightened people's awareness worldwide of natural history and science and the role they played in Earth's survival. He began that job long before he entered the White House.

There are several TR quotes inscribed inside the Roosevelt Memorial rotunda at the American Museum of Natural History. Perhaps the one that best sums up his philosophy about natural history is this: "The nation behaves well if it treats the natural resources as assets which it must turn over to the next generation increased, and not impaired in value."

There was never a stage in TR's life in which he pushed natural history into the background. His love for nature and the need for protecting it is inherent in his books and articles; the laws he wrote and enacted as assemblyman, governor, and president; and the numerous monuments and memorials dedicated to him. His legacy in that respect is practically unparalleled in American history.

A Unique President

Some U.S. presidents have been specialists or dabblers in different areas of science and natural history. George Washington had an amateur interest in scientific experiments. Herbert Hoover and Jimmy Carter were engineers. Thomas Jefferson was a scientist. TR was more eclectic than his predecessors, though. That explains why he formed alliances—and ultimately friendships—with so many specialists in his lifetime.

The connection between the American Museum of Natural History and the Roosevelt family is still strong. Thee helped found the museum. It still offers Theodore Roosevelt Memorial Grants to support research on North American fauna in any phase of wildlife conservation or natural history, and graduate, doctoral, and postdoctoral fellowships to students interested in natural history.

TR's partnerships with specialists such as John Muir, Jacob Riis, Alfred Thayer Mahan, Gifford Pinchot, and John Burroughs contributed to his and their legacies. His talent for picking the best people to help him accomplish a project was notable. TR did not always get the credit for the results, nor did he necessarily want it.

Despite his sometimes supersized ego, TR was willing to give credit where credit was due. Kermit received a lot of the kudos for his exploits during the River of Doubt expedition. TR cited Gifford Pinchot for his conservation efforts. Results were the primary goal for TR. Who got the credit was secondary. The results from his many successes are nevertheless a major part of his legacy.

Donating Specimens

TR's generosity in donating specimens became legendary. He supplied them to the Smithsonian Institution, the American Museum of Natural History, the San Francisco Museum, and other facilities after his various expeditions. When he was not collecting specimens, he was saving lands on which other nature lovers could gather their own or at least enjoy the unspoiled beauty of parks and preserves.

A great portion of TR's legacy remains in people's minds, history books, and other tangible and intangible forms: a quote here, a statue there. The most visible, however, are the specimens and writings displayed in the museums of which he was fondest. They stand as tributes to a man whose love of nature knew no bounds—a love that has been passed down from generation to generation of nature lovers worldwide.

Role in History

Theodore Roosevelt earned his spot as one of the most efficient and effective U.S. presidents and caring citizens—and will most likely remain at the top of both lists as long as history is recorded. The fact that Americans vote consistently to include TR on the list of "top ten or better" U.S. presidents is proof of that.

Chapter 20: TR's Legacy

Candid portrait of a laughing Theodore Roosevelt

Rankings by themselves do not mean much. Often, people vote for the best or worst presidents without knowing what they accomplished, how it affected the country, and when they served. The factors and biases that go into the polls ranking presidents change from day to day or event to event. But, Theodore Roosevelt's name is almost always near the top of the list on any poll.

FACT

Historian Arthur Schlesinger, Sr. began the fad of ranking presidents in 1948. He asked fifty-five other historians to rate each president. He listed five categories from which they could choose: great, near great, average, below average, or failure. TR finished near the top, as he usually does.

Significantly, TR's name is nowhere near the bottom of any poll ranking presidents. That may not be the best thing anyone can say about a U.S. president: "He is never near the bottom." But, it is a tribute to TR that he is always near the top. That is a high compliment for any president's legacy.

The Road to Relevance

In the final analysis, TR was not just "any" president. He was the right person to be in office at the turn of the twentieth century, when the United States needed a "modern" president. Theodore Roosevelt fit that need, even though it took a human tragedy, the assassination of William McKinley, to get him into the White House. TR started the United States down the road to international relevance.

Ten years after he left the White House, he passed away. His January 6, 1919, death saddened millions of people around the world.

Farewell to TR

In the end, TR suffered the fate of all mortals and received the same sendoff: a funeral. And, like so many other funerals, it was a dignified, simple affair. Even though TR led a full public life, he had managed to keep much of what really mattered to him private. So it was with his funeral.

FACT

Pallbearers led by TR's son Archibald carried him into the church. He rested in an oak coffin covered with the American flag, two Rough Rider regimental banners, and a wreath of laurel and yellow acacia sent by the Rough Riders. The yellow, the color of the cavalry, symbolized one of TR's most cherished memories—and the enduring love of the men he led in war.

Two days after he died, 500 hundred invited guests assembled in Christ Church (Episcopal) at Oyster Bay for a 1 P.M. celebration of his life. Another 3,000–4,000 people stood outside. The number of mourners was limited by the size of the church.

Given the opportunity, countless more would have been in attendance to say goodbye to their hero, the man known affectionately as the "American Lion." Even in death, his name lived on, as did his list of "firsts." After his funeral, the British held memorial services at Westminster Abbey in London, marking the first time a non-British person received that honor.

FACT

The funeral ceremony was simple. There was no music and no one delivered a eulogy. Even prayers were limited. Church rector Father George E. Talmage read TR's favorite hymn, "How Firm a Foundation," and said a prayer written by Cardinal John Henry Newman, which was allegedly Quentin's favorite. It was a simple sendoff for a complex man.

Following the conclusion of the ceremony, TR's coffin was placed in the hearse and carried slowly to the top of a hill at Youngs Memorial Cemetery. There, he lies in solitary repose looking out on the sea he loved—and the world he did so much to bring together.

The fortunate 500 mourners in the church at Oyster Bay and the thousands of people who stood outside might have buried their friend that day, but they could not—and did not—bury their memories of him. They remain, in the form of TR's legacy, which may never be buried.

20-1 William G. Steel fought for seventeen years to earn a national park designation for Crater Lake in Oregon. As a reward he became the _____ superintendent of the park.

A. fourth
B. seventh
C. second
D. he never became superintendent

20-2 Speaker of the House David F. Henderson decided abruptly not to run again for Congress only six weeks before the election in 1902. Why?

A. He could not get along with TR, even though they were both Republicans.
B. repercussions from his Civil War wounds
C. to avoid a looming scandal
D. No one knows for sure.

20-3 TR may have averted a major world war in 1906 when he negotiated a settlement between Germany and France over the rule of what country?

A. Morocco
B. Brazil
C. Ethiopia
D. Peru

20-4 Thomas Jefferson became vice president in 1797. That week, he presented a research paper to the American Philosophical Society. What was the subject?

A. The role of the vice president in American politics
B. Paleontology
C. George Washington's false teeth
D. The quasi-war between the United States and France in 1797

20-5 TR is listed near the top of the category "Most Overrated" in recent presidential ranking polls.

A. True
B. False

20-6 TR could not use income tax revenues to fund the large number of national parks he created when he was president. Why not?

A. Congress banned him from using the funds.
B. There was no income tax in place at the time.
C. Income tax revenues could only be used for military purposes between 1901 and 1909.
D. The president did not have the authority to designate how income tax revenues were distributed.

20-1. C: He was not appointed superintendent until 1913. The first superintendent was a Klamath Falls, Oregon, rancher, William F. Arant.

20-2. D: There was solid speculation that he had been dallying with a "certain lobbyess" and was getting too reckless in the process.

20-3. A: Britain claimed jurisdiction over Egypt. France claimed control of Morocco. Britain agreed to France's claim and France agreed to Britain's. Germany felt left out and challenged France's claim. TR negotiated a settlement between them, which upheld the British and French rules in Egypt and Morocco, respectively. Germany still did not have any control over either country, but at least TR made the Germans feel better. And he averted a war.

20-4. B: Paleontology, the study of fossils, helps people understand different forms of life on Earth.

20-5. False: TR's name is not listed in any of the categories such as "Overrated," "Controversial," or "Underrated."

20-6. B: The income tax was not introduced until 1913. Technically, it became law as part of the Sixteenth Amendment to the U.S. Constitution, although there had been attempts to implement one previously.

ANSWERS

Books by Theodore Roosevelt

"Among those men whom I have known the love of books and the love of
outdoors, in their highest expressions, have usually gone hand in hand."

1882	*The Naval War of 1812*
1885	*Hunting Trips of a Ranchman Parts 1 & 2*
1887	*Thomas Hart Benton*
1888	*Essays on Practical Politics*
1888	*Gouverneur Morris*
1888	*Ranch Life and the Hunting Trail* (An abbreviated version is available as *Ranch Life in the Far West*)
1889	*The Winning of the West, Vol. 1 "The Spread of English Speaking Peoples" Vol. 2 "In The Current of the Revolution" Vol. 3 "The War in the Northwest"*
1891	*New York*
1893	*The Wilderness Hunter*
1893	*American Big Game*, with George Bird Grinnell
1894	*The Winning of the West, Vol. 4 "The Indian Wars" Vol. 5 "St. Claire and Wayne"* (unknown publication date) *Vol. 6 "Louisiana and Aaron Burr"* (unknown publication date)
1895	*Hero Tales from American History*, with Henry Cabot Lodge
1895	*Hunting in Many Lands*, with George Bird Grinnell
1897	*American Ideals*
1897	*Some American Game*
1897	*Trail and Campfire*, with George Bird Grinnell
1899	*The Rough Riders*
1900	*Oliver Cromwell*
1900	*The Strenuous Life*
1902	*The Deer Family*, with T. S. Van Dyke, D. G. Elliot, and A. J. Stone
1904	*Addresses and Messages*
1905	*Outdoor Pastimes of an American Hunter*
1905	*The Winning of the West, Vol. 5 "Louisiana and Aaron Burr"*

1907	*Good Hunting*
1909	*Outdoor Editorials*
1910	*African and European Addresses*
1910	*African Game Trails*
1910	*American Problems*
1910	*The New Nationalism*
1910	*Presidential Addresses and State Papers*, 8 volumes
1912	*The Conservation of Womanhood and Childhood*
1912	*Realizable Goals*
1913	*Autobiography* [one of several versions under several titles]
1913	*History as Literature*
1913	*Progressive Principles*
1914	*African Game Animals*, with Edmund Heller
1915	*America and the World War*
1916	*A Book-Lovers Holiday in the Open*
1916	*Fear God and Take Your Own Part*
1917	*The Foes of Our Own Household*
1917	*Social Justice and Popular Rule*
1917	*National Strength and International Duty*
1918	*The Great Adventure*
1919	*Theodore Roosevelt's Letters to His Children*

Publication Date Unknown

Colonial Policies of the United States (Earliest publishing seen is 1937). Most likely written by Theodore Roosevelt Jr.

Hunting Trails of the West (Possibly titled *Ranch Life in the Far West*, by Roosevelt and edited by Gerard T. Altoff and contains selections from *Ranch Life and the Hunting Trail* and others)

The online versions of many of these books can be accessed via the Internet at:
www.frfrogspad.com/writings.htm
http://books.google.com

Resources

"The one thing I want to leave my children is an honorable name."

Places to Visit

Badlands Home (Medora, North Dakota)

Birthplace (New York City; 28 East 20th Street, between Broadway and Park Avenue South, a block west of Gramercy Park)

Inaugural Site—Wilcox Mansion (Buffalo, New York)

Mother's Home—Bulloch Hall (Roswell, Georgia)

Mt. Rushmore Memorial (Keystone, South Dakota)

American Museum of Natural History (New York City)

Presidential Retreat—Pine Knot (Keene, Virginia)

Roosevelt Study Center (Middleburg, the Netherlands)

Sagamore Hill Home (Oyster Bay, New York)

Theodore Roosevelt Collection/Library (Harvard University, Cambridge, Massachusetts)

Theodore Roosevelt Bird Sanctuary/Gravesite (Oyster Bay, New York)

Theodore Roosevelt Island (Washington, D.C.)

Theodore Roosevelt National Park (near Medora, North Dakota)

USS *Theodore Roosevelt CVN-71* (wherever it is at any given time)

Online Resources

The Theodore Roosevelt Association

The Theodore Roosevelt Association is a national historical society and public service organization that has perpetuated the memory and legacy of TR through historical and cultural activities.

www.theodoreroosevelt.org

The Theodore Roosevelt Collection, Harvard College Library

This collection, housed in Harvard University's Houghton and Widener libraries, is a major resource for study of the life and times of TR.

http://hcl.harvard.edu/libraries/houghton /collections/roosevelt.cfm

The U.S. National Park Service

The National Park Service safeguards nearly 400 places across the United States and welcomes more than 275 million visitors every year. You can learn more about TR and plan visits to Sagamore Hill, the Theodore Roosevelt Birthplace, and Theodore Roosevelt National Park, among many other sites.

www.nps.gov

Photography Credits

Cover: "Colonel Theodore Roosevelt of the Rough Riders, circa 1898"
Studio portrait photograph of TR in his riding uniform, by George G. Rockwood circa 1898. Published in *The Man Roosevelt* by Frances E. Leupp, 1904. Restoration by Steven Wynn.

Page 5: "Theodore Roosevelt, about four years old"
Studio photo of TR as a boy, probably 1862. From carte-de-visite of "Teedie" standing. Photo by Wenderoth & Taylor. Theodore Roosevelt Collection, Harvard College Library (520.11-003).

Page 9: "Portrait of Theodore Roosevelt Sr."
Portrait of TR's father, Theodore Roosevelt Sr. as it appeared in TR's 1913 autobiography and displayed at the Sagamore Hill home. Restoration by Steven Wynn.

Page 9: "Portrait of Martha Bulloch"
Portrait of TR's mother, Martha Bulloch, as it appeared in TR's 1913 autobiography and displayed at the Sagamore Hill home. Restoration by Steven Wynn.

Page 11: "Theodore Roosevelt at Harvard Boat House, circa 1877"
Roosevelt in a sculling outfit at the Harvard Boat House. Photo circa 1877. Theodore Roosevelt Collection, Harvard College Library (520.12-002).

Page 25: "Theodore Roosevelt, Harvard graduate, circa 1881"
Portrait by Pach Brothers, circa 1880–1881. Theodore Roosevelt Collection, Harvard College Library (Roosevelt R500.P69a-003).

Page 39: "Theodore Roosevelt in the New York Legislature"
TR posing with a group of his friends while a member of the NY Legislature, circa 1884. Clockwise from back right: TR, Walter Howe, Isaac Hunt, William O'Neill, George F. Spinney of the *NY Times* (center). Theodore Roosevelt Collection, Harvard College Library (520.13-008).

Page 52: "Alice Hathaway Lee Roosevelt"
Photo taken between 1880–1884. Library of Congress, LC-USZ62-25802.

Page 65: "Theodore Roosevelt with Wilmot Dow and Bill Sewall at Elkhorn Ranch, 1886"
From left to right: Dow, TR, and William Wingate Sewall in fur coats, Elkhorn Ranch, Medora, ND. Theodore Roosevelt Collection, Harvard College Library (520.14-005).

Page 74: "Edith Carow Roosevelt"
Photo taken in 1902 by J. Schloss. Library of Congress, LC-USZ62-17631.

Page 83: "Edith Carow Roosevelt with Quentin on chair, 1903"
Photo taken in 1903 by Frances Benjamin Johnston. Library of Congress, LC-USZ62-96678.

Page 90: "Theodore Roosevelt pulling an elephant's tail in political cartoon, 1889"
Cartoon showing Benjamin Harrison on a Republican Party elephant labeled "Tannerism," which is tearing down civil service rules, as TR, Thompson, and C. Lyman try to restrain the elephant by pulling on its tail. Caption reads "This is the 'pull' that civil service reform has with this administration." Appeared in *Puck*, October 2, 1889. Illustration by Louis Dalrymple (1866–1905). Library of Congress, LC-USZC4-3826.

Page 109: "Portrait of Colonel Theodore Roosevelt, 1898"
Colonel TR in portrait photo, August 1898. Photo by Frances Benjamin Johnston (1864–1952). Library of Congress, LC-USZ62-17532.

Page 111: "Theodore Roosevelt and Rough Riders atop San Juan Hill, 1898"
Photo of the victorious Rough Riders atop San Juan Hill, with TR at the center. By William Dinwiddie (1867–1934). Library of Congress, LC-USZC4-7934.

Page 129: "Governor Theodore Roosevelt after nomination as VP in 1900"
Photo of Governor TR after his nomination to VP, in August 1900. Library of Congress, LC-USZ62-28397.

Page 137: "Theodore Roosevelt delivers speech in Hannibal, Missouri, 1903"
President TR delivers a stump speech standing on a table in the middle of a street as a crowd gathers. Photo by Underwood & Underwood. Theodore Roosevelt Collection, Harvard College Library (560.51 1903-048).

Page 148: "Theodore Roosevelt operates an American steam shovel at Culebra Cut, Panama Canal"
Photo of President TR operating a steam shovel at the Panama Canal construction site. Photo by Underwood & Underwood. Library of Congress, LC-DIG-stereo-1s02355.

Page 156: "Santa brings Theodore Roosevelt the Nobel Prize in cartoon"
Newspaper cartoon between 1906–1907 with the caption "The Christmas Surprise Teddy—wonder if old Santa Claus could have made any mistake?"

The Norwegian Parliament is dressed as Santa Claus delivering the Nobel Prize in a Christmas stocking to TR, who's shown in a child's body. Illustration by Charles Lewis Bartholomew. Library of Congress, LC-USZ62-8666.

Page 175: "Theodore Roosevelt camping with John Burroughs at Yellowstone Park, 1903"
President TR and noted naturalist John Burroughs (with beard) stand at their campsite in Yellowstone Park. Billy Hofer is seated, and an unidentified man stands in the background. Theodore Roosevelt Collection, Harvard College Library (560.51 1903-028).

Page 181: "Theodore Roosevelt and his big bull rhino"
TR posing with his trophy bull rhino, 1909. Photograph by Kermit Roosevelt. Library of Congress, LC-USZ62-10308.

Page 209: "Theodore Roosevelt pointing at a map of South America"
Photo of TR pointing at a map of South America toward the area explored during the Roosevelt-Rondon Scientific Expedition in Brazil as another man looks on. Photo was published in TR's 1913 autobiography. Restoration by Steven Wynn.

Page 240: "Theodore Roosevelt with Chief Forester Gifford Pinchot on river steamer *Mississippi*, 1907"
TR stands with Gifford Pinchot. This picture was taken on the trip of the Inland Waterways Commission down the Mississippi River in October, 1907. Photo by the U.S. Forest Service. Library of Congress, LC-USZ62-55630.

Page 243: "Theodore Roosevelt with General Leonard Wood"
TR stands with the general, circa 1916. Library of Congress, LC-USZ62-28470.

Page 253: "President Theodore Roosevelt with his boys, 1904"
Boys pose with their father. Photo by Arthur Hewitt. Theodore Roosevelt Collection, Harvard College Library (Roosevelt R500.P69a-083).

Page 255: "President Theodore Roosevelt and Family, 1903"
TR as president in 1903, surrounded by his family. Possibly on the lawn at the Sagamore Hill residence. Library of Congress, LC-USZ62-113665.

Page 273: "Candid portrait of a laughing Theodore Roosevelt"
Photo of TR with hearty laugh and smile, circa 1914–1919. Photo by M. J. Leclerc. Restoration by Steven Wynn.

Index

We Have
EVERYTHING
on Anything!

The Everything® list spans a wide range of subjects, with more than 500 titles covering 25 different categories:

Business	History	Reference
Careers	Home Improvement	Religion
Children's Storybooks	Everything Kids	Self-Help
Computers	Languages	Sports & Fitness
Cooking	Music	Travel
Crafts and Hobbies	New Age	Wedding
Education/Schools	Parenting	Writing
Games and Puzzles	Personal Finance	
Health	Pets	